THE BATTLE FOR MANCHURIA AND THE FATE OF CHINA

TWENTIETH-CENTURY BATTLES
Edited by Spencer C. Tucker

THE BATTLE FOR
MANCHURIA
AND THE FATE OF
CHINA

Siping, 1946

HAROLD M. TANNER

INDIANA UNIVERSITY PRESS

Bloomington & Indianapolis

This book is a publication of

INDIANA UNIVERSITY PRESS
601 North Morton Street
Bloomington, Indiana 47404-3797 USA

iupress.indiana.edu

Telephone orders   800-842-6796
Fax orders   812–855–7931

Manufactured in the
United States of America

Library of Congress
Cataloging-in-Publication Data

Tanner, Harold Miles.
  The battle for Manchuria and the fate of
China : Siping, 1946 / Harold M. Tanner.
  pages cm. — (Twentieth-century battles)
  Includes bibliographical references and
index.
  ISBN 978-0-253-00723-0 (cloth : alkaline
paper)—ISBN 978-0-253-00734-6 (ebook)
  1. China—History—Civil War, 1945–
1949—Campaigns—China—Siping Shi.
  2. China—History—Civil War, 1945–
1949—Campaigns—China—Manchuria.
  3. Siping Shi (China)—History, Military
—20th century. 4. Manchuria (China)
—History, Military—20th century.
  I. Title.
  DS777.5425.S77T36   2013
  951.04'2—dc23   2012036057

1 2 3 4 5   17 16 15 14 13

For Sophia

If it is all right not to write about
[the Second Battle of Siping],
then don't write about it.

—*Zhou Enlai*

CONTENTS

ACKNOWLEDGMENTS

This project has taken me to Stanford University; Washington, D.C.; Lexington, Virginia; and College Park, Maryland; to Beijing, Shanhaiguan, Xingcheng, Jinzhou, Shenyang, Siping, Changchun, Dalian, and Taipei. I could not have done it without the help of numerous friends, chance acquaintances, and hard-working librarians and archivists. A special word of thanks goes to my friend Bruce Elleman. This book would not exist if not for Bruce's well-placed questions and suggestions. I would also like to express my appreciation to Spencer Tucker, editor of the Twentieth Century Battles series, and to Editorial Director Robert Sloan of the Indiana University Press.

In Beijing, Wang Chaoguang of the Chinese Academy of Social Sciences' Institute of Modern History has been generous with his advice and with arranging the institutional support necessary when doing research in China. He Jiangfeng contributed his enthusiasm and knowledge of sources in Republican-era history as a research assistant in Beijing. Chen Yung-fa, Chang Jui-te, and the Institute of Modern History at Academia Sinica in Taipei provided assistance and a comfortable base for research in Taiwan. In Siping, Zhao Zilun and Wang Haichun of the Standing Committee of Siping's People's Congress and Wang Yongxing of Siping Television shared both insights and material of (they made very clear) an unclassified nature, as well as many excellent meals, accompanied by locally produced beer and *baijiu* (white lightning). A number of elderly citizens of Siping and Jinzhou graciously allowed me to intrude on otherwise restful mornings and afternoons in parks or along the streets with my incessant questions about the events of the 1940s. I also benefited from conversations with Liu Tong and Zhang Zhenglong, both noted historians of the People's Liberation Army. Finally, I thank the anonymous reader who went over the entire manuscript at the request of Indiana University Press for his or her valuable suggestions.

I conducted research for this book at the following libraries and archives: in China, the National Library in Beijing, the Jilin Provincial Archives, the Liaoning Provincial Archives, the Liaoning Provincial Library, and the Liao-Shen Campaign Memorial Hall; in the United States, the National Archives and Records Administration in College Park, Maryland, the Asian Reading Room of the Library of Congress, the Research Library of the George C. Marshall Foundation, the Hoover Institution Library and Archives, Stanford University's East Asia Library, and the University of North Texas Libraries. In Canada, Sr. Huguette Turcotte of the Missionary Sisters of the Immaculate Conception, Fr. Gilles Dubé of the Société des Missions-Étrangès, and Wilfrid Bernier of Les Clercs de Saint-Viateur du Canada kindly supplied me with material from the archives and publications of their respective organizations.

I had the pleasure of presenting various parts of the research for this book as conference papers at meetings of the Southwest Conference for Asian Studies, the Association for Asian Studies, the Chinese Military History Society, and the Military History Society, where my fellow panelists and the panel audiences helped me with their questions and comments. The Chinese Military History Society and its core leadership of David Graff, Ken Swope, and Peter Lorge in particular have offered a supportive professional network. I would also like to acknowledge the generous financial support that I have received from all levels of the University of North Texas: the Department of History and its Military History Center, the College of Arts and Sciences, and the Office of the Provost. Without institutional support for research trips and travel to conferences, this kind of research would not be possible. I hope the results of the research—which include not only conference papers, articles, and a book but also the incorporation of new content and perspectives into both undergraduate and graduate classes—represent an adequate return on the university's investment.

Finally, I would like to thank my long-suffering family: my wife, Jiang Yiyun, who bravely keeps a home running during many (too many) short and long conference and research trips, and my children, Sophia and William, who may wonder if I have any interests other than work. The answer is, of course, "yes," though it often does not look that way!

A NOTE ON CHINESE NAMES

In the main text, Chinese names have been written in the pinyin Romanization system. Most words are pronounced roughly the way an English-speaker would guess. There are a few important exceptions to this rule: "c" is pronounced as "ts," "q" as "ch," and "x" more or less like "s." I have used non-pinyin spellings for the names of a few individuals and entities whose names have become universally recognized under those earlier spellings. For example, Chiang Kai-shek (pinyin Jiang Jieshi), Kwantung Army (pinyin Guandong Army), and T. V. Soong (pinyin Song Ziwen).

THE BATTLE FOR MANCHURIA
AND THE FATE OF
CHINA

1

Siping, 1946

Decisive Battle or Lost Opportunity?

Siping (pronounced SUH-ping) is a small city of 3.2 million people. On a contemporary map, it lies just inside Jilin Province in China's great Northeast, or Manchuria, on the main rail line, roughly halfway between the provincial capital cities of Changchun to the north and Shenyang to the south. The railway line itself bisects the city, dividing it into two districts, Tiexi (west of the railway, pronounced "tia-see") and Tiedong (east of the railway, pronounced "tia-doong"). In the economic development zones on the outskirts of town are the construction companies, warehouses, factories, and a state-of-the art brewery that make the backbone of Siping's modern industrial economy. At night, the city's main shopping district comes alive with stalls and vendors selling clothing, fruit, vegetables, snacks, household goods, electronics, and more. Along the boulevard running west from the railway station, elderly men offer to tell your fortune (always good) for a moderate fee. Around the corner, down a nondescript street, a restaurant serves up the city's local culinary specialty: Li Liangui's Big Marinated Pork Buns, praised by Communist Party leaders including Deng Xiaoping ("economical, simple, and tasty!") and former premier Li Peng ("Comrade Xiaoping likes them. I like them too.").

In the spring of 1946, this city, home of the delicious (and economical) big pork buns, was the scene of a bitter month-long siege. In the summer of 1945, in the last weeks of the Second World War, Soviet troops

1

had entered Manchuria to drive out the Japanese, who had occupied the region since 1931. With the Soviets in occupation, forces of the Chinese Communist Party gained a foothold in Manchuria, which they hoped to use as a base area for their political and military struggle with Chiang Kai-shek's Kuomintang (Nationalist Party). Beginning on 18 April 1946, Chinese Communist troops, who had only captured Siping in March, defended the city against the northward-advancing armies of the Nationalists. For the Communists, more accustomed to mobile operations and guerrilla warfare, the task of digging in and defending a city to the bitter end was a new challenge. General Lin Biao, commander of the Northeast Democratic United Army (NDUA), as the Communist forces were called, rose to the occasion only because Communist Party leader Mao Zedong insisted on defending the city.

For the Nationalist commanders, the prolonged struggle for control of Siping was something of an embarrassment. In March, when he first sent his forces marching north from Shenyang toward Siping, Nationalist general Du Yuming predicted that he would capture the city by the second of April.[1] Du and his officers appear to have been sure that their armies, trained and equipped by the Americans during World War II, would easily defeat the poorly armed ragtag Communist "bandits."[2] In fact, it was not until 18 April that General Du's forces even reached the outskirts of Siping and put the city under siege. The battle for control of the city itself took another full month. On 18 May, the Communist troops abandoned the city and withdrew north toward the Songhua (Sungari) River. Nationalist units under General Du gave pursuit, hoping to cut off and annihilate Lin Biao's main forces, and thus to achieve complete control of Manchuria.

While Communist and Nationalist soldiers were fighting and dying at Siping, their political leaders were deep in negotiations for a ceasefire agreement. The prime mover behind these negotiations was President Harry Truman's special representative to China: General George Marshall. Since his arrival in China in December 1945, Marshall had been laboring mightily to get the Communist and Nationalist parties to step back from the brink of civil war, to amalgamate their armies into a single national army, and to enter into a political power-sharing agreement.

With the fighting in Manchuria threatening to destroy all that he had worked to achieve in China, Marshall threw himself into what must have seemed endless rounds of meetings with the Nationalist leader, Generalissimo Chiang Kai-shek and with the Communists' lead negotiator, Zhou Enlai. It was a thankless and clearly frustrating task, but finally, Marshall brokered a compromise: a fifteen-day ceasefire in Manchuria, to go into effect at noon on 7 June 1946. General Du's pursuit of the Communist forces came to an end. Lin Biao's armies withdrew north of the Songhua, to Heilongjiang Province and its capital city, Harbin, while Du Yuming controlled the south bank of the river. The ceasefire in Manchuria was extended for another eight days on 21 June and then held for the rest of the summer and on into the fall.

Notable as it was, the ceasefire that General Marshall had negotiated for Manchuria did not mean the end of armed struggle between the Communist and Nationalist parties. Chiang Kai-shek initiated campaigns against Communist units in central and northern China on 26 June, 1946.[3] In October, Du Yuming launched an assault against the remaining, isolated Communist forces along the Korean border in southern Manchuria. By 8 January 1947, General Marshall had given up all hope of achieving a peaceful settlement and returned home. Civil war was in full swing, with Nationalist and Communist operations under way across Manchuria and northern and central China.

The rest of the story is well known. In November 1948, Lin Biao's armies eliminated and drove off the last Nationalist forces in Manchuria. To the south, between 6 November 1948 and 10 January 1949, another Communist army utterly destroyed key Kuomintang forces in the Huai-Hai Campaign, a victory that left them poised to cross the Yangzi River.[4] In December 1949, Chiang Kai-shek fled to the island of Taiwan. In 1950, as a consequence of the outbreak of the Korean War, the United States undertook to defend the island from the Communist regime on the mainland. There on Taiwan, Chiang Kai-shek planned for a triumphant return to the mainland even as he assessed the causes of his defeat. As he did so, his thoughts turned to the spring and summer of 1946, to the month-long battle at Siping, to General Marshall's mediation mission, and to the ceasefire in Manchuria.

Looking back on his life, Chiang Kai-shek described his experience in dealing with the Chinese Communist Party both in terms of his personal struggle to build a strong, united Chinese nation-state and as a part of the international ideological conflict between the "free world" and Soviet socialism. In 1956, he set forth his views on these events in a book, *Soviet Russia in China: A Summing-up at Seventy.*[5] *Soviet Russia in China* is a Cold War classic in which Chiang calls upon the United States and the "free world" at large to engage the Soviet Union in "total war," using political and military tactics in a fight to the finish, with Asia becoming a battlefield in the "wars against the Communists."[6]

With regard to China, Chiang described the Soviet Union's policies as an extension of Czarist imperialism, with its eyes on Manchuria, Mongolia, Xinjiang, and Tibet.[7] These border areas, extending in an arc from Manchuria in the northeast to Xinjiang in the northwest and south to Tibet in the west were ethnically and geographically distinct from "China Proper," the area of settled agriculture bounded roughly by the line of the Great Wall in the north and the Tibetan Plateau in the west. Although linked to China Proper through trade, cultural interaction, and war for over two thousand years, this periphery had only been firmly knit into an empire administered from Beijing in China Proper in the seventeenth and eighteenth centuries under the Qing Dynasty, whose ruling house and military elite were Manchu, rather than Han people from China Proper.[8]

From the mid-nineteenth through the first decade of the twentieth century, as the Qing lost power in the face of Western and Japanese imperialism, leaders of the Mongols, Tibetans, and the Muslims of Xinjiang attempted to use the support of Britain and Russia to pry themselves away from the control of the Qing empire and establish independent states. The Qing successfully resisted such attempts, and when the Manchu emperor was overthrown in the nationalist revolution of 1911, the new Republic of China claimed the territory of the former Qing empire as its own and continued to resist any moves from within its frontiers or on the part of foreign powers that would lead to the alienation of any of these border regions. Nonetheless, Mongolia, with the active involvement of Russia and, after 1917, the Soviet Union, was effectively separated from the Republic of China. In 1931–1932, Japan had occupied Manchuria and declared it to be the independent state of "Manchukuo," installing the last Manchu Qing emperor, Aisin Gioro "Henry" Puyi (1906–1967) as emperor of the new country.

In *Soviet Russia in China,* Chiang interpreted Soviet involvement in Manchuria in light of this historical experience. The Soviet government, led by Joseph Stalin, was engaging in the latest round of imperialist aggression against China and its territorial sovereignty. In Chiang's mind, however, this Soviet imperialism and his nationalist response to it were linked to an ideological conflict with international ramifications. Unlike the imperialist powers of the past, the Soviet Union desired to change China's entire social, political, and economic structure through violent internal struggle that would be a part of a global socialist revolution. Chiang's struggle in China was, then, a part of the greater battle between the capitalist west and the socialist camp. The Chinese Communists were merely agents of the Soviet Union, helping the Soviets to further their imperialist schemes (which would compromise China's territorial integrity) and to carry out a violent sociopolitical revolution in China itself. Chiang and the Republic of China, on the other hand, were loyal allies of the United States, and deserved the full and unquestioning support of the American government.

Chiang Kai-shek saw the Second Battle of Siping in this context: as a part of the war to defend China against the imperialist ambitions of the Soviet Union, in which the Chinese Communist forces were merely Stalin's stooges. This was a war that Chiang had lost in 1949, but which might have come out very differently, Chiang argued, if the Second Battle of Siping and its aftermath had been handled differently. The battle itself, Chiang said, had been "another decisive battle against the Communist troops." As he described it, the three hundred thousand men under Lin Biao's command had been utterly defeated: "More than half the Communist effectives became casualties." Reports from the front, he said, "all agreed that barring some special international complications the Chinese Communists would not be able to fight anew after the terrific punishment they had just taken at the hands of the Government forces."[9]

Then there came the ceasefire and the suspension of Du Yuming's pursuit of the Communist forces. Chiang believed that if his armies had continued their pursuit, "Communist remnants in northern Manchuria would have been liquidated." Without a base area in northern Manchuria, the remaining Communist forces in Manchuria would have been deprived of Soviet support and "a fundamental solution to the problem of Manchuria would been at hand." Instead, "the morale of Government troops in Manchuria began to suffer" and Lin Biao rebuilt his forces in northern Manchuria. "The subsequent defeat of Government troops in Manchuria in the winter of 1948," said Chiang, "was largely due to the second ceasefire order."[10] In this view, Siping was the decisive battle that could have been—if only a ceasefire, negotiated by George Marshall, had not intervened. Defeat had been snatched from the jaws of victory.

Chiang did not explicitly blame George Marshall for his failure to follow up on the "decisive battle" of Siping. Indeed, Chiang portrays himself as the prime mover behind the ceasefire, in which he, acting out of a misplaced confidence in the better side of human nature, had generously given the Chinese Communists "another chance to prove their loyalty to the nation"—a generosity of spirit which, he saw afterward, had been a mistake.[11]

Some of Chiang's American supporters were more forthright in their assessment of events and of George Marshall's responsibility. Chiang Kai-shek's defeat on the mainland gave rise to much anguish and heated recriminations in Washington D.C. Many on the political right accused the Truman administration of having committed serious strategic errors that had led to Chiang's fall and what seemed to them, at the time, as Soviet hegemony over China in the context of the Cold War. None were more vehement in their accusations than Senator Joseph McCarthy. Strongly implying that Marshall was purposely manipulating Truman's China policy for the benefit of the Soviet Union, McCarthy described Marshall as having been captivated by Zhou Enlai's charm and deceived into thinking that the Chinese Communists were merely agrarian reformers. Referring to the Second Battle of Siping, McCarthy wrote, "The Nationalist forces defeated the Reds in a battle south of Changchun and, with the Reds in flight to the northward, the Nationalists easily retook Changchun on the 23rd of May. At this time the advantage lay with the forces of the Republic." Then, Marshall having been bamboozled by the suave Zhou Enlai and sympathetic to Soviet Communism, his efforts to achieve a ceasefire "reached a frenzy." When agreed upon, the ceasefire "checked the victory of the Nationalists at Changchun, halting them in their tracks and giving the Reds a chance to regroup, retrain, and prepare for more decisive action later."[12]

Professional historians lack the late Senator McCarthy's flamboyance, his talent for demagoguery, and his remarkable ability to make utterly baseless accusations and still be taken seriously (at least for a while). But a number of them, while not sharing in any way McCarthy's political chicanery, twisted logic, and bizarre conspiracy theories, do agree with key aspects of his analysis of George Marshall's mission in China and the significance of the Second Battle of Siping and the Manchurian ceasefire of June 1946. Arthur Waldron, for example, asserts that the Chinese Communist forces at Siping had incurred forty thousand casualties and were on their last legs. Describing Marshall as a naive American hero who was hopelessly out of his depth in the intricacies of Chinese politics, Waldron suggests that Marshall's decision to push for a ceasefire in June 1946 led to Chiang's defeat in the Northeast.[13] In the introduction to their translation of Zhang Jia'ao's diary, Donald Gillin and Ramon Myers blame General Marshall for "denying Chiang Kai-shek's government the fruits" of the victory at Siping. Marshall was thus responsible, they assert, for Chiang's loss of Manchuria in November 1948 and, because Manchuria was a crucial battlefield, for the ultimate loss of the mainland in 1949.[14]

In their best-selling biography *Mao: The Unknown Story,* Jung Chang and Jon Halliday echo the themes that appear in Chiang's *Soviet Russia in China,* in Joe McCarthy's ideological rants, and in the more sober and responsible work of Waldron, Gillin, and Myers. Chang and Halliday argue that by pressuring Chiang into the ceasefire agreement of June 1946, George Marshall in effect saved the Chinese Communist Party from certain defeat. China's fate, which could have been decided at Siping, was irrevocably changed when a foolish American general prevented Chiang Kai-shek from completing a pursuit-and-annihilation operation that would have sealed his victory in Manchuria.[15] For Chang and Halliday, too, Siping was the decisive battle that could have been.

THE MYTH OF DECISIVE BATTLE

Mao Zedong also saw the Second Battle of Siping as a potentially deci-sive encounter. From his point of view, all the Communist forces needed to do was to defend Siping stubbornly until a combination of Commu-nist resistance on the ground and American diplomatic pressure at the negotiating table forced Chiang Kai-shek to agree to a ceasefire. With that, the Communist position in Manchuria north of Siping would be assured. Northern Manchuria, bordering the Soviet Union and North Korea, would become the core of a strong Communist base area spread-ing across Manchuria, Inner Mongolia, and northern China, with its capital in the city of Changchun. As the defense of Siping unfolded, Mao even had a model in mind: the Battle of Madrid.

The Battle of Madrid loomed large in the imaginations of socialist and Communist movements around the world. In early November 1936, the leftist Republican government of Spain (a combination of anarchists, socialists, and communists) prepared to defend the capital city of Ma-drid against an assault by General Francisco Franco's Nationalist armies. With support from the Soviet Union, the Left held tenaciously to Madrid for four months. The decision to defend Madrid inspired the forces of the Left to many acts of bravery. The siege was also accompanied by a ruth-less hunting out and execution of real and imagined "fifth columnists" within the city. Both in Spain and around the world, the fight for Madrid was represented as a decisive struggle between the forces of Franco's Nationalists and the leftist Republicans.[16]

In fact, as it slogged on, the battle of Madrid turned out to be tragi-cally indecisive: after four months of brutal combat for control of the city, the battle ended in a stalemate. General Franco's victory over the forces of the Left came in battles elsewhere on the peninsula. Military historian George Hills acknowledges that the loss of Madrid in 1936 would have been a serious psychological blow to the Republican forces, and that its capture would have been a great boost to Nationalist morale. But at the same time, he argues that in strategic terms, the Left's decision to defend Madrid was a mistake. Withdrawal from the city, which was of no strategic value, would have allowed the Republicans to focus their forces elsewhere while giving Franco's Nationalists the added burden of administering and defending a large city with a hostile population. The Republicans' decision to defend Madrid, Hill suggests, was determined less by strategic calculation than by an ideological and fundamentally romantic view of the significance of decisive battles to defend great cities, a view that may have been inspired by the sieges of Petrograd and Tsaritzyn during the Russian Revolution—sieges already highly romanticized in the collective imagination of the international socialist movement of the 1920s and 1930s.[17]

The leaders of the Chinese Communist Party shared in the intellectual and emotional heritage of the international socialist movement. While they did far more than merely imitate the Soviet Union, they did, in a fundamental sense, owe their Marxist-Leninist ideology and the basic principles of their political organization to the Soviet Union, whose agents, working through the Communist International in the 1920s and early 1930s, had played a crucial role in inspiring, organizing, and funding the Chinese Communist Party. Even during the Anti-Japanese War of 1936–1945 (i.e., the Chinese theater of the Second World War), Chinese Communist leaders had held up the battle of Madrid as a model for imitation. In 1938, as the Japanese advanced toward the city of Wuhan, Mao Zedong suggested that Wuhan would be "China's Madrid." At Wuhan, the Chinese would hold firm and halt the enemy advance. Of course, in Mao's imagination, China's Madrid, unlike the real thing, would actually be a decisive battle, and the defenders would go on to win the war. As it turned out, Wuhan fell. China and the Chinese Communist Party would have to search elsewhere for their "Madrid." For Mao, that moment seemed to come with the Second Battle of Siping. Here, finally, his men would draw the line. The enemy would advance no further. Siping would be a decisive battle, the turning point of the Chinese Communist Party's long and bitter revolutionary civil war against Chiang Kai-shek's Kuomintang-dominated national government.[18]

In the way that they imagined and then sought to assess the Second Battle of Siping, Mao Zedong, Chiang Kai-shek, and later observers and historians all shared the assumption that Siping had been, or could have been, a "decisive battle." Before we look at the Second Battle of Siping, judge the ideas and actions of the political and military leaders responsible for the battle, and seek to draw lessons from their experience, we should ask: what is a decisive battle? What is it like? How do we recognize it when we see it? What makes it decisive? We might even ask: is there really such a thing as a decisive battle at all?

The *idea* or the *ideal* of the "decisive battle" clearly does exist. It is an attractive idea, first, because the goal of war is to destroy the enemy's ability or at least his will to continue the fight, and second, because war is suffering, and even the winning side would like to have it done in as fast and efficient a way as possible. The thought of accomplishing all of that in one glorious, epic encounter is understandably seductive. To make it even more appealing, the "decisive battle" functions as the context in which grand deeds of individual heroism are framed. There is something undeniably flashy and memorable about actions that lead to the utter downfall of the enemy as opposed to months or years of attrition, or a long, bitter standoff in the trenches in which neither side seems to make any significant progress. For some historians and for many fans of military history, the "decisive battle" serves as a symbolic representation of the inherent superiority of the winning side. And perhaps most insidiously, a focus on "decisive battles" is all too often a convenient way of reducing complex historical events into a single, morally charged "turning point" which explains everything, all too conveniently.[19] But, for all its attractiveness, is there, or was there ever, such a thing as a decisive battle?

The Hapsburg field marshal Raimondo Montecuccoli (1609–1680) argued that "conquests and decisions can only be achieved by combat and battle and to believe otherwise is a delusion."[20] Furthermore and perhaps most pertinently to Chiang Kai-shek's analysis of his failure at Siping, Montecuccoli insisted on an immediate and aggressive follow-up to a decisive battle: "The remnants of the routed army must be hunted down and annihilated."[21] Napoleon, whose spirit has hung over the planning, prosecution, and history of war since the eighteenth century, sought to put Montecucolli's ideas into practice. Napoleon actively sought the decisive battle. His many followers and admirers developed ways of war that "emphasized numerical strength, deep strategic penetration, and rapid concentration of force on the decisive point."[22]

Politicians, generals, military historians, and the general public share a love of the idea of the decisive battle. But in practice, while battles may be easily found and bitterly fought, decisiveness has proved to be more elusive. Indeed, historian Russell Weigley argues that even between 1631 and 1815, the "age of battles," the decisive battle remained an ideal: in practice, "the age of battles . . . proved to be an age of prolonged, indecisive wars, wars sufficiently interminable that again and again, the toll in lives, not to mention costs in material resources, rose grotesquely out of proportion to anything their authors could hope to gain from them."[23] Weigley adds that the failure to achieve the hoped-for decisive defeat of the enemy in battle is related to the difficulty, *in practice,* of successfully pursuing and annihilating the enemy's retreating forces in the immediate aftermath of the (hopefully) decisive battle. Because the victor's mobile forces were often so severely weakened in the battle itself, "Even the greatest generals have rarely followed up triumphant battles with devastating pursuit."[24]

Whether or not the "decisive battle" ever existed in fact, the technological developments in warfare in the nineteenth and twentieth centuries put an end to the quest for dramatic decision in a short, sharp battle of annihilation. In the American Civil War and in the First and Second World Wars, the general's task was to wear the enemy down in a long war of attrition in which his rear areas, including civilian industry and civilian population, became legitimate targets in a "total war." In mid-nineteenth-century China, the imperial armies of the Qing Dynasty dealt with massive uprisings like the Taiping and Nian Rebellions (1850–1864 and 1851–1868, respectively) by progressively securing one sector after another, slowly and methodically drawing the circle ever tighter around the enemy, a technique that Chiang Kai-shek adapted to his own use to defeat the Chinese Communist party's rural base areas in the 1930s.[25] Mao Zedong, for his part, was known for avoiding decisive battle in favor of fighting smaller engagements designed to weaken the enemy over time. Both Mao and Chiang Kai-shek were familiar with the practice of falling back before a superior enemy, giving up space in order to gain time for a long war of attrition in which the enemy's need to administer and defend his newly acquired territory and its hostile population would weaken him in the long term. Still, Mao Zedong, his generals (many of them formally educated in the military arts), and Chiang Kai-shek and his generals were also familiar with the concept of the decisive battle. When they saw the opportunity, both Mao Zedong and

Chiang Kai-shek sought a resolution of conflict through overwhelming victory in battle.

For the Western historian and the Western reading public, the idea of the decisive battle remains as attractive as it was to Mao Zedong and to Chiang Kai-shek as they thought about the Second Battle of Siping. To be sure, Mao and his comrades in the Communist Party's Central Committee did not imagine that Lin Biao would annihilate the Kuomintang forces as they attacked Siping. In their view, the decisiveness of the battle would come when Lin broke Chiang Kai-shek's will to continue the fight, thus leading to a decisive victory at the negotiating table. As we will see, they hoped that George Marshall would contribute toward that goal by encouraging Chiang to agree to a ceasefire on terms acceptable to the Communists. Chiang, for his part, and particularly in hindsight, clearly viewed the Second Battle of Siping in more traditional "decisive battle" terms as the place and time in which his armies should have destroyed his enemy's *ability* to wage war. Observers from Joseph McCarthy to Jung Chang and Jon Halliday share this more traditional understanding of "decisive battle" when they lament that Siping was the decisive battle that could have been.

"WHAT IF?" AND THE LESSONS OF HISTORY

When Chiang Kai-shek and others suggest that the civil war in Manchuria would have turned out otherwise if not for Marshall's negotiation of a ceasefire in the aftermath of the Second Battle of Siping, they are engaging, if only in a small way, in a brand of "what if" history that attributes tremendous historical influence to the decisions made by key individuals in the context of specific "turning point" events. It is a form of history that professional historians are very uncomfortable with, but one which makes for compelling reading and is therefore tremendously popular. "What if" scenarios and a focus on individual responsibility are particularly common in discussions of military history. After all, common sense and our own daily experience tell us that individuals do have at least a degree of freedom of choice, and that our choices do have concrete consequences. This gives us the confidence that we can (if we wish) learn from our mistakes and do better the next time around. By extension, "what if" history and a focus on personal responsibility are attractive because they seem to provide us with stories that may be comparable to contemporary or future events.

That, indeed, is the purpose of "what if" history. A plausible alternative scenario that hinges on a single individual or a small group of individuals making a different decision at a key moment in history is, in fact, a commentary on the present.[26] It also serves as a powerful example to be applied by analogy to future crisis moments when it seems that the fate of an enterprise, a nation, or humankind itself depends on a single person making the correct decision. For Westerners, the best-known "what if" scenario is that of British Foreign Minister Neville Chamberlain at Munich in 1938. In his negotiations with Adolf Hitler, Chamberlain famously agreed to allow Hitler to take the German-speaking Sudetenland from Czechoslovakia. This, he said, would achieve "peace in our time." When Hitler later continued to push to bring Austria under German rule, and then to invade Poland, leading to World War II, critics accused Chamberlain of "appeasement," suggesting that if he had stood firm against Hitler in Munich, events in Europe might have turned out very differently. Ever since, Western diplomats who negotiate with states that are popularly perceived as being aggressive run the risk of being accused of "appeasement." The fact that historians have pointed out that Hitler himself was disappointed with the outcome of the Munich Conference, that he had expected the British to stonewall and thus give him an excuse for war—a war for which Britain was not prepared—simply does not register on the popular consciousness.[27] That is the key to the power and the popularity of "what if" scenarios focusing on personal responsibility: they provide clear, unambiguous historical lessons.

This is precisely where professional historians and popular histories part ways. The general reading public looks to history for clear lessons that will explain the present and offer guidance or even predictions for the future. Knowing that command decisions do make a difference, the reading public wants to know about who made what decisions, why they made them, and what they could have done differently. This is especially attractive to those who have lost a war. They (and their descendants for generations) find some solace in the idea that they could have won if not for the foolishness of a particular commander or politician. But when a non-academic reader looks to the work of historians for answers she or he does not find a clearly sign-posted road to the future. Instead he sees, in the words of Sir Michael Howard, "workmen, busily engaged in tearing up what he had regarded as a perfectly decent highway; doing their best to discourage him from proceeding along it at all; and warning him, if he does, that the surface is temporary, that they have no idea when it will be completed, nor where it leads, and that he proceeds at his own risk."[28]

In this study of the Chinese Communist and Nationalist forces, their leaders, and the American negotiators before, during, and in the aftermath of the Second Battle of Siping, I hope to strike a happy medium between the general public's desire to learn lessons from history and the professional historian's concern with scholarly rigor, nuance, and context. As we look at the unfolding of events in Manchuria, we will consider the roles of the major leaders: Mao Zedong, Chiang Kai-shek, and George Marshall. We will also introduce and consider the roles and significance of other leaders including the general Lin Biao, commander of the Communist forces in Manchuria, Nationalist general Du Yuming, and some of the officers serving under both men. As we look at the road to battle, at the Second Battle of Siping itself, and at how the war developed afterward, we will want to consider the organization, capabilities, and leadership of the forces on both sides, the goals that the men in the field were expected to achieve, and the ways in which commanders on the ground did (or did not) learn and apply lessons in the process of battle. In the long run, we will also be asking what broader lessons military leaders, political leaders, and historians would suggest that we learn from the Second Battle of Siping, and why.[29]

2

The Manchurian Chessboard

August–September 1945

Chinese chess, or *xiangqi*, like Western chess, is a game of strategy, based on war and played with pieces laid out on a board.[1] But while the kings, queens, bishops, knights, castles, and pawns of Western chess move from square to square, Chinese chess is played on a grid of ten horizontal and nine vertical lines, with the vertical lines interrupted in the middle by a space representing a river. The players move their generals and advisors, ministers, elephants, chariots, horses, cannons, and soldiers along the vertical and horizontal lines of maneuver, advancing and retreating, blocking, pinning, capturing, and skewering in an attempt to checkmate or stalemate their opponent.

To understand Chinese chess, it is important to understand the board, the pieces, and their positions. The same holds true for understanding the civil war in Manchuria. Siping became a focal point in that war in the spring of 1946 not because of its size, but because it happened to be located at a key strategic point on the map. In order to understand the battle of Siping and the lines of retreat and advance that brought the Communists and the Nationalists to a showdown in this otherwise unremarkable railway town, we need to look carefully at the major natural and manmade geographical features of China's great Northeast, or Manchuria. We need also to consider the ways in which Japanese and Soviet occupation established the context in which the Communists and Nationalists took their initial positions on the map and in which the early days of the struggle for control over Manchuria was played out.

FORTRESS MANCHURIA

From a strategic point of view, Manchuria seems to have been designed specifically as a launching pad for invading China. In 1945 Manchuria consisted of the three provinces of Heilongjiang, Jilin, and Liaoning (see map 2.1). At the time, these provinces included parts of what is, on a modern map of the People's Republic of China, the northern corner of the Nei Mongol (Inner Mongolia) Autonomous Region.[2] To the north and east are the Russian Federation's Siberia and Far Eastern Province, both parts of the Soviet Union in the 1940s. To the south, bordered by the Tumen and Yalu Rivers and the Changbai Mountains, is North Korea, a client state of the Soviet Union from 1945 through 1991.

From the mouth of the Yalu River the Manchurian coastline swings down around the Liaodong Peninsula and on to the Chinese border town of Shanhaiguan, giving Manchuria several important seaports: Andong (now called Dandong), Dalian, Lüshun, Yingkou, and Huludao. The Liaodong Peninsula, pointing south toward the Shandong Peninsula, is home to two of these ports (Lüshun and Dalian), thus giving the Liaodong Peninsula special strategic importance and making it a traditional point of entry into Manchuria for Chinese migrants coming by boat from Shandong. Andong, relatively remote, played little role in the events of 1945 through 1948. Yingkou, Huludao, Lüshun, and Dalian, however, were all key areas in the Civil War. Also important was Qinhuangdao, a port located in Hebei Province just south of the Great Wall, not far from Shanhaiguan.

On land, the Southwestern Highlands and the Greater Xing'an (Khingan) mountains set the core areas of Manchuria off from China Proper (that is, the agricultural areas below the line roughly demarcated by the Great Wall) and from Inner and Outer Mongolia. The mountainous terrain between China and Manchuria is pierced by several passes. The most important, Shanhaiguan, the "First Pass Under Heaven," consists of a narrow strip of land, only a few kilometers wide, between the sea and the mountains. Shanhaiguan was the endpoint of the Ming Dynasty's Great Wall. Because it is the most direct route from the North China plain to Manchuria, a major road and, in modern times, the Beijing–Shenyang railway line passed through Shanhaiguan. The road and

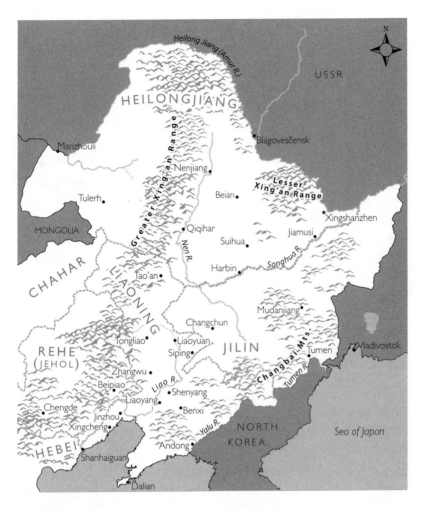

MAP 2.1. The three northeastern provinces (Manchuria) and neighboring areas, 1945. *Map by Tracy Ellen Smith.*

railway follow a narrow strip of coastal plain (less than fifty kilometers wide) known as the Liaoxi Corridor from Shanhaiguan up to the railway junction city of Jinzhou (see map 2.2).

Around ten kilometers north of Shanhaiguan another pass, Jiumenkou, offers a more difficult but still feasible invasion route between Manchuria and China. The terrain around Jiumenkou is so mountainous and the pass so narrow (only four meters or so wide in some places) that it never became a major road or rail transportation route. But by virtue of its position Jiumenkou, as we shall see, poses a particular challenge to any force (whether based in Manchuria or in China Proper) hoping to defend Shanhaiguan because it does provide a route through which an opposing force can try to go around Shanhaiguan and approach it from the rear.[3] Much farther north, another road and railway route connected the northern Chinese city of Chengde (the capital of Rehe Province) to the Manchurian city of Jinzhou. Because Chengde itself lies 230 kilometers northeast of Beijing, the route from Chengde to Jinzhou, though a possible line along which an army could invade Manchuria, was too remote and thus not a realistic alternative to Shanhaiguan. Nonetheless, if one controlled both Rehe Province and Liaoning, Chengde could serve as a staging point from which to send troops into Manchuria. Control of Rehe and of the Chengde–Jinzhou railway line thus became important to both the Communist and Nationalist forces.

Historically, the mountains and the seas kept Manchuria politically, culturally, and economically distinct from China Proper, whose people saw themselves as living "within the pass" (i.e., "inside," on the Chinese side, of Shanhaiguan). They were agricultural people who identified themselves as "Han people" after the Han Dynasty, which had ruled China from 206 BCE to 220 CE. Manchuria itself was the home of various tribal peoples, most notably the Jurchens and, in the eastern parts of the region (now allocated to Inner Mongolia), pastoral Mongol tribes. Large parts of Liaoning Province were at times under the control of kingdoms based in Korea and had Korean populations. In pre-modern times, the people of Manchuria subsisted on a mixed economy including farming (particularly in the river valleys of central Manchuria), hunting, fishing, trade, animal husbandry, and, in the Mongolian areas, pastoralism. Although not nomadic, many Jurchens raised horses and were known for their cavalry skills.

Chinese imperial regimes like the Qin, Han, Tang, Song, and Ming Dynasties exercised little if any control over the territory and people of Manchuria. Some sent armies into Manchuria, often on the way to campaigns on the Korean peninsula. More generally, some Chinese regimes, notably the Ming, controlled the Liaoxi Corridor and extended a loose control, when they could, over the agricultural regions of Liaoning most easily accessible via Shanhaiguan. Otherwise, they used trade privileges, gifts, and occasional, limited military interventions as carrots and sticks in an attempt to "use barbarians to control barbarians" and prevent the formation of large, powerful tribal confederations that might come through the passes to raid—or even conquer—Chinese territory.

The concern about invasion was more than justified. While Chinese regimes found it impossible to project military force very far into Manchuria for very long, several empires operating from Manchuria invaded and occupied parts of China. Manchuria's hybrid culture of nomads, hunters, and farmers and its being close to, but geographically distinct from, China Proper made it possible for the dominant groups in Manchuria to absorb elements of Chinese culture and technology, create confederations within Manchuria itself, and mobilize resources to launch successful military campaigns "south of the passes."[4] In 937 the Khitans, based in eastern Inner Mongolia and Manchuria, incorporated into their Liao Empire a slice of Chinese territory stretching from the town of Datong to modern Beijing to the sea. In 1129 the Jurchens, a tribal people in Manchuria, having conquered the Liao in 1123, captured all of northern China from the Song Dynasty (960–1279). Northern China remained under the control of the Jurchen Jin Dynasty (1115–1234) until it, and eventually the Song, and Manchuria itself, were incorporated into the Mongol Yuan Dynasty (1271–1368).

The Yuan Dynasty's successor, the Ming Dynasty (1368–1644), whose rulers were Han Chinese from the Yangzi valley, found it impossible to control any of Manchuria other than the Liaoxi Corridor and the agricultural areas of Liaoning. In the sixteenth century, in an attempt to fend off invasions from the nomadic and hunting peoples of Mongolia and Manchuria, the Ming built a system of walls and fortresses, often following the natural contours of the terrain. This "Great Wall," as it is now known, became the effective boundary between Ming China and Manchuria.[5] The defenses at Shanhaiguan, Jiumenkou, and other passes, and a system of walls and garrisons to protect the Liaoxi Corridor, were key parts of this system.

In the end, neither the Great Wall nor the Ming government's attempts to keep the Jurchen tribes divided and weak by "using barbarians to control barbarians" achieved the desired goal. In the late sixteenth and early seventeenth centuries, a Jurchen chief named Nurhaci (1558–1626) and his son Huangtaiji (1592–1643) knit the Jurchens together, gave them a writing system, re-named them "Manchus," organized them into a powerful fighting force of eight units, or "Banners," and established a Chinese-style dynasty, the Qing, in 1636. In 1644, with the Ming reeling from popular rebellions, the Manchu leaders incorporated key Ming armies into their own forces, came through Shanhaiguan and Jiumenkou, and proceeded to incorporate all of China into their Great Qing Empire, which remained in power until 1912.

As Manchus, the Qing, ruling from the former Ming capital of Beijing, were the first to incorporate all of Manchuria into an empire administered from China.[6] However, the Manchus did not want to see their ancestral homeland settled by and dominated by Chinese. Chinese farmers had been settled in southern Manchuria (i.e., Liaoning Province) for generations, but laws and a line of demarcation known as the Willow Palisade prohibited Chinese from settling in the northern and western regions, which were to be preserved as areas for Manchus and Mongols, respectively.[7] Small communities of Koreans, whose presence dated back to earlier times when large parts of Manchuria were parts of the Korean kingdoms of Goguryeo (also spelled "Koguryo," 37 BCE–668 CE) and Balhae (also spelled "Parhae," 628–926), lived in the areas near the Korean border.

Despite the ban on migration into the Manchu homeland (which ended in 1902), hunger for land and trade brought waves of Han Chinese migrants across the Bohai Gulf from Shandong and through Shanhaiguan from northern China to "adventure east of the pass" to seek their fortunes in Liaoning and beyond. By 1912, the Manchus, who had been minority rulers over their vast Chinese population from the beginning, were also a small minority in Manchuria itself. Very few Manchus, either in China or in Manchuria, spoke, read, or wrote the Manchu language. The wealthy Manchu elite still dominated the government and the military, but ordinary Manchu soldiers, known as Bannermen, often lived in poverty.

Manchu weakness in 1912 was reflected not only in their numerical inferiority and the loss of much of their cultural identity, but also in debilitating political decline. From the mid-nineteenth century onward, the Qing empire had been hit internally by environmental degradation, population pressure, and rebellions, and externally by aggression from the industrialized European nations and Japan. As a result, the Manchu Qing rulers had lost the loyalty of the Han Chinese elite who made up the bulk of their intellectuals, their government bureaucrats, and the soldiers and officers of their new, modernized army units. In 1912, a republican revolution overthrew the Qing Dynasty and established a new state: the Republic of China. As the successor state of the Qing Empire, the Republic of China inherited Qing territory, including Manchuria. By this time, new economic developments and new trends in the international situation had combined to put a new twist on Manchuria's strategic significance.

When looked at from within, Manchuria can be thought of as a series of concentric circles (see map 2.1). The inner circle is the Manchurian plain, a vast area of flat arable land including the cities of Harbin, Changchun, Siping, and Shenyang. The Manchurian plain is watered by the Liao, Songhua (Sungari), Nen, Xiliao, Zhuoer, and other rivers and extends one thousand kilometers from north to south and four hundred to five hundred kilometers from east to west. Surrounding the Manchurian plain are the Eastern Highlands, the Greater and Lesser Xing'an ranges, and the Southwestern Highlands. The Songhua River valley, extending northeast from Harbin to Jiamusi, separates the Eastern Highlands from the Lesser Xing'an and offers a transportation route from the Central Plain to Russia (formerly the Soviet Union).[8]

In pre-modern times, Manchuria's plains, mountains, rivers, and ports had supported an economy that featured a combination of agriculture, animal husbandry, hunting, trapping, fishing, and trade. By the late nineteenth century, massive waves of Han Chinese migration and the advent of the industrial revolution had given Manchuria new significance as a center of agricultural production, forest products, and industry. Chinese farmers converted the Manchurian plain into one of the world's greatest producers of soybeans. The mountains of the Lesser and Greater Xing'an ranges held vast reserves of timber. The mountains of the eastern and southwestern highlands held great reserves of coal, iron, and other minerals. The great Northeast, regarded in the Qing as the spiritual homeland of the Manchus, had the potential to be a modern agricultural and industrial powerhouse. Investment, intervention, and outright occupation by two foreign powers, Russia and Japan, played a major role in building modern Manchuria's infrastructure and economy.

MANCHURIA UNDER FOREIGN OCCUPATION

Manchuria's strategic importance and economic potential had attracted the attention of foreign powers even before the fall of the Qing in 1912. By the eve of the Battle of Siping in 1946, Manchuria had experienced nearly a century of influence by Russia and Japan, fourteen years of Japanese occupation (1931–1945), and, at the end of the Second World War, a Soviet invasion and occupation (August 1945–March 1946). Foreign influence, invasion, and occupation were crucial in shaping the human geography, the transportation infrastructure, and the economy of the Northeast. The historical, diplomatic, and strategic context in which the struggle for Manchuria was played out in 1946 was the product of nearly a century of foreign influence which shaped everything from the roles of the foreign powers to the layout of the streets of Manchurian cities, including Siping itself.

The Russians were the first foreign power to force their way into Manchuria. In the eighteenth and nineteenth centuries, the Russian empire expanded deep into Turkic Central Asia and across Siberia to the Pacific coast and the port of Vladivostok (an area that they acquired from the Qing). As a result, nineteenth-century Russian strategists were deeply concerned about the defense of their borders with China. How could the far-flung Asian territories of the empire be knit more closely to European Russia? How could supplies and troops be quickly and efficiently transported to potential trouble spots along the border with China and of the port of Vladivostok? The answer was simple: railways.[9]

Building the railways was not so simple. The politicking, the jockeying for power, the choice of routes, the raising of funds, and the surveying, mapping, and engineering of the Trans-Siberian railroad is a fascinating story in and of itself.[10] By 1899, one could travel by rail from Moscow to Lake Baikal. A ferry across Lake Baikal took the traveler to a short line from the lake to Chita, a trading town about eight hundred kilometers east of Irkutsk. From here, the Russian railway engineers faced a severe challenge. The route from Chita around Chinese Manchuria and down to Vladivostok was circuitous, and the terrain forbidding. In 1896, the engineering challenges alone had convinced the Russian railway engineers to look into the shorter and technically less difficult route straight across Manchuria to Vladivostok.

The practical requirements of engineering were reinforced by concern about a new strategic threat. In 1894–1895, Japan had fought and won a war with the Qing Dynasty over control of Korea. It was clear to Moscow that an expanding Japanese empire on the Asian mainland posed a threat to Russian Siberia. The fastest way to link Vladivostok to the Trans-Siberian railway and to extend Russian influence into Manchuria (thus building strategic depth) would be to build a railway line from Chita across Manchuria to Vladivostok. In 1895, in what is known as the "Triple Intervention," Russia, Germany, and France forced Japan to give up the Liaodong Peninsula, which it had captured during the Sino-Japanese War of 1894–1895. Subsequent negotiations with the Qing Empire (and a large bribe to the Chinese diplomat representing the interests of the Qing court) resulted in the signing of a secret alliance and a railway contract in 1896.[11] Under the agreement, the Russians built the Chinese Eastern Railway. Completed in 1903, this rail line ran from the Siberian border across northern Manchuria through the city of Harbin and onward to Vladivostok. In further negotiations, Russia also acquired the right to use the ports of Lüshun (known in the West as Port Arthur) and Dalian on the Liaodong Peninsula and to construct another rail line, the South Manchurian Railroad. This line ran north from Lüshun through Shenyang, up to Siping, Changchun, and then to Harbin, where it connected with the Chinese Eastern Railway (see map 2.2).

The coming of the railways brought Russian railway workers and managers, soldiers, banks and bankers, businessmen, and all the accoutrements that went along with the expatriate communities that European imperialism generated across the globe. In Harbin, "the Moscow of the East," Russian buildings, Russian orthodox churches with their distinctive onion domes, and Russian restaurants, newspapers, nightclubs, and shops catered to a substantial expatriate Russian community.[12] In smaller places like Siping, the Russian influence was also felt, though to

MAP 2.2. The Manchurian railway system, 1945–1948. *Map by Tracy Ellen Smith.*

a lesser degree. The first Russians in Siping were railway workers, who came in 1899—along with a police station. Over the next four years, the railway line gave shape to the town itself.[13] A railway station, hotels, various and sundry businesses, and three main streets were built in front of the railway station.[14] The construction of the railway and the railway station also dictated that the town would develop in two parts, with the Tiexi (west of the tracks) area toward which the station faced being the main business and administrative district, while Tiedong, east of the tracks and behind the railway station, was more working-class.

The Chinese Eastern Railway, the South Manchurian Railway, and various smaller branch lines built over the years generated considerable economic growth in Manchuria. Railway construction and associated economic activity contributed to the incentives that drew wave upon wave of Chinese migration into Manchuria. Population centers and mining activity grew up along the railway lines.[15] The railways also brought economic benefits to the Russian workers, railway employees, and Russian businesses that sprang up along with the railways. But for the Russian government, the Trans-Siberian, the China Eastern Railway, and the South Manchurian Railway were economic dead weights. These expensive rail lines, built with borrowed money, never generated enough revenue in trade, in freight charges, or in taxes to pay their way.[16] Nor did Russia's Manchurian railways fulfill their strategic function of enabling Russia to fend off the advance of Japanese power. In the Russo-Japanese War of 1904–1905, Japan defeated the Russians not only at sea, but also in land battles fought in Manchuria.

Most of the Russo-Japanese War was fought over control of ports, railways, and railway cities—the same ones that would play key roles in the fighting between the Communist and Nationalist forces some forty years later. The war began on 8 February 1904 with Admiral Togo's stunning surprise attack on the Russian fleet as it lay at anchor at Port Arthur (Lüshun). The Japanese goal was to control the sea and then strike the Russians hard and fast, before they could send reinforcements from Russia to Manchuria.[17] Converging on the South Manchurian Railway south of Shenyang (then known in the West as Mukden), three Japanese armies fought their way north. The last major land battle of the war, the Battle of Mukden, (20 February–10 March 1905) ended when the Russians withdrew to Siping.[18] There, they hastily constructed a new line of fortifications, gathered their substantial reserve forces, and prepared for what they hoped would be the decisive battle that would stop the Japanese in their tracks and even turn the tide of the war in favor of Russia.[19]

Russian and Japanese advance scouting parties, probing south and north, respectively, had minor encounters in the Siping area. These maneuvers must have been disconcerting to the Chinese residents of Siping and the surrounding towns and villages, who are said to have sabotaged railroad and telegraph lines in order to obstruct both Russian and Japanese military maneuvers.[20] In the end, the decisive battle at Siping that the Russian commanders hoped for never came. The Japanese, exhausted by their rapid advance to the north of Shenyang, were not prepared to attack. Political unrest back in Russia, and Japan's spectacular sinking of the Russian Baltic fleet in the Straits of Tsushima (27–28 May 1905), convinced Russia to agree to peace negotiations.[21] The war formally came to a close with the signing of the Treaty of Portsmouth on 5 September 1905.

The Treaty of Portsmouth brought Japan into Manchuria as a second foreign power, competing with Russia for influence. As part of the peace agreement with Russia, Japan acquired a long-term lease on the port cities of Lüshun and Dalian, the South Manchurian Railway, and all the interests and privileges that came with having an imperialist toehold in Manchuria. South Manchuria, with its coal, iron, and steel industries, railways, and ports, came under Japanese domination. The Russians remained powerful in the north, with Harbin still the home to a large Russian expatriate community. Siping lay in between. Japanese influence in Manchuria grew steadily over the next two decades and more. Before and after China's Nationalist Revolution of 1911, Japanese railway personnel moved into cities and towns from the port of Dalian to Shenyang to places like Siping. The last Russian military train pulled out of Siping station on 11 May 1906, and the Japanese military moved in.[22] In 1908 Japan officially gained the right to a railway concession area in Siping in which Japanese law—not the laws of the Qing Dynasty—would reign supreme.

As Japan continued to strengthen its presence in Manchuria, Japanese and Korean banks (the latter run by Japanese, who had made Korea a Japanese colony in 1910) gained control of financial markets. A Japanese army, the Kwantung Army, moved in to guard the railways and Japanese interests generally. Tensions with Russia and with its successor, the Soviet Union, continued to build. At the same time, ultra-nationalists and some elements of the Japanese military believed that Japan needed to be more aggressive about asserting its interests on the Asian mainland, and particularly in Manchuria. On 18 September 1931, young officers of the Kwantung Army set off an explosion along the railway line near Shenyang (then known as Mukden) in order to manufacture an excuse to take over all of Manchuria. In the wake of this "Mukden Incident," Manchuria was transformed into "Manchukuo," ostensibly an independent country ruled by the last Qing emperor Aisin Gioro Puyi, but in reality a Japanese colony.

The Japanese Kwantung Army hoped that under Japanese management, Manchuria would become an economic lifeline for Japan.[23] Japanese business conglomerates known as "zaibatsu" were encouraged to invest in agriculture, mining, railways, and industry.[24] Private enterprise proved unwilling to invest as much as was needed; therefore, Kwantung Army officials initiated a government-sponsored Five-Year Plan to boost economic development. In late 1937, the government established a close partnership with one of the newer zaibatsu: Nissan. With government sponsorship and control of the South Manchurian Railway Company, Nissan's newly inaugurated Manchurian Heavy Industries Corporation played a major role in turning Manchukuo into one of the top ten industrial bases in the world. The driving force behind the development of Manchukuo was to establish a rational, state-controlled exploitation of the area's agricultural, mineral, and other resources to strengthen Japan's strategic position in the world.[25] By 1940, Manchurian industries supplied Japan with "significant amounts of coal, pig iron, steel ingots, gold, chemical fertilizers, and other essential commodities."[26] This industrial base, developed under Japanese administration, would later play an important part in the civil war between the Chinese Communist and Nationalist parties between 1945 and 1949. In addition, the Japanese colonial administration's extensive state-owned industrial and agricultural enterprises, confiscated by the Chinese Communist Party when it took control of Manchuria in 1948, formed the beginnings of the People's Republic of China's state-owned enterprises in the Northeast.

Japan's colonial administration of Manchuria was an economic success, but it was not unopposed by the Chinese population of the area. Chiang Kai-shek had ordered armies formally under his command, including the Manchurian warlord Zhang Xueliang's Northeast Army, to withdraw in the face of the Kwantung Army's aggression on 18 September 1931. It galled Chiang to do so, but he knew very well that his forces were not capable of taking on the vastly superior Japanese army. Furthermore, Chiang was, at the same time, engaged in a series of campaigns in which he hoped to defeat Mao Zedong's Communist guerrilla forces in southern China. Believing that he should first deal with the internal (and, from a military point of view, weaker) threat and achieve stability within China before tackling the external threat, Chiang swallowed his pride and negotiated withdrawal and disengagement with the Japanese.[27]

Most of the Chinese population of Manchukuo did little or nothing to resist the Japanese. Ordinary farmers and workers could not afford to indulge in politics, protest, or rebellion: they needed to make a living and support their families regardless of who was in power. Urban elites generally collaborated with the Japanese.[28] But a hodgepodge of unofficial forces chose to fight. At first, the resistance forces were spontaneous, local in character, and had no overarching leadership or coordination.[29] Some were members of the Young Marshall's army who had stayed behind. Others included all types of people, from ordinary farmers to wealthy landowners to bandit gangs. The operations undertaken by these resistance groups generally ended in defeat and posed relatively little threat to the Japanese. Anti-Japanese forces quickly grew to around three hundred thousand, but by 1933, most of them had been defeated, dispersed, or surrendered.[30]

THE COMMUNIST ANTI-JAPANESE RESISTANCE
AND THE SOVIET RED ARMY

To the degree that there was any attempt to forge the disparate resistance groups into larger coalitions, it was done by former officers from Zhang Xueliang's Northeast Army. The Chinese Communist Party played no significant role in the initial stages of resistance against the Japanese. At the time, the Party Center was not willing to enter into "united front" relations with non-Communist organizations.[31] In addition, the Party had only a small presence in the major cities of the Northeast, and virtually none at all in the rural villages.[32] Only after 1933, when the Soviet Union advocated a harder line against Japan, did the Chinese Communist Party get involved, sending a number of agents including Zhou Baozhong (1902–1964).[33] Communist Party agents then began to work with a large number of disparate guerrilla organizations across Manchuria, none of them yet under any form of unified command. Zhou and other Communist Party members worked to integrate a number of the resistance forces into a Communist-led "Northeast United Anti-Japanese Army" in 1937.[34] In practice, however, lack of communications between the central command and the individual units of the Northeast United Anti-Japanese Army meant that the various units of the army remained highly independent.[35]

These Chinese forces used guerrilla tactics—small-unit operations, surprise attacks, ambushes, misdirection, and sudden strikes followed by rapid withdrawal—against the Japanese.[36] In 1937, following the Marco Polo Bridge Incident of 7 July, which marked the beginning of all-out war between Chiang Kai-shek's Republic of China and Japan, the Communist guerrilla forces in Manchuria were expected to coordinate their actions with those of the Communist resistance in China Proper, primarily to tie up Japanese troops in the Northeast so that they could not be spared for action against Chinese Communist base areas south of the Great Wall. This coordination was virtually impossible, however, as there was no direct contact between the Communist leaders in the Northeast and the Communist Party Center in Yan'an.[37]

The Japanese responded with a carefully planned, cruel, and effective counter-insurgency effort.[38] They moved farmers into protected villages in order to deprive the Communist guerrillas of popular support and inflicted heavy casualties on the resistance forces. In the absence of any direct contact with the Chinese Communist Party Central Committee in Yan'an, the Communist forces in the Northeast had to rely on the Soviet Union for leadership and for a place of refuge where they would periodically retreat, reorganize, and then return to Manchuria. In late 1940, at the request of the Soviets, Zhou Baozhong and other leaders withdrew a large portion of the guerrilla forces to the Manchuria-Soviet border, where the Soviet Union, concerned about its relations with Japan, insisted on keeping them.[39] The remaining Communist troops in Manchuria withdrew to the Soviet Union in 1942, where they were reorganized as an "International Brigade." From 1942 through August 1945 these Chinese Communist forces remained in the Soviet Union, training and infiltrating small teams into Manchuria to conduct guerrilla attacks and sabotage operations against the Japanese.[40]

In strictly military terms, the Chinese resistance forces in Manchuria, numbering perhaps three hundred thousand at the height of their strength, were of little significance. However, the presence of Communists among them and the continued, though very small-scale, guerrilla and sabotage operations carried out between 1942 and 1945 played an important part in the Communist Party's propaganda campaign after Japan's surrender. By exaggerating the roles played by Communists in the resistance, and downplaying the roles of non-Communist fighters, the Party could portray itself as having been on ground in Manchuria, leading fourteen years of resistance to Japanese rule. This in turn was presented to the general public, to the Soviets, and to the Americans as evidence that the Communist Party—and not the Nationalists—deserved to take control of the Northeast in the wake of the Japanese defeat in 1945.[41]

In the end, it was the Soviet Union, not Communist guerrillas, that defeated Japan's Kwantung Army, putting an end to fourteen years of Japanese control over China's three Northeastern provinces. The Soviet Union had inherited imperial Russia's economic and strategic interests in Manchuria. At the Yalta Conference of 4–11 February 1945, Franklin Roosevelt had agreed to give the Soviet Union control over the Manchurian railways, the commercial port of Dalian, and the military port of Lüshun (Port Arthur). In return, Joseph Stalin agreed to enter the war against Japan three months after the defeat of Germany. Then, the American atomic bombing of Hiroshima and Nagasaki convinced the Soviets to move ahead of schedule, lest the Japanese surrender before the Soviets could establish a physical presence in Manchuria.

The Soviet invasion of Manchukuo, described in detail by historian David Glantz, was a carefully prepared and professionally executed operation.[42] Nobody (including the Chinese Communist Party) had advance notice of when and how the attack would take place.[43] Secretly deploying overwhelming force to the Far East and advancing along every possible axis of invasion, the Soviets took advantage of rough terrain, poor weather, and darkness, taking the Japanese by surprise.[44] Soviet operations began on 9 August 1945. Within six days, the Red Army had achieved its objectives. And as the Soviets were crushing the Kwantung Army, Japan surrendered. As Mao Zedong observed, "The Americans dropped two atomic bombs on Japan, and they didn't surrender. Then the Soviets invaded Manchuria and that took care of it."[45]

The arrival of the Soviet Red Army marked the beginning of yet another episode of foreign occupation, this time one designed to advance the strategic and economic interests of the Soviet Union. In the short term, this meant the organized looting of Manchurian industry and raw materials for the benefit of the war-ravaged Soviet economy. From the Soviet point of view, confiscation of enemy (Japanese) wealth was simply well-earned compensation for the tremendous losses that the Soviet Union had incurred during the war against Japan's European ally, Nazi Germany. Soviet experts were sent to all the major industrial centers to assess the industrial base. Entire factories were dismantled. For example, the Hitachi works, which manufactured machinery and castings and employed over 1,125 workers in 1945, had only 37 of its original 333 pieces of machinery in place when Colonel Robert Rigg, an American officer, inspected it in 1946. The Manchurian Electric Wire Company, employing 2,342 people in 1945, lost 96 percent of its machinery as well as finished and unfinished goods, most of it taken by the Soviets, who shipped it out on 260 railway cars.[46] Equipment, raw materials, and finished products were shipped to the Soviet Union by rail and by sea. If the machinery was too large to fit through the doors, walls would be torn down. When the workload became greater than the limited number of Soviet technicians could handle, Japanese technicians were forced to help to take industrial machinery apart and move it out.

The Soviet occupation undoubtedly caused some serious short-term damage to industries in Manchuria. The Americans, the Nationalist government, and even the Chinese Communist Party's Northeast Bureau (the Party's leadership organ in Manchuria—see below) were concerned about the Soviet Union's actions.[47] Nonetheless, the raw materials, railways, roads, ports, and other resources and infrastructure that had formed the basis of Japanese-occupied Manchuria's economic system remained in place and contributed to making the area a valuable prize in the eyes of both the Nationalist government and the Chinese Communist Party.

The Soviet occupation also had some negative effects on the Chinese residents of the Northeast (to say nothing of Japanese and other foreign civilians). As they entered the Northeast, Soviet soldiers were deeply impressed with the poverty of the rural areas. Their officers, as would be expected, warned them to respect the customs, persons, and property of the Chinese people, whom they were liberating from Japanese imperialism.[48] In Shenyang, Chinese citizens were initially thankful to the Soviets for having defeated the Japanese. The Soviet commander even allowed Chinese to join in the looting of Japanese property—after making sure that his men had taken what they wanted.[49] Foreign nationals—Japanese and Germans—were not so fortunate. A German merchant in Mukden described how Russians searched his house, threatening to shoot his whole family, if he did not turn over "secret military plans." Then, acknowledging that that a merchant would not have such plans in the first place, the Russians insisted that the German drink beer with them.[50]

By September, relations between the Soviet Red Army and the people of Shenyang had taken a turn for the worse. Soviet soldiers, perhaps unable or unwilling to distinguish between Chinese and Japanese, searched everywhere for items of value, entering homes and holding up civilians on the streets. Chinese were drafted as forced labor to help to dismantle and move industrial goods and equipment from the factories. Instances of Russian soldiers harassing and raping Japanese and Chinese women were common enough to have had a particularly negative impact on the reputation of the Red Army and the Soviet Union. As an elderly resident of Jinzhou recalled, the Russian soldiers "loved to drink and chase women."[51] City residents blocked off small residential streets at night in order to keep the Russian soldiers out. According to some accounts, there were even instances in which Chinese killed Russian soldiers who threatened their safety. This may have contributed to the initial suspicion with which many residents of the Northeast viewed the Chinese Communist Party as it tried to establish a military and political presence.[52] The Soviet dismantling of industry also put large numbers of Chinese factory hands out of work. This both led to social instability and created a pool of potential recruits for the Chinese Communist armies.[53]

Soviet looting of industry and the criminal misbehavior of poorly disciplined soldiers were of great concern at the time and to those Chinese individuals directly involved, but had relatively little long-term effect on China in general or the Northeast in particular. The real significance of the Soviet Red Army's occupation of Manchuria was that it created ideal conditions for the Chinese Communist Party to gain a foothold in an area in which, despite their claim to having led fourteen years of resistance against the Japanese, they had no organizational presence at the beginning of August 1945. As we will see below, the Soviet Union assisted the Chinese Communists in the Northeast in a number of important and sometimes very complicated ways. But their help to their Chinese comrades began in a very simple and straightforward manner. When the Soviet Red Army invaded Japanese Manchukuo, it brought along with it the first contingent of Chinese Communist soldiers to be active in Manchuria since the early 1940s.

These first Communist units on the ground in Manchuria were none other than Zhou Baozhong's resistance forces, which had retreated from Manchukuo to the Soviet Union in 1941–1942. Six hundred of these Chinese soldiers were parachuted into key cities in Manchuria to do reconnaissance and intelligence-gathering for the Soviet Red Army as it commenced its operations against the Japanese.[54] These and subsequent teams worked the Soviets to establish control of scores of strategic points across Manchuria. As they did so, they also established a Communist party presence in these areas, organized local, Communist-dominated governments, and re-activated Communist Party members who had remained behind, living under Japanese occupation. As his troops became established in Manchuria, Zhou Baozhong changed their name to the Northeast People's Self-Defense Army. Recruiting new soldiers, his forces quickly grew to seventy thousand.[55] But in those early days of the Soviet invasion of Japanese Manchukuo, it was still not clear exactly what role the Northeast would play in the Chinese Communists' plans for the rapidly approaching post-war era.

THE COMMUNIST PARTY STAKES
ITS CLAIM TO MANCHURIA

The sudden Japanese surrender on 15 August 1945 gave the Kuomintang and the Communist Party new opportunities, accompanied by new challenges. Both sides—and the Chinese people as a whole—had suffered deeply since the Japanese takeover of Manchuria in 1931 and the Japanese invasion of China Proper in 1937. At the same time, the Communists and Nationalist armies had both acquired new strengths during the years of war against Japan.

The Nationalists had borne the brunt of Japanese aggression. Chiang Kai-shek's government had lost extensive territory to the Japanese, including the capital of Nanjing, Manchuria, and most of eastern China—in other words, the most economically and industrially advanced parts of the country. As late as 1945, Japan's Ichigo offensive had inflicted substantial casualties on Chiang's forces and had captured crucial rice-producing and army recruiting areas in Hunan Province. On the other hand, the war had brought Chiang new strengths in the form of American military aid and advisors. American aid was not enough to enable Chiang to defeat the Japanese. Nonetheless, it did enable him to build several armies either wholly or partly outfitted with American arms and equipment. Many of these American-trained and -equipped armies would play important roles in the post-1945 Civil War, and particularly in the Northeast.

The Communists, for their part, had also endured losses and setbacks at the hands of the Japanese. As noted above, Japan's Kwantung Army had successfully cleared Manchuria of Communist-led resistance forces. In northern China in 1941, the Japanese turned back a major Communist offensive, the Hundred Regiments Campaign.[56] The next year, Japanese troops followed up with the infamous "three alls" campaign: "Kill all, burn all, destroy all." This brutal but effective counter-insurgency operation was designed to clear entire areas of northern China of Chinese Communist power by destroying the rural agricultural economy and communities on which Communist guerrilla forces relied for intelligence, logistical support, recruits, and supplies. Then, from April 1944 to February 1945, the Ichigo offensive in South China drew Nationalist troops away from the Communist areas in North China and inflicted massive casualties on the Nationalist armies.[57]

Though hard-pressed by the Japanese, the Communists emerged from the war with new strengths. The simple fact that they were not the government of China allowed the Communists to score propaganda victories by portraying Chiang's government as weak and themselves, the Communists, as the party that was willing to stand up to the Japanese no matter what the sacrifice. The struggle against Japan provided the Communist party with perfect conditions for recruiting, both in the rural areas and from among patriotic urban intellectuals who found themselves frustrated with the Nationalist government's corruption and with its evident inability to mount effective resistance against Japan. Operating from Yan'an in the remote mountainous fastness of northern Shaanxi Province, far beyond the control of the Nationalist government, Mao Zedong's Communists were able to build extensive base areas in northwestern and northern China and Inner Mongolia. By the summer of 1945, the Communist base areas extended across northern China and Inner Mongolia from Ningxia and Shaanxi Provinces in the west to Shandong Province in the east and Rehe and parts of Liaoning Province in the north (see map 2.3). The Communist Party's two armies, the Eighth Route Army and the New Fourth Army, had a combined strength of 470,000 regulars and 2,100,000 militia.[58]

Together, simply by continuing to resist Japanese occupation, the Chinese Nationalist and Communist forces tied down Japanese troops and placed demands on Japanese military resources. But neither the Communists nor the Nationalists, separately or (occasionally) working together, were able to defeat the Japanese armies in China. When the Japanese surrender came, it was the result of the American Pacific campaign and American attacks on the Home Islands, including the atomic bombings of Hiroshima and Nagasaki and the Soviet invasion of Manchukuo. As these events were unfolding in the final months of the war, neither the Communists nor the Nationalists chose to risk their forces in any major operations against the Japanese. Instead, both were looking ahead to the likely resumption of their struggle for control over China. For the Nationalists, this meant preserving their strength, being ready to move into Japanese-occupied areas as soon as possible after the Japanese surrender, preventing the Communists from expanding beyond their base areas, and, ultimately, invading those base areas to eliminate the Communist threat once and for all. For the Communists, the pressing tasks of a post-Japanese surrender era would be to preserve their base areas and to establish a presence in the Japanese-occupied areas before the Kuomintang could get there.

In late 1945, acting on the assumption that the war against Japan would last into 1946, the Communist leadership made two choices in order to accomplish those tasks.[59] In northern China, that is, north of the Yangzi Valley, the Communist forces would make the transition from guerrilla to conventional warfare. Communist guerrilla forces would be reorganized into conventional units and begin to engage the Japanese (and, ultimately, the Kuomintang armies) in what the Chinese called "mobile warfare" (*yundongzhan*). In mobile warfare, army units maneuvering in the field would cut off and annihilate enemy forces. This transition from guerrilla to conventional warfare was very much in line with Mao Zedong's theory of guerrilla warfare and had his approval. But its chief proponent was Zhu De, the commander-in-chief of the Communist forces. Zhu had helped Mao to establish the Red Army in their guerrilla days in the remote mountains of Jinggangshan back in 1927. Unlike Mao, who was self-taught in military affairs, Zhu was a product of professional military training, having attended the Yunnan Military Academy in China and the University of Göttingen in Germany. Zhu's education and experience had made him a critic of guerrilla tactics and a strong proponent of conventional warfare and army professionalism—positions that had sometimes put him at loggerheads with the more romantic, amateurish, and intellectually adventurous Mao.[60]

The second part of the Communists' strategy in 1945 was more typically Maoist. It called for the development of new rural base areas south of the Yangzi, behind Japanese lines. Starting in 1944, Mao had begun sending crack regular units south to link up with small guerrilla forces and build these new base areas. As historian Christopher Lew points out, the Communist strategy, if successful, would have forced Chiang Kai-shek to fight both Communist guerrillas in the south and regular Communist forces in the north in the wake of the anticipated Japanese surrender. These plans did not come to fruition because Japan surrendered earlier than expected.[61]

As they planned for the transition from the war against Japan to the resumption of their civil war with Chiang Kai-shek, Mao and his comrades in the Communist Party leadership did not focus on Manchuria.

MAP 2.3. (*Opposite*) Chinese Communist base areas, August 1945. *Map by Tracy Ellen Smith.*

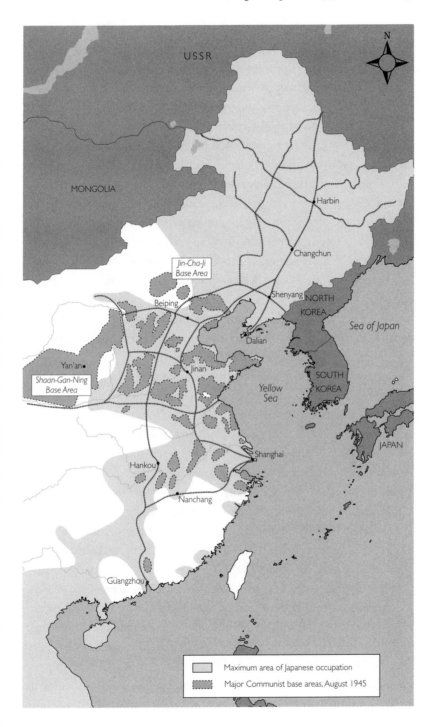

USSR

MONGOLIA

Harbin

Changchun

Jin-Cha-Ji
Base Area

Beiping

Shenyang   NORTH
KOREA

Dalian

Sea of Japan

Yan'an

Shaan-Gan-Ning
Base Area

Jinan

Yellow
Sea

SOUTH
KOREA

Hankou

Shanghai

JAPAN

Nanchang

Guangzhou

Maximum area of Japanese occupation

Major Communist base areas, August 1945

Nonetheless, they were aware that Japan's surrender would leave a power vacuum in Manchuria, and that both they and the Nationalists would want to move into that power vacuum. The Party had been actively looking at the Northeast in 1944, when they sent agents to the major cities to make contact with workers and to gather intelligence.[62] The Northeast had certainly acquired an important place in Mao's strategic thinking at least as early as May–June 1945. Mao noted the importance of Manchuria at the Seventh National Congress of the Chinese Communist Party in May 1945. In June, he remarked at a Party meeting that with Soviet assistance, the Communists could establish a secure base area in the Northeast, and that "we might lose our current bases, but so long as the Northeast is in our hands, the Chinese revolution is on an unbeatable foundation."[63] After 8 August 1945, the Communists were also keenly aware that the Soviet Red Army's presence in Manchuria could give them an advantage in gaining a foothold there.[64] Still, their attention remained concentrated, for the moment, on developing base areas in the south and preparing to defend existing base areas in the north. Manchuria was still regarded as a sideshow, but the Party leaders, particularly Liu Shaoqi, were keeping one eye on the developments in the Northeast.[65]

The Communists' first moves from their northern Chinese base areas into Manchuria were tentative and depended heavily on Soviet cooperation. On 11 August, Zhu De issued "Seven Orders of the Day," in which he called for the dispatch of four Communist units to the Northeast to assist the Soviets in their fight against the Japanese.[66] Three of these were units originally from Zhang Xueliang's Northeast Army, whose commanders (including one of Zhang Xueliang's younger brothers, Zhang Xuesi) had joined forces with the Communists—in other words, native sons of Manchuria whose involvement could add legitimacy to the Communists' argument that they were simply reasserting Chinese sovereignty over the northeastern territories lost to Japan in 1931. However, Zhu De's highly publicized orders were not meant to be carried out—at least not immediately. They were a propaganda move, a formal announcement to friends and enemies alike that the Communist Party intended to compete for a role in Manchuria. The Party leadership was keenly aware that the Soviet presence and the Soviet Union's international obligations made it impossible for them to simply send large numbers of troops directly into the Northeast. Also on 11 and 12 August, Zhu De issued separate, secret orders instructing three of the four units ordered into Manchuria to hold back until the Party Center at Yan'an could get a better understanding of the situation.

Of the four units publicly ordered into Manchuria, the closest, geographically, were forces stationed near the Rehe-Liaoning border area and under the command of Li Yunchang. Li, a graduate of the Whampoa Military Academy and a member of the Chinese Communist Party since 1925, had rich experience both in political organization and in combat against the Japanese. In August 1945, when Zhu De's orders were issued, Li's unit was too far from Yan'an to make direct contact with their under-powered radio equipment. As a result, Li first heard his orders through news reports. Re-establishing radio contact, Li soon found that in fact, his unit alone was to dispatch forces to Manchuria immediately in order to gather information and report back to the Party Center.[67] Li and his commanders formulated plans to advance toward Manchuria in three columns—west, central, and east—and awaited further orders.

The Communist Party's central leadership, too, was waiting. While the Chinese Communists were planning their advance into Manchuria, their international patron, the Soviet Union, was in the midst of nego-tiations with their enemy, Chiang Kai-shek's Nationalist Party govern-ment. Joseph Stalin, who was playing all sides of the power equation, wanted to ensure that Chiang's government would recognize Soviet eco-nomic and strategic interests in China, and particularly in Manchuria, in the post-war era. Like imperial Russia before it, the Soviet Union was intensely interested in the railway lines and ports of Manchuria. Chiang Kai-shek, for his part, hoped to play a balancing act in the emerging ri-valry between the Soviets and the Americans, giving limited privileges to each in order both to maintain China's independence and to link the interests of both foreign governments to the continuation of his own power.

Chiang's representatives and the Soviets signed the Sino-Soviet Treaty of Friendship and Alliance and an accompanying agreement on railways on 26 August. In return for port and railway privileges, the So-viet Union undertook to transfer sovereignty over Manchuria only to the armed forces and civilian government personnel of Chiang's Republic of China. The agreements left the Communist Party leadership uncertain as to whether or not they could send troops into Manchuria without causing a major diplomatic crisis for the Soviet Union. The Soviet Union, having reached an agreement with Chiang Kai-shek's government, was cutting back its support for the Communists in the Northeast and insisted that Mao respond to Chiang Kai-shek's invitation to come to Chongqing for peace talks (this is discussed further in chapter 3).[68] The Soviet Union's treaties with Chiang's government and the fact that the Soviets had occupied the major cities of the Northeast limited the Communists' freedom to operate in the area. As late as 23 August—on the eve of his departure for Chongqing—Mao Zedong had doubts as to whether the international situation would allow the Communist Party to send troops into the Northeast.[69]

Nonetheless, the Party Center felt confident enough of Soviet indulgence that even if troops could not be sent, it could send small numbers of cadres (Party/army officials) and troops on an exploratory basis.[70] Of the forces publicly ordered into Manchuria, only Li Yunchang's western column, commanded by Zeng Kelin and political commissar Tang Kai, was authorized to advance into Manchuria. On 28 August, Liu Shaoqi (who was acting as leader of the Party Center in Mao's absence) had decided that small numbers of troops could enter Manchuria.[71] On that day, Zeng and Tang's men entered Manchuria. They did not come through Shanhaiguan, which they feared would be too difficult to take from the two thousand Japanese and Manchukuo forces still stationed there. Instead, they slipped quietly through the smaller pass of Jiumenkou in the rain and proceeded posthaste toward the main rail line that led from Shanhaiguan to Jinzhou and Shenyang.[72]

On 29 August, the Party Center issued new instructions for Communist units advancing into Manchuria. Because the Soviets were bound by treaty to transfer sovereignty in Manchuria to the Nationalist government, there were strict limits as to what the Soviets could do and what kind of contact they could have with the Chinese Communist forces. Chinese Communist units were to proceed with caution, not to force the issue of direct, official contact with the Soviet Red Army, not to ask the Soviet forces for assistance, and not to use the railways to enter major cities. Chinese Communist forces entering Manchuria were to do so under

FIGURE 2.1. Zeng Kelin and Soviet officers planning the attack on Shanhaiguan, August 1945. *Courtesy of the Liao-Shen Campaign Memorial Hall.*

the guise of local, volunteer forces, with a minimum of publicity, to focus on rural areas and smaller towns and cities, and not to do anything that might cause diplomatic problems for the Soviets.[73]

In theory, Zeng Kelin and Tang Kai's men should have been bound by these orders. But when they advanced into Manchuria, they found themselves out of radio contact with Li Yunchang's headquarters. As a result, Zeng Kelin did not receive the new orders issued on 29 August. So, around nine o'clock in the morning on 30 August, when a Soviet patrol unit of some seventy-six men approached their position, the Communists hurriedly organized some buglers into a military band to make a proper welcome, complete with applause and heartily shouted slogans. The Soviets, unexpectedly encountering a group of unidentified armed men without uniforms, quickly maneuvered their cars, jeeps, and artillery, surrounded the welcoming Chinese Communists, and ordered them to surrender their weapons. After a few tense moments, Zeng and Tang, speaking through a Soviet interpreter, convinced the Soviet officers that they were indeed forces of the Chinese Communist Eight Route Army. Hugs and handshakes followed as a matter of course.

Since they could not be bound by orders that they had not received, Zeng and Tang proceeded to establish a working relationship with the Soviets. First, they convinced their new comrades to undertake a joint attack on the remaining Manchukuo "puppet" forces at Shanhaiguan. With the Soviets providing tanks and artillery support and the Chinese storming the walls, Shanhaiguan fell at nine o'clock on the night of 30 August. The capture of Shanhaiguan gave the Communists control over the main land route and railway line from China Proper to the Northeast. This would make it far easier for the Communists to transfer troops into the region, and even raised the possibility that they could successfully deny access to Chiang Kai-shek's armies.

With Shanhaiguan under control, Zeng and Tang hoped to get the Soviets to go one step further and capture the nearby port of Qinhuangdao, to which many of the Japanese had fled. The Soviet commander had been able to justify the attack on Shanhaiguan on the grounds that it lay directly on the border of Manchuria and China Proper, but Soviet involvement in an attack on Qinhuangdao, which was firmly in Hubei Province, would have been too open a violation of the Sino-Soviet treaty. Chiang Kai-shek's government forces soon took the surrender of the Japanese at Qinhuangdao, which the American Seventh Fleet would later use as a place to land Nationalist troops on their way to fight the Communists for control of Manchuria.

Unable to launch an attack on Qinhuangdao, Zeng Kelin and Tang Kai, stationing a garrison force at Shanhaiguan, moved by train (driven by a Japanese locomotive engineer) up the Liaoxi Corridor to Jinzhou toward Shenyang, leaving small forces at key towns along the rail line, including at Jinzhou, where the local Soviet commander welcomed them on 4 September. When Zeng, Tang, and two thousand men and officers arrived at Shenyang on 6 September, the Soviets were not so friendly. Soviet troops refused to allow the Chinese off their train, and the Soviet commander demanded to know who the men were, where they had come from, and who had sent them. Even when he understood that they were part of Mao Zedong's Eight Route Army, the Soviet officer told them, "According to the Yalta Agreement and the Sino-Soviet Treaty, the high command cannot agree to your entering Shenyang." After hours of nego-tiation, hampered by inept translators and losses of temper on both sides, the Soviets finally agreed to allow the Chinese to disembark and to set up a headquarters in the city. In order to minimize any potential diplo-matic embarrassment for the Soviet Union, Zeng Kelin, on Soviet advice (and with the approval of the Party Center) had his men remove all Eighth Route Army insignia and adopted the name "Northeast People's Autonomous Army" as the official designation of Chinese Communist troops in Manchuria.[74]

Zeng Kelin and Tang Kai's actions, although in violation of the or-ders of 29 August (which they had not received), were crucial in estab-lishing a Chinese Communist presence in Manchuria. They had cap-tured the key city of Shanhaiguan, created Communist military and political presence in key towns and cities along the Liaoxi Corridor, and asserted their right to be in the city of Shenyang. In the meantime the Communist Party Center had not remained idle. Small Communist reconnaissance teams from Shandong had crossed the Bohai Gulf, land-ing on the Liaodong Peninsula on 26 and 29 August. As reports came in from these units, from Zeng Kelin and Tang Kai, and from other sources, the Party Center began to attach more importance to the Northeast. In the aftermath of the victory at Shanhaiguan, Li Yunchang led three regiments and a battalion (a total of five thousand men) to the city. On 10 and 11 September, the Party Center ordered its forces in Shandong to transfer four divisions and twelve regiments (between 250,000 and 300,000 men) to the Northeast. Many of these soldiers had been looking forward to returning to their homes once Japan had been defeated and were less than enthusiastic about their new assignment.[75]

The fact that the Chinese Communists were making a bid to es-tablish a significant presence in Manchuria was increasingly obvious to Chiang Kai-shek, to the Americans, and to the Soviets. For the Soviets, it represented a diplomatic conundrum. The Soviet Union sympathized with and supported the Chinese Communist Party, but for global diplo-matic and strategic reasons, it had to act, or at least appear to act, more or less within the constraints of the Yalta Agreement and the Sino-Soviet treaty in which they had promised to transfer sovereignty over Manchu-ria to Chiang Kai-shek's government. As the Communist Party began to move its troops toward and into Manchuria, the ambivalence of Soviet policy was a major concern. Until they understood the Soviet position and the situation on the ground in the Northeast more clearly, the Communist Party's leaders in Yan'an preferred to act with caution. As a result, their goals in late August and early September were limited: take control of the railway line from Shanhaiguan to Shenyang and occupy Chahar and Rehe, the two provinces adjacent to Manchuria. A more ambitious move into the Northeast would need to await a clarification of Soviet policy.[76]

A NEW STRATEGY: MARCH ON THE NORTH, DEFEND IN THE SOUTH

On 14 September, a Soviet Douglas twin-engine airplane took off from Shenyang headed for Yan'an. On board were Zeng Kelin and a Soviet officer, Dmitri Belorussov.[77] Zeng's task was to give the Communist Party leadership a firsthand report on the events and conditions on the ground in Manchuria. Belorussov's job was to clarify the Soviet Union's attitude. Landing in Yan'an the next day, after an overnight refueling stop in Inner Mongolia, the two were hustled off to a meeting of the Communist Party's Politburo. Mao Zedong and Zhou Enlai were then in Chongqing for peace negotiations with Chiang Kai-shek. In charge of the Politburo was Liu Shaoqi, a veteran Communist Party leader and the author of an influential propaganda pamphlet entitled "How to Be a Good Communist." As second-in-command to Mao Zedong, Liu was responsible for making a decision based on Zeng's report and the statements of the Soviet officer.[78]

Zeng's report was highly encouraging. Communist cadres and troops were established in Shanhaiguan, Shenyang, and other strategic points. The Soviet Red Army was basically stationed along the main line of the China–Changchun railroad and the major cities. Most of Manchuria was in chaos and therefore available for the Communists to move in. Large supplies of Japanese weapons and ammunition were there for the taking, and it would be easy to build troop levels through recruitment and by incorporating former Manchukuo soldiers into the Communist ranks. Belorussov's news was not as good. The Soviet officer began by delivering a formal written message from General Malinovsky: neither Communist nor Chinese Nationalist troops would be allowed to enter the Northeast until the Soviet Red Army had ended its occupation and withdrawn from the territory. Any Communist units already on the ground must withdraw from the areas that they had occupied, particularly in major cities such as Shenyang, Dalian, and Changchun. In conversation, Belorussov was willing to be more flexible. The Communist units on Shenyang and other cities would not need to withdraw immediately, though they should be prepared to do so whenever asked, and the Soviets would not prevent the Chinese Communists from sending more forces from China Proper into areas of Manchuria not under Soviet occupation, as long as it was done discreetly and without using the names of the Eighth Route and New Fourth Armies.[79]

On the same day that Liu Shaoqi and the Politburo met with Zeng and Belorussov, they had received a report from Huang Kecheng, then leading the New Fourth Army's Third Division far to the south in Jiangsu Province. Huang was deeply concerned about the difficulties that Chinese Communist units had been experiencing as they tried to establish base areas in the mountainous rural areas of southern China in the weeks before and after the Japanese surrender. Knowing that the Soviet Red Army and some Chinese Communist units were already in Manchuria, Huang suggested that Communist forces withdraw from their many small base areas in the south and, instead, send large numbers of troops into the Northeast, whether the Soviet Union liked it or not.[80] Huang Kecheng's suggestion echoed other reports of the tremendous challenges and weak positions of the many small Communist units dispersed in isolated base areas in southern China, where they were vulnerable to attack from government forces.

Taking the situations in the Northeast and in the south into consideration, Liu Shaoqi and the Politburo decided to make a fundamental change in the Communist Party's strategy. Instead of focusing on mobile warfare in northern China and building guerrilla base areas in southern China, the Communists would now "march on the north, defend in the south." This strategy, formally articulated by Liu Shaoqi on 19 September with the agreement of Mao Zedong and Zhou Enlai (still in Chongqing), was announced to the Party on 29 September.[81] Under this new strategy, the Communist Party, acting with the Soviet Union's full approval, would assert complete control over Rehe and Chahar Provinces and Shanhaiguan, giving them control over the land routes into Manchuria.[82] With these routes in their hands, the Communists would make a strong bid to control Manchuria itself, moving as many cadres and troops into the region as the Soviets would allow. At the same time, Liu and the Politburo decided that the Communist forces in the south should retreat from their widely dispersed and extremely vulnerable positions—a decision that fit nicely with Mao Zedong's negotiations in Chongqing, since he could represent the withdrawal from the south as a concession to the Nationalists.[83] On 17 September, the Party Center ordered the New Fourth Army units then deployed in the south to move immediately to the north of the Yangzi River, and from there, to prepare for redeployment to the areas of eastern Hebei and Rehe in order to be in position to advance into Manchuria as soon as the Soviet Red Army should return home.[84]

With the "march on the north, defend in the south" strategy, the Communist Party had completely changed its approach to the coming battle with the Kuomintang. The Communists would pull back and take up defensive positions in the south. In northern China, the Communist Eighth Route and New Fourth Armies would continue to defend their established base areas, not simply for their own sake, but in order to set the stage for an advance into Manchuria, which would become a new base area (to whatever degree the Soviets would allow). These new tasks confirmed and reinforced the Chinese Communists' move away from guerrilla warfare and toward mobile warfare conducted by standard army units. If the Communists were to assert unquestioned control over eastern Hebei, Chahar, and Rehe and to make a bid for control of Manchuria, they would not be able to give up territory, allow the enemy to become over-extended, and then use small-scale guerrilla and sabotage operations to weaken him. Sabotage, particularly railway sabotage, would still have an important role to play. But instead of using classical Maoist guerrilla tactics, the Communists would need to maneuver divisions and armies on the field of battle, engaging the enemy in large-scale decisive battles designed to inflict massive casualties and halt the enemy's advance. Beyond that, the goal of controlling access to

Manchuria implied that if the Nationalists reached a key point—such as Shanhaiguan—the Communists would need to defend it if at all possible. Ideally, the Communists would stop the Nationalists in Eastern Hebei, even before they reached Shanhaiguan.

This determination to hold territory by seeking decisive battles and, if necessary, by defending key strategic points would lead to a series of events culminating in the battle to defend Siping. But as matters stood in September 1945, the Communists had grounds for optimism. They had achieved control of the key land routes from northern China to Manchuria, including Shanhaiguan. Large Communist armies in northern China itself stood ready to carry out railway sabotage and mobile warfare in order to slow the inevitable Nationalist advance toward the Northeast. Communist troops had already gained a foothold in the Northeast, and more were on their way by land and by sea from Shandong Province. Communists in the Northeast were also beginning to establish a political presence, organizing local governments and establishing party organizations. The Nationalists, though they had some agents and sympathizers in the Northeast, were still on the outside. Chiang Kai-shek's best armies were far away in southwestern China and Vietnam, his government had no administrative presence in Manchuria, and the Soviet Union was purposely placing obstacles in the way of his attempts to reassert Chinese sovereignty over the three Northeastern provinces that he had lost to the Japanese in 1931. Chiang, conscious of the limits of his military power, had to consider his next move carefully: Should he focus on regaining control of China within the Great Wall first? Or should he send some of his armies directly to Manchuria?

3

The Communist Retreat

October–December 1945

While the Communists were staking their claim to the Northeast, they were also conducting a series of negotiations with the Nationalist Party leaders in China's wartime capital of Chongqing. No real agreements were reached there. The negotiations are significant because they established a pattern of "talking and fighting" in which each side tried to use the peace talks in order to gain advantage on the battlefield while, at the same time, they used military operations to gain leverage at the negotiating table. The military operations of this period, in which the Nationalists drove Communist forces out of the Liaoxi Corridor, are interesting for what they reveal about both Communist and Nationalist strategic thinking and operational capabilities, and for the insights they give us into the relationship between Mao Zedong and his commander in Manchuria, General Lin Biao.

THE CHONGQING NEGOTIATIONS

If they had been left to their own devices, Chiang Kai-shek and Mao Zedong would not have attempted to negotiate with each other. The fact that the talks took place at all was due to the fact that both sides felt that both the Soviet Union and the United States wanted them to avoid an all-out civil war.[1] Chiang initiated the talks on 14 August 1945 when he sent a telegram to Mao:

With the surrender of the dwarf pirates, the realization of an extended period of world peace is within sight. As a range of weighty international and national questions urgently await resolution, I especially invite you to set a date to honor the temporary capital with your presence for mutual discussion. On matters relating to the future of the nation, I hope that you will not delay.[2]

Mao's response was a brief acknowledgement of the message and a longer telegram, sent out in Zhu De's name, outlining the Communist Party's conditions for talks: joint acceptance of the Japanese surrender, no civil war, an end to the Kuomintang's one-party rule, and organization of a coalition government. Mao's assumption was that the Kuomintang would reject the Communists' positions, and that the talks could thus be avoided.[3] Chiang followed up with two more invitations, on 20 and 22 August.

Chiang's messages, which were couched in the language of a commanding general and Confucian patriarch speaking from a position of moral superiority to a misbehaving inferior, were hardly the thing to convince the Communist leadership to send Mao to Chongqing. Indeed, the members of the Politburo were concerned for Mao's safety. As late as 13 August, and probably later, Mao's position was that civil war was inevitable.[4] What apparently changed Mao's mind were two messages from Joseph Stalin, delivered sometime around 20 August. Stalin, who did not believe that the Chinese Communists could win a war with the Nationalists, ordered Mao to negotiate with Chiang Kai-shek and warned him that civil war would drive the Chinese people to the brink of extinction.[5]

Mao did not necessarily agree with Stalin, but since both the Soviets and the Americans were determined to see negotiations take place, he did as Stalin asked. On 23 August Mao was telling the Politburo that neither the Americans, the British, nor the Soviet Union wanted to see civil war break out in China; if there was civil war, and the Soviets openly supported the CCP, the result might be a nuclear third world war, which the Soviets could ill afford.[6] With comments like these—so different from his rhetoric of only ten days previous—Mao was laying the foundations for the opening of negotiations with Chiang Kai-shek. On 28 August Mao, accompanied by Zhou Enlai, flew to Chongqing with American ambassador Patrick Hurley and the talks began.

Neither side entered the Chongqing peace talks with any degree of sincerity. In addition, each side felt that the other had military weaknesses that could be exploited at the negotiating table, and that the negotiations would in turn help to create conditions conducive to their own military advantage. Chiang Kai-shek went into the talks having just concluded two new treaties with the Soviet Union. In the Sino-Soviet Treaty of Alliance and Friendship, signed 14 August 1945, the Soviet Union and China agreed to respect each other's territorial sovereignty and to cooperate on matters of economic development.[7] A Sino-Soviet railways agreement, signed on the same day, gave the Soviet Union joint ownership and management of the Chinese Eastern Railway and the South Manchurian Railway (collectively renamed as the China Changchun Railway). The Soviet Union also gained thirty-year rights to the military port of Lüshun (Port Arthur) and the commercial port of Dalian, as well as various economic privileges in Manchuria. What Chiang Kai-shek gained was the Soviet Union's reaffirmation that the "Three Eastern Provinces" of Manchuria were a part of China, which the Soviet Union would turn over to Chiang's central government.

Chiang's hope was that international pressure would limit Soviet support for the Communists and force the Soviets to give his troops access to Manchuria. This would allow him to attack the Communist forces in North China from two directions.[8] Mao and the Communists, for their part, aware that Chiang's armies were stretched thin and would need to be transferred from the Southwest to the Northeast, planned to continue to press their advantage in Manchuria as far as the Soviet Union would allow them. Firmly believing that Chiang Kai-shek still intended to eliminate them from China, the Communist leadership went into the Chongqing talks with the attitude that they would "adopt the position that conditions for civil war were not good for the benefit of Chiang and the Americans in order to resolve things in our favor in the negotiations."[9] To complicate the issue, Mao, a hard-drinking, chain-smoking man who habitually used rough language, and the austere, formal, Confucian/Christian Chiang Kai-shek were two mutually incompatible personalities.[10] Chiang thought that Mao was "shameless and gutless."[11] Mao believed that "Chiang Kai-shek only understands fists—he doesn't understand reason."[12]

With neither side sincerely interested in reaching a peaceful resolution, the Chongqing talks were doomed to failure from the beginning. The Nationalists insisted that the Communist Party incorporate its armed forces into the national army under Chiang's command as a precondition for Communist participation in coalition government. The Communists insisted on achieving recognition of their political control of North China and Manchuria before they would discuss the tricky issue of military reorganization. Mao was willing to give up his South China base areas simply because they were already a liability.[13] Things went so poorly that in late September, the Central Committee advised Mao and Zhou Enlai to drop the negotiations.[14] Mao's talks with Chiang Kai-shek concluded on 10 October, having achieved nothing more than a face-saving mutual agreement calling for a Political Consultative Conference. Further rounds of talks between Zhou Enlai and Kuomintang negotiators from mid-October through late November were similarly inconclusive.

As the talks unfolded both sides continued with military maneuvers and fighting. Chiang Kai-shek, with the help of the United States, began the tremendous logistical task of transferring some of his best armies from their positions in the remote south and southwest toward Northern China in preparation for an invasion of Manchuria. The Communist Party continued to strengthen its position in the Northeast. As Mao Zedong remarked later, "We didn't allow the peace talks to affect our military maneuvers [and] we concentrated our forces to fight three big battles."[15] The Communist Party worked to obstruct Nationalist troop movements by sabotaging the north–south railway lines and by fighting the Nationalists in several encounters, most notably the Shang-Dang Campaign (10 September–12 October), and the Ping-Han Campaign (also called the Handan Campaign, 22 October–2 November). Communist victories in these campaigns (both fought over control of the north-south railway line from Wuhan to Beijing) made it very difficult for Chiang Kai-shek to use roads and railroads to move his armies northward from the Yangzi valley toward Manchuria: his only recourse was to rely on American naval and (to a lesser extent) air transport.

LIN BIAO AND PENG ZHEN

The longer it took for Chiang Kai-shek to move his troops north, the more time the Communists had to consolidate their position in the Northeast. From mid-August through mid-October, the Communist forces in the Northeast were compelled to act with a greater degree of restraint than they would have liked. As discussed above, the Soviet Union did not want to see civil war break out in China, nor did it want to unnecessarily complicate its relations with Chiang Kai-shek and with the United States by actively sponsoring the creation of a Chinese Communist Party base area in Manchuria. As Mao later recalled, the Soviet Union (much to his dissatisfaction) "did not allow us to make revolution."[16] From August through mid-October 1945, the Communist Party Center followed Stalin's wishes. At first, in early to mid-September, the Party ordered that heavy troops be concentrated in eastern Hebei and in the Rehe and western Liaoning area, and along the Bohai gulf coast in order to fight Chiang's armies there, before they could reach Manchuria.[17] But by around 24 September, they took a much more conservative attitude toward the Northeast. At this point the Party Center, still hoping that forces in eastern Hebei could halt or delay the progress of Chiang's armies toward Manchuria, ordered the Northeast Bureau to disperse its troops widely across the region and to place its emphasis "first and foremost on the cities and rural areas that can be supported and concentrated on because they back onto the Soviet Union, Korea, Outer Mongolia, and Rehe."[18] The idea was to build rural base areas which the Communists could use if they were later forced to fight the Nationalists in Manchuria. On 10 October, the Party Center even told its leaders in the Northeast, "Under the present circumstances you should absolutely not concentrate your forces—do not be afraid of people laughing at you for not having cast off the guerrilla mentality."[19]

In order to carry out its policies in Manchuria, the Communist Party's Central Committee had established a "Northeast Bureau"—a kind of branch office that originally consisted of five men from the Party Center: Peng Zhen, Chen Yun, Cheng Zihua, Wu Xiuquan, and Lin Feng.[20] Peng Zhen was chosen to chair the Northeast Bureau. Peng was an experienced man and a full member of the Central Committee,

FIGURE 3.1. Peng Zhen (second from left) and other members of the Northeast Bureau looking over war plans. *Courtesy of the Liao-Shen Campaign Memorial Hall.*

had previous experience directing underground work in Manchuria back in the days of the Japanese occupation, and had been a leader in the Party's exploration of possible action in Manchuria as early as May 1945.[21] Flying out of Yan'an on the same Soviet airplane that had brought Zeng Kelin and Belorussov to Yan'an for their meeting with the Party Center, the five men of the Northeast Bureau arrived in Shenyang on 18 September, where they set up their offices in the mansion previously belonging to Zhang Zuolin and his son, Zhang Xueliang—the warlords of Manchuria.

Peng Zhen's job was to translate strategy made in Yan'an into action on the ground in Manchuria, and to keep the Party Center in Yan'an apprised of developments in Manchuria so that the leadership could make informed decisions. This was not an easy job. Policies made in Yan'an were not always in tune with actual conditions. As a result, the orders to

disperse Communist troops widely across the Northeast and to empha-
size the areas backing onto the Soviet Union, Mongolia, and Korea were
only partially carried out. In fact, a disproportionate number of Communist troops and Communist Party cadres remained deployed in southern
Manchuria, in and around the cities and the major railway lines.

One reason for this tendency to favor the cities had to do with Peng
Zhen's background and preferences. Peng was not a military leader: his
expertise and experience were in political organization, both within the
Party leadership itself and among the urban working class in cities behind enemy lines. Back in May 1945, when he had been assigned to plan
a strategy for fighting the Japanese in Manchukuo, Peng Zhen argued
that the conditions for rural-based guerrilla warfare and "surrounding
the cities from the countryside" did not exist: the Japanese had already
achieved control over the rural and urban areas and the railway lines.
Instead, Peng argued, "The emphasis of our work should be on the urban
and industrial centers, main transportation routes, points of strategic importance in the rural areas, and on the puppet troops."[22] When he came
to the Northeast in August 1945, Peng Zhen's task was to prepare to fight
the Nationalists, not the Japanese. Nonetheless, it is fair to assume that
he brought with him his earlier ideas about the importance of gaining a
foothold directly in the cities and then expanding Communist influence
into the rural areas, rather than the other way around.

Peng Zhen's emphasis on the cities and major railway lines of South
Manchuria was also related to the distribution of resources. As Peng
later explained, the newly arrived Communist troops, lightly equipped
and facing the onset of the Manchurian winter, were in desperate need
of supplies. This naturally led them to the major railway lines and cities of South Manchuria, where they would find the most resources.
Furthermore, if the Communist Party was to defeat Chiang Kai-shek's
armies in battle, they would need industrial resources—these too were
concentrated in South Manchuria. Another factor that tended to keep
the Communist forces concentrated in South Manchuria was the state
of the railways. Many of the rural and border regions in which the Party
Center wanted to see base areas developed were inaccessible because
the branch railway lines were not functioning or because railway con-
nections simply did not exist.[23] In addition, as part of their attempt not

to appear to be favoring the Communists, the Soviets often refused to allow the Northeast Bureau to use the main railway lines to move troops.[24]

Weapons and equipment (particularly winter gear) were major issues for the Communist troops. Zeng Kelin's initial, optimistic reports had convinced the Party Center that there were huge stockpiles of Japanese weapons and that the Soviets would be happy to turn these over to the Communist forces, along with key factories like the Shenyang Arsenal. As a result, the Party Center ordered units from Shandong and elsewhere to leave their weapons and gear behind and proceed as fast as possible to Manchuria, where they would be re-equipped.[25] When they arrived, many of these veteran troops were bitterly disappointed. The Soviets, it seemed, were not as forthcoming as Zeng Kelin had led everyone to expect. On 21 September Peng Zhen reported to the Party that the Soviets were tightly controlling all military warehouses and factories, and that whether they would release any material at all "remain[ed] a mystery."[26]

Did the Soviets eventually release Japanese weapons and factories for the production of military supplies to the Chinese Communists? And if so, did they do so in amounts significant enough to make a difference to the outcome of the fight for control of Manchuria? The answer to both questions is a qualified "yes." Evidence from Chinese Communist, Nationalist, and Soviet sources and from American intelligence reports all indicate that at least some Communist units were equipped with Japanese weapons. According to some reports, the Eighth Route Army men were particularly fond of the Japanese Arisaka 38 rifle—a 6.5×50 mm bolt action weapon that was easily re-chambered to take Russian-made 7.32×39 mm rounds.[27] Some of the transfers were done in a way that would give the Soviets "deniability." American intelligence reports described how Soviet units guarding Japanese military warehouses would stage fake firefights with Chinese Communist forces in order to claim that the weapons had been taken by force.[28]

It is indisputable that some Communist units were armed with weapons from the warehouses of the Japanese Kwantung Army. For example, American military observers in Shenyang noted a force of around three thousand Chinese Communist troops, well-armed with "captured

Jap material" supplied by the Soviets.[29] This kind of anecdotal evidence is suggestive, but there is not enough hard data to give us a complete picture of the extent to which supplies of Japanese weapons and other Soviet assistance may have contributed to the combat strength of the Communist forces. Record-keeping was probably dodgy at best, and if there are any accurate accounts of the number of Japanese rifles, artillery pieces, rounds of ammunition, tanks, and other equipment released by the Soviets, they are sealed up in Russian or Chinese archives and not available to the average researcher. Russian sources suggest that the Soviet Union gave substantial aid to the Chinese Communist forces: 700,000 rifles, 12,000–14,000 machine guns, 4,000 artillery pieces, 600 tanks, and 679 ammunition stockpiles.[30] Chinese historian Yang Kuisong, using both these Soviet and Chinese sources, suggests that even when taking into account possible exaggeration in the Russian sources, the Soviets provided enough weapons to equip several hundred thousand Communist troops. These weapons, some of them used in Manchuria and some shipped out to Shandong, "significantly shortened the Chinese Communist Central Committee's original timetable for achieving complete victory over the Kuomintang."[31]

If the Soviets did indeed transfer substantial amounts of captured Japanese weapons and equipment to the Chinese Communists, then why did Peng Zhen complain on 21 September that the Soviet attitude was "a mystery"? And why did Communist commanders complain bitterly about the lack of Soviet support, both at the time and decades later in their memoirs?

The fundamental reason is that the attitude of the Soviet forces on the ground in Manchuria shifted along with changes in Moscow's strategy for securing its interests in the region (in other words, Moscow's strategy for minimizing Chiang Kai-shek's control over the region and for keeping the Americans out entirely).[32] From late August through mid-September, the Soviets hoped to foster a Communist political presence in Manchuria. Therefore, they worked with Communist troops, cooperated with them in capturing Shanhaiguan, welcomed them into the cities, and gave them generous access to Japanese military supplies. This was precisely when Zeng Kelin formed the optimistic impressions that he relayed to the Party Center in mid-September. But by late September, the Soviets were worried that open support of the Communists in Manchuria would give the Americans an excuse to get further involved in North China or even in Manchuria itself. Soviet diplomats emphasized their commitment to honor treaty obligations to Chiang Kai-shek's government. In Manchuria, the Red Army reasserted control over Japanese arms dumps and factories. As a result, newly arrived Communist troops were left out in the cold.[33]

From early October through mid-November, continued American military presence in North China and American transport of Nationalist troops headed for Manchuria heightened Soviet concern and led them to encourage the Communists to take a stronger stance. Military supplies once again became available. Then (as we will see below) from 17 November 1945 through February 1946, Moscow returned to a strategy of giving lip service to its promises to transfer Manchuria's railways, cities, and factories to Chiang Kai-shek. The level of cooperation and support for the Communist troops dropped to a new low. Finally, when they began to withdraw from Manchuria in March 1946, the Soviets once again threw their support behind the Chinese Communists and gave them access to Japanese military warehouses.

These shifts in Soviet policy meant that Chinese Communist military units had different experiences with the Soviets, depending on where they were and when they were interacting with Soviet officers. In the long run, Japanese weapons and other Soviet assistance helped the Communist forces to make the transition from guerrilla warfare to successful large-scale mobile operations.[34] But all that lay in the future. In October 1945, the Communists had received some Japanese weapons, but they were still vastly inferior to the Nationalist armies in terms of equipment and training. In fact, a relatively small number of Communist troops and cadres had entered Manchuria from the Soviet Union and North China, including Shandong. In October, following orders from the Party Center, they began an ambitious recruitment program. Factory and mine workers, idealistic students, and former Manchukuo soldiers and police were rapidly incorporated into the Communist ranks, with little regard for anything other than their physical ability to serve.[35] More forces were on their way from North China and from Shandong. However, the logistical challenges of moving troops either by land or by sea meant that the Communists were not able to bring troops into the Northeast nearly as fast as Liu Shaoqi wanted to.[36]

Also en route to Manchuria in October 1945 was one of Mao Zedong's most experienced and talented commanders: Lin Biao. Lin (1907–1971) was a member of the Socialist Youth League and a cadet at the Kuomintang's Soviet-supported Whampoa Military Academy in 1925. He quickly rose to the rank of colonel in Chiang Kai-shek's National Army and participated in the Northern Expedition (Chiang's campaign to defeat the warlords and unite China under Kuomintang rule) in 1926–1927. When the "United Front" between the Kuomintang and the Communists collapsed in 1927, Lin joined Mao Zedong in developing the Communist Party's own Red Army in the countryside. By 1945, Lin was a highly experienced and talented field commander, a veteran of the Long March and of many battles against both Kuomintang and Japanese forces. Although he exposed himself to danger time and again, Lin had never been wounded—until 1937, when he went riding, wearing a recently captured Japanese cloak and with a Japanese sword at his side. A Chinese soldier, mistaking Lin for a Japanese officer, shot him in the abdomen. Severely wounded, Lin spent three years (1939–1942) in Moscow. Very little is known of Lin's sojourn in the Soviet Union. It seems likely that he used the opportunity to observe and learn from the Soviet military, but what, if any, influence this may have had on his understanding of the art of war is not clear.

Personally, Lin was an intense, reserved man, subject to fits of nervousness. In terms of his military thinking, Lin was often at odds with Mao Zedong. Mao, the self-taught amateur, is best known for his theories of guerrilla warfare and for his willingness to take bold action. The Whampoa-trained Lin favored standard maneuver warfare, but he was also more inclined to caution than Mao. As a result, the relationship between the two men was at times difficult. Nevertheless, Mao not only disagreed with but also respected and trusted Lin Biao. At any rate, Mao was far away in Yan'an. In the first year of the struggle for the Northeast, it was Lin Biao's clashes with his immediate superior Peng Zhen that would be the most troublesome.

Lin arrived in Shenyang on 29 October 1945 to take over as commander of the Communist forces in the Chahar-Rehe-Liaoning area.

Lin's orders were to "assist Peng Zhen with military matters."[37] This was the beginning of a difficult relationship. Peng Zhen outranked Lin Biao in the very hierarchical Chinese Communist Party leadership, and he was the Secretary of the Northeast Bureau. Lin was to serve as commander of the Party's armed forces in Manchuria, but he was not even a member of the Northeast Bureau. Lin was not happy with his status, but he did have one political advantage: he was in the Northeast on Mao's orders, and he maintained direct contact with Mao and with Liu Shaoqi even while he took his orders from Peng Zhen, who was his direct superior in the Northeast.[38]

Lin's transfer to the Northeast coincided with yet another shift in the attitude of the Soviet Union and, consequently, with a corresponding change in the Communist Party's strategy. In October and early November, as Chiang Kai-shek's armies (transported by the American Seventh Fleet) landed at the port of Qinhuangdao, just south of Shanhaiguan, the Soviets became worried about the extension of Nationalist (and, by implication, American) influence in Manchuria. As a result, the Soviet Union urged their Chinese comrades to adopt a more aggressive policy in the Northeast.[39] As early as 3 October, the Soviets were telling Peng Zhen to be more aggressive about controlling South Manchuria and promised to help in any way that they could.[40] At this point, the Party Center was not prepared to be as aggressive as the Soviets apparently wanted them to be. Liu Shaoqi told Peng Zhen, "Absolutely do not concentrate forces, do not be afraid of people [i.e., the Soviets] mocking you for not having transcended guerrilla warfare, because we don't have airplanes or heavy artillery, we cannot part from guerrilla warfare, otherwise we will be wiped out." Liu believed that the Communists would need to give up Shanhaiguan, allow the Nationalists to extend their forces into Manchuria, and then "deploy [their] main forces in battles of annihilation."[41]

By the time Lin Biao arrived in Shenyang, Mao Zedong had taken control of strategic planning for Manchuria. Mao proposed a course of action far more aggressive than Liu Shaoqi had advocated. On 16, 21, and 28 October, Mao, writing for the Communist Party Center, told the Northeast Bureau to oppose any attempt by Chiang Kai-shek's forces to enter Manchuria by land or by sea, stating that "our Party must resolutely mobilize all its forces, control the Northeast, protect north China and central China, smash their offensive in the next six months, then force Chiang to the negotiating table and make him accept the autonomous status of northern China and the Northeast. Only then can there be a transition to peace: otherwise, peace is impossible."[42]

The strategy of dispersing troops widely across the Northeast to build base areas in preparation for protracted war was now abandoned. Mao was pushing hard for a campaign to either control all of Manchuria or, at the very least, force Chiang's armies into a standoff in order to give Zhou Enlai more leverage in the negotiations in Chongqing. Lin now had over eighty thousand poorly armed troops, of which only thirty thousand were seasoned veterans from the New Fourth and Eighth Route Armies. The rest were raw, politically unreliable recruits from Manchuria.[43] Under the new strategy, Lin was to use these forces at Shanhaiguan, along the line from Jinzhou to the port of Yingkou and up to Shenyang, in order to prevent the Nationalist armies from gaining a foothold in Manchuria.

ENTER THE NATIONALISTS

In August 1945, the Nationalist government had no comprehensive strategic plan for the inevitable post-war struggle with the Communists. Whatever strategy there was emerged directly from Chiang Kai-shek's own mind. Chiang, who saw the Communists as roving "bandits," believed that the key to "bandit" pacification was to control key cities and transportation lines.[44] Chiang and his government initially approached the problem with a tremendous amount of confidence: their belief was that their vastly superior military forces would defeat the Communists in three to six months.[45]

This belief was based on two assumptions. The first was that Chiang's armies would defeat the Communist forces in a series of quick, decisive battles. The second was that Chiang would be able to use diplomacy rather than military force to get control of Manchuria. On 28 July 1945, he reflected in his diary that a civil war with the Communists in Manchuria would be an extremely difficult conflict, and one that the Communists, with Soviet support, might win.[46] Chiang's concerns reflected the opinion of some of his key military advisors. Bai Chongxi, an experienced former warlord now serving Chiang, advised against deploying troops to Manchuria.[47] But from the Americans, Chiang was getting contradictory signals. On the one hand, as the Joint Chiefs of Staff put it on 18 September 1945, "It is U.S. policy to assist the Chinese Government in the establishment of essential Chinese troops in liberated areas, particularly Manchuria, as quickly as practicable."[48] On the other hand, the United States was determined not to commit its own troops to a ground war in China and not to help the Kuomintang to pursue "fratricidal war" against the Communists.[49] The United States would help move Nationalist troops to Manchuria and support their efforts to assert military control over the area, but would not send American troops there and would not support war with the Communists.

The inherent contradiction in the American position and the clearly limited support that the United States was willing to give to Chiang's troops led General Wedemeyer to recommend a United Nations–sponsored guardianship for Manchuria.[50] Wedemeyer (whose views were shared by some members of the State Department) simply did not believe that Chiang had the ability to take Manchuria by force. In his view, a better choice would have been for Chiang to consolidate control over North China before turning his attention to the Northeast.[51] On the other hand, the Truman administration's policy was that Manchuria should be united with China Proper under Chiang's control—this amounted to at least an indirect, if not a direct, encouragement to Chiang to commit troops to the Northeast.[52] Furthermore, there were both political and economic factors at work. Politically, Chiang could ill afford not to reassert Chinese sovereignty over the Northeast, which he had lost to Japan under such humiliating circumstances in 1931. From an economic point of view, Manchuria's resources were a concern: Shanghai and other eastern cities depended on Manchurian coal for their electricity generating stations. The combination of domestic political considerations and American encouragement led Chiang to conclude that he would need to assert his government's rights in Manchuria, by force if necessary, but preferably through negotiations with the Soviets.

If he were to recover control of Manchuria, Chiang would need to establish both a political and a military presence in the area. Even before his troops began moving into position, Kuomintang agents were operating openly in Shenyang and other cities, recruiting supporters and preparing public opinion for the return of the central government and its armies. In this regard, the Nationalists had an advantage: both Nationalist and Communist sources suggest that initially, the people of the Northeast supported Chiang's government and looked forward to Manchuria's returning to Kuomintang control. Under his treaties with the Soviet Union, Chiang could, and did, take some steps toward establishing political control over the Northeast. He re-organized the three provinces of Manchukuo into nine new provinces and appointed provincial governors. With Soviet permission, he set up a "Northeast Command" in Changchun, with General Xiong Shihui in charge. But in order to really recover sovereignty, Chiang would need to put boots on the ground.

This was not easy. Communist sabotage and military operations made it impossible to use the north–south railways to move troops. The Soviets purposely imposed limits on air transport of Nationalist troops and officials in order to prevent them from achieving a smooth transfer of political authority over provincial and city governments.[53] The American Seventh Fleet stood ready to transport Nationalist troops by sea on a schedule that suited the Americans, but which Chiang found far too slow for his liking. Sea transport also depended on the goodwill of the Soviet Union, which controlled the Manchurian ports. The Soviets refused to allow troops to land either at the Soviet-controlled military port of Lüshun or the commercial port of Dalian. In addition, the Soviets had turned Yingkou and Huludao over to Chinese Communist forces, which likewise refused to allow the Americans to land. This "sea denial" on the part of the Soviet Union put Chiang Kai-shek at a severe disadvantage.[54] Instead of being able to enter Manchuria from multiple points, the Nationalists were forced to land at Qinhuangdao, just south of the Great Wall, and to fight their way into Manchuria via Shanhaiguan and the Liaoxi Corridor. The process began in late October when over twenty American ships brought the Nationalist Thirteenth Army to Qinhuangdao. The Thirteenth Army was one of Chiang's crack armies, an American-trained and -equipped force of three divisions. The commander was the Whampoa-trained General Shi Jue (1908–1986).

In Shi Jue's estimation, his forces were not ready to attack the Communists at Shanhaiguan immediately after landing. The Thirteenth Army had only been issued three months of ammunition for training purposes, most of which had been used up by the time they got to Qinhuangdao. In his memoirs, Shi Jue implies that the Americans were slow to follow up on their promise to deliver more ammunition as needed. Also, when being transported by sea from Kowloon to Qinhuangdao, the Thirteenth Army had transferred their draft animals to the central command and had not been able to gain a new supply of draft animals. This posed significant problems for their mobility. In addition, hundreds of Shi Jue's men were ill.[55]

In light of these difficulties, Shi Jue was not willing to carry out any action other than reconnaissance and preliminary probing of Communist defenses in the area south of Shanhaiguan. In these operations, Shi Jue worked with American forces that had secured Qinhuangdao prior to Shi Jue's arrival and had been repairing the railway from Qinhuangdao to Shanhaiguan—a railway that the Communists in the area had sabotaged. The presence of American and Chinese Communist troops in the same area made for a tense situation, but one in which both sides exercised a degree of restraint. American policy was to assist the Nationalists in their attempt to recover Manchuria, but not to get directly involved.[56] The Communist side was constrained by orders not to engage the Americans—for neither Mao nor the Soviet Union wanted to give the United States a reason to expand its presence at Qinhuangdao or, worse yet, to advance into Manchuria itself.[57] In one incident on 4 November, Communist soldiers fired on five American sailors who were driving toward Shanhaiguan in a borrowed Nationalist army jeep, slightly wounding one. When they realized who they were firing on, the Communists took the Americans into custody and then released them to a French hospital in Shanhaiguan for transfer back to their ship.[58]

When they encountered Nationalist forces, the Communists were not so restrained. In one exploratory probe, the Thirteenth Army had lost an entire company at a place called Shahe. The commander escaped and returned to headquarters to report that the Communists had Japanese weapons, ample supplies of ammunition, and formidable firepower, and had destroyed an entire village. This alleged demonstration of Communist power is said (by Shi Jue's detractors) to have given Shi Jue doubts about the wisdom of attacking Shanhaiguan.[59] Chiang, too, still had reservations about the wisdom of advancing into the Northeast. On 8 November, reflecting on the difficulty of using the single route through Shanhaiguan, he wrote, "This is, as the saying goes, curing a dead horse as if it was a live horse." Perhaps, he thought, it would be a better idea to "first gain control of North China and Inner Mongolia and then attempt the Northeast."[60] Nonetheless, the next day, Chiang decided to follow through with the idea of advancing through Shanhaiguan toward Jinzhou in order to at least gain a foothold in South Manchuria. The commander in charge of the operation would be Du Yuming.

Du Yuming (1903–1981) arrived at Qinhuangdao to take up his position as commander of the Northeast Peace Preservation Headquarters on 8 November, taking command of Shi Jue's Thirteenth Army and the Fifty-second Army. He would ultimately be in command of these and the Thirtieth, Thirty-second, Ninety-second, and Ninety-fourth armies, all of which were to be transferred to the Northeast.[61] Du, like Lin Biao, was a graduate of Whampoa Military Academy and a veteran of the Northern Expedition of 1926–1928. Unlike Lin, Du felt a deep loyalty to Chiang Kai-shek and continued his career in the Nationalist military. Du participated in General Joseph Stilwell's ill-fated Burma Campaign in 1942, and then spent the rest of the war in command of reserve forces in southwestern China.[62]

Accounts of the Battle of Shanhaiguan indicate a deep sense of rivalry between Du Yuming and Shi Jue. Whether their mutual animosity was there at the time or was a product of later events is hard to say. Accounts published on the mainland tend to follow Du Yuming's own memoir, written after his release from prison and clearly influenced by the political climate of China in the 1950s. Du was highly critical of Shi Jue and the Thirteenth Army. In his memoirs, Du describes how he arrived at Qinhuangdao and then went to inspect the place where the Thirteenth Army's company had been wiped out, and he concluded that the Communists did not have the firepower that the defeated company commander had claimed and that the village which had allegedly been destroyed by the Communists was, in fact, unharmed.[63] After giving the unfortunate company commander a suspended death sentence (to give him a chance to redeem himself in battle), Du began to lay plans for the assault on Shanhaiguan. He now had two armies to work with: in addition to the Thirteenth Army, the U.S. Seventh Fleet had now landed the Fifty-second Army at Qinhuangdao. The Fifty-second was mixed—half American equipment, half Chinese—but its men, unlike those of the Thirteenth Army, had been battle-hardened in the Burma campaigns against the Japanese. With these two armies, Du Yuming had some sixty thousand well-armed, well-trained, experienced troops at his command. Chiang Kai-shek had now decided to fight his way into Manchuria, at least as far as Jinzhou, which would give him a foothold in Manchuria itself and a base from which to assert control over Rehe province. Du Yuming would begin that struggle with an attack on Shanhaiguan.

THE BATTLE OF SHANHAIGUAN

When they had taken Shanhaiguan, the Communist Party leaders realized that Chiang Kai-shek was bound to land troops at Qinhuangdao and attack Shanhaiguan in order to open the path to Jinzhou and on to Shenyang. From late September to mid-October 1945, the Communist Party Center issued multiple directives concerning the importance of holding Shanhaiguan.[64] Mao and the Party Center were confident that if the Americans did not get directly involved, Lin Biao would be able at a minimum to prevent Du Yuming from capturing Shenyang, and that he would be able to hold the Nationalists off at Shanhaiguan for at least half a month while more Communist troops entered the Northeast from Shandong and via Hebei and Rehe.[65]

The Communist Party's local commander in the area including Shanhaiguan was Li Yunchang. Li himself was not in the city: Shanhaiguan was garrisoned by ten thousand troops under the command of Yang Guofu. The men were poorly armed, with an average of one rifle for every two soldiers, and completely unfamiliar with the requirements of fighting a positional defense.[66] Yang Guofu's forces at Shanhaiguan were not only outgunned: they were also outnumbered by a ratio of one to six. Given the small number of troops and weapons available to him, Yang Guofu had to spread out his forces thinly over a long line of defense in order to defend both Shanhaiguan and the smaller passes to the north, including Jiumenkou. Nonetheless, as of 9 November the Nationalists had done no more than send small probing expeditions in the direction of Shanhaiguan. This led Li Yunchang to give Lin Biao and Mao Zedong an utterly unrealistic report, claiming that his forces had driven back several Nationalist attempts to attack Shanhaiguan. Li opined that with their large armies confined in the small Qinhuangdao area, the enemy would be like a turtle in a jar as soon as their transport ships had departed, and that they could be easily annihilated.[67] In fact, the only reason the Communists were still in Shanhaiguan on 9 November was that the Nationalists had not yet completed their preparations. When they did, Li Yunchang's underestimation of the enemy would quickly become apparent.

Du's strategy for taking Shanhaiguan was in some respects similar to that followed by the Chinese Communist forces of Zeng Kelin and Tang Kai when they had first entered Manchuria back in September. Du would send the Fifty-second Army's Twenty-fifth Division into Manchuria through the small pass of Yiyuankou north of Shanhaiguan. They would then swing to the right and capture the railway town of Zhongqiansuo, thus cutting off Li Yunchang's line of retreat. The Thirteenth Army would mount a frontal attack against the Communists at Shanhaiguan, with the Fifty-fourth Division going through another pass at Jiumenkou to swing around and attack Shanhaiguan from the rear. Du's goal was not merely to drive Yang Guofu out of Shanhaiguan and capture the main point of entry into Manchuria, but also to pin the Communist troops against the coast and annihilate them.[68]

What saved Yang Guofu and his men from annihilation was that Du's plan began to go awry almost from the beginning. On 12 November, the Twenty-fifth Division began moving into position to cross the Great Wall, which it did the next day. But as they entered Manchuria, the Kuomintang troops failed to completely seal off the area, so that news of their advance reached the Communists at Shanhaiguan. At the same time, the Thirteenth Army mounted its attack on Shanhaiguan ahead of schedule—before the Twenty-fifth Division had been able to reach Zhongqiansuo and cut off Yang Guofu's route of retreat.[69]

Realizing that they were in serious danger, Yang Guofu's forces withdrew before the Twenty-fifth Division could get into position to cut off their retreat. On 16 November, the Nationalists occupied Shanhaiguan. But Du Yuming's plans had already begun to unravel. While the Communists retreated, using time and terrain to their advantage, the Nationalist forces failed to cut them off.[70] Division headquarters were unable to maintain reliable communications with units in the field, key forces moved too slowly, and commanding officers on the front lines carried out standing orders rather than respond flexibly to changing circumstances on the ground. For example, when it became clear that the Communist main forces had already cleared Zhongqiansuo, the Nationalist unit responsible for capturing that railway town could have changed its plans and tried to cut the Communists off at the next key point to the east. Instead, they followed their original plan and captured the now useless Zhongqiansuo. Another unit, pursuing the retreating Communists through the night, had to cross a series of small, shallow, but very cold streams. Unwilling to get wet, they laid down planks for bridges, which they had to cross slowly, in single file. This involved a delay of half an hour to an hour each time, so that the troops only advanced fifteen kilometers that night.[71]

While the exhausted Communist forces retreated from Shanhaiguan and on up the Liaoxi Corridor, their leaders far away in Yan'an remained strangely confident. On 14 and 15 November, while Li Yunchang's situation at Shanhaiguan was falling apart, Mao seems to have been envisioning a progressive bleeding of the Nationalist armies, culminating in a decisive battle for the control of Manchuria.[72] On 14 November he instructed, "Take Jinzhou as a core area, making it the strategic pivot for operations in which we focus our entire strength."[73] While he realized that Lin Biao had other forces in western Liaoning, Mao urged Lin, "Use the main force cautiously, so that in the future with a decisive battle, one battle will resolve the problem."[74] In Mao's mind, the issue of Manchuria would be resolved in a single, climactic decisive battle to occur at or near Jinzhou.[75] This search for a decisive battle would eventually lead him to order his forces to make a firm stand at Siping in the spring of 1946. But for the moment, as Du Yuming's forces made their inexorable way up the Liaoxi Corridor, Mao's vision of a decisive battle in which Lin Biao, with seventy thousand poorly armed and exhausted men, would cleverly wipe out three well-armed Nationalist armies was evidence of just how out of touch—or impossibly romantic—Mao Zedong could be.

THE LIAOXI CORRIDOR CHANGES HANDS

In Yan'an on 16 November, Mao Zedong had heard via a United Press report the news that his troops had lost Shanhaiguan. He immediately telegraphed Li Yunchang to tell him to hold the line along which the major towns of the Liaoxi Corridor were strung out—from Shanhaiguan to Suizhong, from Suizhong to Xingcheng. These were the keys to the defense of the major railway junction of Jinzhou and the port of Huludao. Li responded that he had only ten thousand regular combat troops with limited combat capability on the line between Shanhaiguan and Xingcheng. It would be impossible for him to keep Du Yuming from advancing from Suizhong to Xingcheng. In response, the Party Center revised its plans. On 17 November, the Center ordered Li, Huang Kecheng, and other officers under Lin Biao to attempt a mobile defense of the Jinzhou area: "Conduct a determined fighting retreat stage by stage, neither defending territory to the death nor lightly giving it up." Two units, those of Huang Kecheng and Liang Xingchu, were to concentrate their forces at Jinzhou as fast as possible and prepare to launch a sudden attack on the enemy from his left flank and rear.[76]

While the Communist Party Center and its forces on the ground in Manchuria prepared to defend Jinzhou and (perhaps) seek the conditions under which Mao's vision of a decisive battle might become a reality, Du Yuming, Lin's fellow Whampoa Military Academy graduate, was seeking to achieve the goal that had eluded him at Shanhaiguan: the utter destruction of Lin's forces. By 18 November, Du's forces had reached Suizhong. They had also outrun their logistical tail and had to pause for four days while their supply lines caught up with them. When they were ready to move forward again, the next targets were the Communist forces at Xingcheng, Jinxi, Jinzhou itself, and the port of Huludao. Xingcheng was a walled city along the railway line, not far from the coast. Here again, Du ordered a portion of his force to outflank the city, cut off the Communists' route of retreat, and pin them against the beach while his main force attacked Xingcheng from the south.[77]

Xingcheng stands at a critical chokepoint along the Liaoxi Corridor, with mountains to the north, south, and west and the ocean to the east. Its thick, high city walls date back to 1428, when the city was built as a part of the Ming Dynasty's defenses against the Jurchens. Some of Du's officers feared that if Lin Biao were to choose to make a stand in the Liaoxi Corridor, this would be the place. Consequently, they approached the city with care. Du Yuming urged them forward.[78] Once again, the Communists anticipated Du's plans and retreated while they still could, although not without being severely mauled in an encounter with a Nationalist unit.

When he entered Xingcheng, Du Yuming would have passed under an elaborate stone memorial archway. This archway, still standing today, was erected in 1638 in honor of the meritorious deeds of the Ming emperor Chongzhen. Less than ten years later, the Manchus had captured Xingcheng, pushed the Ming out of the Liaoxi Corridor, entered China through the pass at Shanhaiguan, and begun the conquest of China Proper. At the time, this historical lesson would not have seemed relevant to Du Yuming; he had grasped the initiative and had the Communists on the run. After taking Xingcheng, his troops aggressively pressed their advantage. On 21 November, they pursued the Communists to Jinxi, which they took, along with the nearby port of Huludao, the next day.

At Xingcheng, Jinxi, and Huludao, the Nationalist forces once again demonstrated that they had the sheer force and firepower to capture territory, while the Communists proved that, although weak, they were clever enough to survive to fight another day. As they made their way up the Liaoxi Corridor, the Kuomingtang forces continued to be slowed down, not by Lin Biao, but by the challenges of moving a large modern army up the thirty-kilometer-wide corridor between the sea and the mountains. Five divisions, says Shi Jue, were stretched out in a long line of march extending fifty kilometers in length, with motor vehicles and horse- and mule-drawn carts from various units all mixed together, presenting Lin Biao with a vulnerable target if he had only been capable of turning and launching an attack at the time.[79]

Fortunately for Shi Jue and Du Yuming, Lin Biao did not have the means to counterattack. Instead, he had an intelligence network good enough to warn them of the enemy's intentions and positions so that he could flee successfully. The Nationalists, for their part, still suffered from poor communication and delays in movement that gave the Communists time that they otherwise would not have had. The Nationalists also had technical limitations that played to the Communists' advantage. Unlike the Communists, the Nationalist forces did not have the experience or equipment needed to destroy railway tracks. As a result, Communist units at Jinxi successfully used the railway to take troops and supplies out of Jinxi under the very noses of Nationalist soldiers. In addition, without flat-trajectory artillery, those same soldiers could do nothing beyond hitting the Communist train with machine-fire, which had little effect.[80]

With Xingcheng and Jinxi lost, and the Nationalists now able to land more troops and supplies at the port of Huludao, the situation was less and less favorable to the Communists. On 21 November, the Party Center ordered Lin and his officers to "hit the enemy army hard as he advances from Shanhaiguan toward Jinzhou, try hard to annihilate one or two divisions, control a section of the railroad, cut the enemy's line of retreat in order to squelch the enemy's power, block his advance, and protect our orderly withdrawal from Shenyang, Changchun, and other major cities."[81] Lin Biao in return described the situation to the Communist Party Center. His troops were exhausted and dispersed. Some units had lagged behind and were actually to the rear of the enemy's front lines. There were serious shortages of weapons, ammunition, food, clothing, and shoes. From the general headquarters on down, the Communist officers did not have maps and were unfamiliar with the terrain, and communications were chaotic at best:

> The enemy uses these weaknesses of ours, advances on us, and surrounds our flanks. In light of this situation, I have one basic opinion, that is: right now, our army should avoid being defeated in detail by the enemy and avoid getting hurriedly rushed into battle. We should prepare to give up Jinzhou and the area 200 to 300 li north of Jinzhou, let the enemy stretch out and become thinly dispersed, then choose weak spots to attack. Therefore our forces in Shenyang and Yingkou need not rush to reinforce us, they should stay where they are and carry out preparations and thorough training, build up their strength, especially build up their artillery capability in preparation for entering battle later.[82]

On 22 and 23 November the Party Center (now headed once again by Liu Shaoqi) approved Lin's recommendation, while adding the hope that Communist forces operating in the enemy's rear would still manage to wipe out one or two divisions and slow Du Yuming's advance.[83] At this point, the Party Center was so disconnected from the situation on the ground that they were still thinking in terms of how Lin might be able to annihilate the Nationalist Thirteenth and Fifty-second Armies.[84] In the meantime, Communist forces worked to transport supplies and materiel out of Jinzhou, and to sabotage hydroelectric and transportation facilities. The Nationalists, however, moved too fast. By the time Lin Biao had moved his troops into position to attack the Nationalist forces, they had already gotten into position to attack Jinzhou. Throughout the night of 25 November, the Nationalists, as they prepared for the attack, could hear loud explosions and see flashes of fire in the city. At seven o'clock in the morning on 26 November, the men of the Nationalist Fifty-second Army entered the city. The Communists had already fled, leaving weapons and supplies behind them.[85]

PENG ZHEN, LIN BIAO, AND THE LESSONS OF DEFEAT

The loss of Jinzhou was a major setback for the Chinese Communist forces in the Northeast. Only a month before, Mao Zedong had been talking confidently about controlling all of Manchuria, and the Soviets had been urging Peng Zhen to take a hard line against the Nationalists. Now, in late November, the Communists were on the ropes. Peng Zhen and Lin Biao had lost territory, key strategic points, men, weapons, and supplies in a series of retreats from Shanhaiguan to Xingcheng to Jinzhou. They had also lost credibility both with the people of southern Manchuria (who had been inclined to support the Nationalists from the start) and with the Soviet "elder brother." As they considered their defeat, the new situation on the ground, and the diplomatic context, Peng, Lin, and the Communist leadership in Yan'an all understood that they would need to make changes in both tactics and strategy if they expected to recover from their setback, defend their remaining positions, and eventually defeat the Nationalist armies. The tactical lessons were relatively straightforward; debate on strategic issues, on the other hand, indicated serious differences of opinion, both within the Northeast Bureau and between the Northeast Bureau's leadership and the Party Center.

The one major tactical lesson from the Liaoxi campaign was that the Communist soldiers were not prepared to conduct defense of static positions or engage in large-scale mobile operations in the field. In a strictly organizational sense, the Eighth Route and New Fourth Armies had already made the transition from guerrilla to standard warfare. But this "transition" had simply been a matter of reorganization of forces into standard army units. Beneath the surface, the men and officers were still guerrilla warriors. In the Liaoxi Campaign, guerrilla tactics had proven completely incapable of standing up to the numerically superior, well-armed, and well-trained professionals of Du Yuming and Shi Jue's armies. Lack of weapons (particularly artillery) had been one factor. But other weaknesses included a failure to build sufficient defensive works, poor coordination of firepower, lack of coordination between units, loose battle discipline, instances of units giving up positions at random, and a tendency to attack in tight formation. All of these led to lost opportunities and needlessly high casualties.[86]

Lin Biao's response to these problems was to articulate two tactical principles: the "three-three system" and "one point, two flanks." Under the three-three system, each squad would be divided into three teams of three or four men each. In combat, the squad would advance with the teams in triangular formation instead of all advancing together in the tight linear formations that exposed too many men to enemy fire. The idea of "one point, two flanks" was that when attacking the enemy, a commander should identify the enemy's key weak point and attack it with overwhelmingly superior numbers and firepower. At the same time, depending on the circumstances, he should attack the enemy with lesser force at one or more other points, both in order to prevent the enemy from understanding where the main point of attack really was and to either envelop, cut off, or pin down enemy forces. "One point, two flanks" was Lin's way of addressing the tendency of many of his officers to divide their forces evenly in order to attack an enemy position from multiple points.[87] These tactical principles, articulated in late December 1945, did not, of course, transform the Communist forces overnight. They represented only the beginning of a long process of tactical innovation, training, and improvement of equipment which enabled Lin Biao's forces to make the transition from guerrilla war to standard warfare over the course of years of combat in Manchuria.

As commander of the Communist forces, Lin Biao was ultimately in charge of tactical issues. But when it came to strategy, the Party leaders, both in the Northeast Bureau and at the Party Center, had the final word. However, in the month after the retreat from Jinzhou, it became increasingly clear that Peng Zhen and the leadership in Yan'an did not see eye to eye on strategy—and that some members of Peng's own Northeast Bureau did not agree with him either. As we have seen, Peng Zhen's background was in urban work, and his strategy for the Northeast focused on taking and holding the "Three Big Cities" of Shenyang, Changchun, and Harbin. But immediately after the retreat from Jinzhou, members of the North Manchuria Branch of Peng's Northeast Bureau held a three-day meeting and concluded that they should stop focusing on the "Three Big Cities." Instead, the Communists should disperse their forces in the medium and small cities and rural areas, concentrate on building base areas, and prepare for a protracted struggle and eventual victory.[88]

Back in Yan'an, Mao Zedong had fallen seriously ill in mid-November. He would spend the next three months or more under the care of Soviet physicians. In the meantime, day-to-day leadership over the Central Committee was once again in the hands of Liu Shaoqi—the same man who, back in September, had overseen the development of the "advance in the north, defend in the south" strategy. Liu and the Central Committee agreed with the North Manchuria Branch's recommendations, which were very much in tune with the Center's thinking. In a series of telegrams from late November through December, Liu Shaoqi and the Central Committee told the Northeast Bureau that the weakness of the Communist forces and the Soviet Union's commitment to transfer authority over the major cities and rail lines to Chiang Kai-shek's government meant that there was now "no possibility of our attempting to control the entire Northeast."[89]

The Party Center had given up the dream of controlling the entire Northeast, but they had not given up the region entirely. The major cities and main rail lines were lost for the moment—the Soviets were already driving the Communist forces away from these areas in preparation for transferring them to Chiang Kai-shek. But the Communists still could, and, they believed, should, do their utmost to control the small and medium towns, the branch railway lines, and the rural areas. The Center accordingly ordered Peng Zhen to disperse most of his forces to these areas in order to build strong base areas and prepare for a protracted struggle. Peng Zhen responded with plans that echoed the Center's directives, but at the same time he continued to raise the possibility of attacking the major cities once the Soviets had withdrawn—apparently over the objections of some of the members of his own Northeast Bureau.[90]

While they instructed Peng Zhen to prepare for protracted struggle, the Central Committee also wanted him to prepare for Chiang Kai-shek's next move. After the capture of Jinzhou, Du Yuming was brimming with confidence: he asked Chiang to give him ten armies, with which he promised he could completely eliminate the Communists in the Northeast in three months, after which he could send armies through the passes to take on the Communist forces in Rehe and North China.[91] Chiang, far more cautious, ordered Du Yuming not to advance any further without explicit orders. Already in the advance to Jinzhou, the Nationalist armies had experienced supply problems.[92] Furthermore, from the beginning of the Liaoxi Campaign, Chiang had harbored reservations about the wisdom of getting drawn further into Manchuria. Back on 15 November he had told his generals that it would be better to put the Northeast to one side and concentrate on consolidating control over North China first.[93] Now, having pushed as far as Jinzhou, Chiang hoped to pause to secure control over the rail line from Jinzhou to Shanhaiguan. His next step would be to attack the Communists in the border province of Rehe in order to cut off the Communists in Manchuria from their old base areas in Rehe and North China. Anticipating this move, the Central Committee ordered Peng Zhen and Lin Biao to deploy a part of their forces to West Manchuria and to strengthen command and control over the troops in that area so that they would be able to help in the defense of Rehe.[94]

While they prepared for war, the Central Committee still held some hope that if they showed enough strength, and if the Soviet Union and the United States got more involved, they could get Chiang Kai-shek to agree to a deal that would acknowledge a Communist political and military presence in the Northeast.[95] In mid-December, these hopes gained more credibility when they learned that President Truman would be sending General George Marshall as his special representative to China in order to mediate between the Nationalists and the Communists.

4

George Marshall's Mission

December 1945–March 1946

The fight for control over the Liaoxi corridor had repercussions not only in China, but also in Washington, D.C. America's grand strategy in the emerging Cold War with the Soviet Union called for a united, pro-American China to help secure American influence in East and Southeast Asia. A civil war between Chiang Kai-shek's government and the Soviet-sponsored Chinese Communist Party threatened to undermine the American vision of China's future. Therefore President Truman asked General George Marshall to go to China as his personal representative and negotiate a settlement between Chiang Kai-shek and the Chinese Communist Party.

George Marshall's mission to China extended from his arrival in Shanghai on December 20, 1945, until the recall of the mission on January 6, 1947. The Marshall Mission itself has been documented and analyzed in a number of excellent books and articles.[1] The purpose of this chapter is not simply to retell the familiar story of the Marshall Mission, but rather to explore the interplay among American, Chinese Nationalist, and Chinese Communist strategic goals, Marshall's negotiations, and the development of the military situation in the Northeast. Marshall's presence in China, his daily, personal assertion of American interests, and his attempts to use diplomacy to influence the course of events in China became important parts of the framework within which both the Kuomintang and the Communist Party made tactical decisions on the ground in Manchuria. Ultimately, both the decision to fight at Siping in April–May 1946 and the handling of the aftermath of the battle were intimately linked to Marshall's negotiations.

HARRY TRUMAN'S CHINA PROBLEM

Harry Truman's attitude toward China can be summed up in two words: apathy and ignorance. That verdict may overstate the case, but in truth, China does not seem to have held much interest for Truman. Like most Americans of his generation, Truman would have grown up knowing very little about China. Given his background and the strong influence of Christianity and of the missionary movement on his knowledge of the world, it is more than likely that before he became president, Truman saw China as did most Americans of his time: as a vast, backward nation of souls to be saved and as a huge market of four hundred million consumers. But practically speaking, there was no profit to be made from saving souls, and as long as China's four hundred million potential consumers were mired in poverty, the huge China market remained no more than a dream. China, accordingly, had never played a significant role in American foreign policy. When the Great Qing Empire faced disintegration in the early twentieth century, President Theodore Roosevelt suggested that imperialism would be a good thing for China. The place was so backward, and the people so inferior, that its only hope for progress was to be ruled by a superior nation. As for Manchuria, Roosevelt was of the opinion that its fate was of little importance to the United States, and that everyone might be better off if it were taken over by the Russians or the Japanese. When Japan really did take over Manchuria in 1931, the United States protested, but did little else. The territorial integrity of the Republic of China was simply not a matter of serious interest or concern to the United States.

Only when Japan took French Indochina—thus encroaching on the interests of a European nation—and then attacked at Pearl Harbor did American leaders begin to link their national interests to those of Chiang Kai-shek's Republic of China in any serious way. But even during the Second World War, China played a distinctly secondary role in American strategy and in American foreign policy. Lend-Lease supplies to China were granted in limited amounts—never enough to make a significant difference to Chiang Kai-shek's ability to fight the Japanese. Joseph Stilwell, the man whom Roosevelt chose to act as commander of the China-India-Burma theater, was a mediocre commander whose incompetence on the battlefield was matched only by his arrogance at the negotiating table.[2] Stilwell made no secret of the fact that he despised Chiang Kaishek. His reports to his superior officer, General Marshall (then Chief of Staff), and to President Roosevelt himself portrayed Chiang Kai-shek as the head of a hopelessly corrupt government and an ineffective military, unwilling to take the fight to the Japanese. On the strength of these reports, and at Marshall's express urging, Roosevelt ordered Chiang Kaishek to put Stilwell in command of China's armies. Stilwell delivered the message in person, in a blunt style purposely calculated to insult the Generalissimo. Stilwell clearly enjoyed making Chiang squirm, but it was Chiang who had the last laugh: he demanded that Roosevelt recall Stilwell and send someone who could be more diplomatic. Stilwell left China's wartime capital of Chongqing unceremoniously on 21 October. Chiang Kai-shek did not see him off at the airport.[3]

    To replace Stilwell as his representative in China, Roosevelt, in a gesture of bipartisanship, chose Patrick Hurley, an Oklahoma (and later New Mexico) Republican who had no experience in China—an advantage from Chiang Kai-shek's point of view. At first, Hurley hoped to build a cooperative relationship between Chiang's Nationalists and the Chinese Communist Party. Optimistic at the outset, Hurley visited the Communist leaders in Yan'an and played an instrumental role in arranging the Chongqing negotiations (as discussed in chapter 3). Hurley soon became disillusioned with the Communist Party—and with many of the State Department's China experts, both those on his staff in Chongqing and those in Washington. On 26 November 1945, Hurley, then visiting Washington, unexpectedly submitted his letter of resignation to President Truman. In the letter (which he released to the press the next day), Hurley complained that professional foreign service men in the State Department sided with the Chinese Communists and/or with European imperialism against freedom, democracy, and the free enterprise system in China, and that when he asked for these career men in China to be relieved, some of them wound up being transferred to Washington and becoming his supervisors.[4]

Hurley's resignation came as a surprise and left Truman in something of a quandary. From a strategic point of view, the United States wanted a strong, united, pro-American Republic of China to function as the linchpin of American interests in East Asia and as a bulwark against the expansion of the Soviet Union. But at the same time, President Roosevelt had been concerned about the patently undemocratic nature of Chiang Kai-shek's regime and about the inefficiency and corruption within the Chinese military.[5] Harry Truman shared these concerns, but hoped that Chiang Kai-shek would in fact bring corruption under control and build a more democratic regime. He was soon disillusioned.[6] In the meantime, with the onset of the Cold War, China policy was becoming highly politicized. The drama of Hurley's resignation was indicative of a deeper split within the American foreign policy and military establishments, in which expressions of negative points of view about the Kuomintang and positive points of view about the Chinese Communist Party were becoming increasingly dangerous.

For the time being, President Truman and Secretary of State Byrnes remained convinced that the key to achieving their strategic goals in China lay in forcing the Kuomintang and the Communist Party into some form of coalition government, but in some quarters, there was serious skepticism—skepticism that was articulated in ways that suggested that those in favor of compromise were in some sense on the side of America's enemy in the Cold War. Admiral Leahy, for example, recording his reaction to Byrnes' stress on achieving coalition government in China, wrote in his diary, "Today for the first time, I sense a feeling that Secretary Byrnes is not immune to the communisticly [*sic*] inclined advisors in his Department."[7] To make matters more complicated, Truman himself had little confidence in Byrnes, commenting in early December, "I would have a pretty good government, don't you think, if I had a good Labor Department and a good State Department?"[8] Thus it was in the context of an increasingly disputed and confused China policy that Truman turned to George Marshall in a last attempt to pull China back from the brink of all-out civil war and to bring Chiang Kai-shek and the Communists together in a democratic coalition government with a professional, apolitical army. Marshall, hailed as the architect of the American victory in the Second World War, had just retired from his position as Chief of Staff. On 27 November, within hours of receiving the news of Hurley's resignation, Truman telephoned Marshall, asking him to lead a mission to China.[9]

DESIGNING MISSION IMPOSSIBLE

Even as they worked on the plans for the Marshall Mission, members of Marshall's staff were convinced that it stood little chance of success.[10] In hindsight, and with access to Chinese as well as American sources, we can see clearly just how hopeless the enterprise was. To begin with, there was a fundamental contradiction between the American government's expansive and idealistic goals in China and the limited means available to achieve those goals. There were contradictions, too, between the ideological zero-sum calculus of hard-line Cold Warriors in the United States and George Marshall's cautious pragmatism. In addition, the attitudes of both the Nationalist government and the Chinese Communist Party virtually guaranteed that the Marshall Mission would end in failure.

The American goal in China was to make the country into a reliable strategic and economic partner. The Truman administration was apparently convinced that democracy could contribute to the realization of this goal by dissolving enmities, eliminating corruption, and laying the grounds for sustained economic growth. In specific terms, the American involvement in China's brewing civil war aimed at achieving a real ceasefire, bringing both sides into a coalition government, and combining the Nationalist Party and Communist Party military forces into a single, national (as opposed to party) professional military. Beyond that, the United States hoped to build the institutions of liberal democracy in China—representative government, a free press, an independent judiciary—in short, to re-make China into at least some approximation of the American model. But at the same time, Truman, Marshall, the State Department, and the American military viewed the situation in China not only through the missionary mindset as a place to be Christianized, democratized, and modernized, but also through the lens of the Cold War as a piece in the strategic puzzle of America's global competition

with the Soviet Union.[11] Thus, their belief in the transformative potential of democracy was tempered by a desire to support Chiang's regime,
however distasteful it might be, in order to prevent the establishment
of a pro-Soviet Chinese Communist regime. As a result, the Truman
administration's goals in China were both ambitious and inherently
contradictory.

To achieve the American goals in China would have required extensive resources and a leader willing to take significant risks.George
Marshall was not a risk-taker. He was methodical, calculating, and inclined to caution. As an officer, his concern for the well-being of his
troops made him particularly interested in logistics, and reluctant to
commit men to situations in which they would not receive the level of
support they needed in order to assure victory. These characteristics
made Marshall a very effective Chief of Staff, but they were antithetical
to the totalistic, all-or-nothing calculus of committed Cold Warriors.
Patrick Hurley's resignation and his angry denunciation of alleged Communist sympathizers in the State Department were clear indicators of
a hardening of the ideological lines in the American government, and
in American society in general. The more strident the rhetoric of the
Cold War, the more difficult it became to formulate and carry out any
policy that settled for anything less than total victory. General Albert
Wedemeyer, then commanding American forces in China, articulated
the "all-or-nothing" approach in a memorandum to the Department of
State in November 1945: "If the unification of China and Manchuria
under Chinese National Forces is to be a United States policy, involvement in fratricidal warfare and possibly in war with the Soviet Union
must be accepted and would definitely require additional United States
Forces far beyond those presently available in the Theater to implement
the policy."[12]

Direct involvement of American forces in the Chinese Civil War—
not to mention a possible war with the Soviet Union—was precisely
what the Truman administration was trying to avoid. After four years
of war in Europe and the Far East, the United States had neither the
material resources nor the will to engage in what could, if the Soviet
Union became involved, become another two-front war. The American
military was stretched thin. The defense of Europe took priority over

any concerns in East Asia. Demobilization was the order of the day, and public opinion was very much against any direct American military involvement in China. On 20 December, Undersecretary of State Dean Acheson, drawing on letters from the public, and especially from labor union members, told Marshall that "the use of US troops in China is unpopular with the American people."[13]

Marshall was, then, to bring an end to the Chinese Civil War without the use of American military power. He would need to rely on his own diplomatic skills and on whatever types of pressure short of direct military involvement he could bring to bear on the Chinese Nationalist Party government and its Communist Party enemy. In return for their cooperation, Marshall had very little to offer the Chinese Communists other than the dubious privilege of being minority members of a democratically elected coalition government on whatever terms Chiang Kai-shek would agree to. As the United States had no significant relationship with the Communists, Marshall had very few "sticks" to use against them. Marshall did have some significant leverage to bring to bear against Chiang Kai-shek's government: economic aid packages, loans, military aid, and American transport of Nationalist armies could all be cut down, or cut off, if Chiang proved uncooperative.

Any tools that Marshall might use to put pressure on Chiang Kai-shek were weakened by the simple fact that in the final analysis, the Truman administration was committed to the survival of Chiang's regime and the incorporation of the Communist Party and army into a coalition under Chiang's leadership, and not the other way around. On 14 December, Marshall told Truman that as he understood it, "In the event I was unable to secure the necessary action by the Generalissimo, which I thought reasonable and desirable, it would still be necessary for the U.S. Government, through me, to continue to back the National Government of the Republic of China—through the Generalissimo within the terms of the announced policy of the U.S. Government." Truman agreed that this was indeed the case. Even if Chiang Kai-shek refused any compromise solutions that Marshall might suggest, the United States would continue to support the Nationalist regime in ways short of direct American involvement in the Chinese Civil War.[14] Someone leaked this conversation to China's ambassador in Washington, who reported to Chiang that "when Marshall asked the President what to do if the Chinese Communists do not knuckle under or if our government is not willing to accept the Communists' conditions for being included in the government, the President answered, support your excellency."[15]

When Marshall left Washington for China, he had a clear understanding of his mission, its goals, and the tools that he had at his disposal —he and his staff, in fact, had contributed substantially to the drafting of his orders. Marshall also came to China with at least some preliminary impressions about China in general and about the Communist and Nationalist parties. Marshall had been to China twice earlier in his career. In 1914 Marshall went to China to study the battlefields of the Russo-Japanese War, which must have given him some impression of Manchuria's geography and strategic significance.[16] Later, Marshall spent three years (1924–1927) as executive officer of the Fifteenth Infantry Regiment in Tianjin. While there, he had tried (evidently with little success) to learn Chinese and had observed the Second Zhili-Fengtian War (1924—a major conflict between two leading warlord factions) and Chiang Kai-shek's rise to power.[17] Whatever personal impressions Marshall may have had of China he kept largely to himself. Like most foreigners, Marshall lived a privileged and comfortable life and had little contact with Chinese people. He did observe, and was struck by, the poverty and suffering of ordinary Chinese citizens, by the rapacity of the warlords, by the brutality of warlord soldiers, and by the lack of any stable, competent government. He also professed himself confused about warlord intentions, observing, during the Second Zhili-Fengtian War, "Chinese methods are too devious for foreign penetration."[18]

Marshall's early impressions of China were supplemented both by his experiences as Chief of Staff during World War II and during his preparation for his mission to China in late 1945. As Chief of Staff, Marshall had received General Joseph Stilwell's acerbic reports on Chiang Kai-shek and was responsible for advising President Roosevelt on the handling of the clash between Stilwell and Chiang—a clash which ended in Chiang's insisting on Stilwell's recall. During these years, Marshall was largely sympathetic with Stilwell and tended to agree with Stilwell's low regard for Chiang and his capabilities.[19] American intelligence tended to reinforce a rather negative image of Chiang Kai-shek with assessments like this one, transmitted to the War Department on November 20, 1945:

> I believe that Generalissimo Chiang Kai-shek is sincere in his desire to bring about stability within the country, to initiate democratic procedures, to unify China and to implement wide sweeping social reforms. Considering his background, training, and experience as a warlord, politician, and his oriental philosophy, his approach to problems presented will probably be inefficient, incomprehensible and unethical by American standards.[20]

It is fair to say, then, that Marshall went to China in December 1945 with a negative impression of Chiang Kai-shek and of the Nationalist government. Marshall's impressions of the Communist Party and its leadership were based less on personal experience and more on second-hand reports. Marshall was certainly familiar with intelligence reports and memoranda suggesting that the Communist Party was more honest and competent, and more likely to win the support of the Chinese people, than Chiang Kai-shek's Nationalists.[21] Whether, or to what extent, Marshall agreed with that assessment is impossible to say.[22] It is clear, however, that Marshall had formed an opinion about the Communist Party's relationship to the Soviet Union: in his view, the Chinese Communists were simply tools of the Soviets.[23] Marshall was accordingly suspicious of Communist intentions. On 30 November 1945, as he prepared for his mission to China, he wrote:

> I assume that the Communist group will block all progress in negotiations as far as they can, as the delay is to their advantage. The greater the delay the more they benefit from the growing confusion of the situation and the serious results that will follow from the non-evacuation of the Japanese military. Also the longer the delay the less probability of the Generalissimo's being able to establish a decent semblance of control over Manchuria, with the subsequent certainty that the Russians will definitely build up such control.[24]

THE EDUCATION OF GENERAL MARSHALL

In late November, when China's Foreign Minister reported on President Truman's plans for the Marshall Mission, Chen Lifu, one of Chiang Kai-shek's top advisors, told him, "This is no good. Anyone else coming here would be better than George Marshall!"[25] Marshall, Chen argued, had no experience with the Communists, who would deceive and manipulate the clueless American. Foreign Minister Wang Shijie countered that it would be "a learning experience" for the Americans to participate in the mediation. Chiang and the Nationalists assumed that Marshall was cold and logical where Hurley had been emotional, that he was naive, and, furthermore, that his understanding of China was deeply influenced by Joseph Stilwell's negative reports, the thinking of Communists and Communist sympathizers in the State Department, and a natural American inclination to side with the underdog.[26] In the eyes of Chiang and his advisors, Marshall was someone who needed to be educated and manipulated in order to better serve Chiang's ultimate goal, which was to consolidate his government's control over all of China and, by implication, to defeat the Chinese Communists.

The Communist leaders, too, regarded Marshall as a target of education and manipulation. As Zhou Enlai saw it, Marshall's imminent arrival did not signal any change in American policy in China.[27] The American goal would still be to create a united, pro-American China under Nationalist Party leadership. At best, the Marshall Mission indicated that the United States would attempt to achieve its goals in China through a combination of diplomatic and economic pressure and negotiations rather than direct military involvement. For the Communist leadership, the American desire to prevent an all-out civil war in China represented an opportunity. The American commitment to peace fit in particularly well with the Communist Party's situation in the Northeast. Lin Biao's defeat in the Liaoxi Corridor had made the Soviet Union very nervous about any further fighting in Manchuria. The Communists could use the negotiations in order to reduce American support for the Nationalists' military advance in North China and Manchuria (in essence, neutralizing the United States) or even to force the Nationalists to recognize the Communist position in the Northeast.[28] In that case, Lin Biao could continue to quietly build military strength in Manchuria behind the screen of Soviet occupation.[29] In order to use the mediation process to their advantage, Communist negotiators would need not only to educate George Marshall, but also to seek common ground with the American envoy. Mao Zedong interpreted Patrick Hurley's resignation and the appointment of Marshall as a sign that "progressive" forces were on the rise in the United States, and that he could work with the

Americans.[30] Unlike the Nationalists, then, the Communist leadership received the Marshall Mission with a good deal of optimism.

Marshall's "education" began directly on his arrival in China on 20 December. Both General Wedemeyer and Walter Robertson, the Chargé of the American Embassy, told him that his mission was hopeless—that there was no way to get the Nationalist and Communist parties to agree to a real coalition government. As Wedemeyer later remembered it, Marshall responded angrily, "I am going to accomplish my mission and you are going to help me."[31] In Nanjing, Chiang Kai-shek, despite previous reservations, received Marshall cordially—the beginning of what became an all-out effort on the part of Chiang and Madame Chiang to use warmth (to the extent that the famously stiff and reserved Chiang was capable of warmth) and hospitality in an effort to win Marshall's sympathies.[32] Gifts, banquets, and birthday celebrations were all a part of the diplomatic effort. The scale of each event probably had to be carefully calibrated, since Chiang and his officials had been warned that Marshall was a man of simple tastes and that banquets should be kept relatively low-key.[33]

Privately, Chiang and his advisors found Marshall to be arrogant and patronizing.[34] They were also deeply worried that Marshall and the Americans in general simply did not appreciate the complexities of China's situation, the nature of the Chinese Communist Party, and the role and intentions of the Soviet Union. Neither Chiang nor his advisors agreed with the American goal of democratizing Chinese politics. As General Bai Chongxi saw it, there was a fundamental contradiction between liberal democratic principles and rule of law on the one hand and the need to suppress the Communist Party on the other. Years later, as he recalled this period, General Bai used same kind of language used by the post-1989 leaders of the Chinese Communist Party when he proclaimed, "The big mistake that America often makes is to force their model of democracy on other countries."[35]

From Nanjing, Marshall then flew on to Chongqing, where Zhou Enlai met him at the airport. Zhou began his part of the "educational" process by telling Marshall that the Communist Party's policies were the same as those of the late Franklin Roosevelt: a ceasefire, a united, democratic China under a coalition government, and a unified military.[36] Mar-

FIGURE 4.1. George Marshall (second from left), T. V. Soong (third from left), and Chiang Kai-shek (far right) at Marshall's birthday party, 31 December 1945. *Courtesy of the Research Library of the George C. Marshall Foundation.*

shall, though favorably impressed, understood that for the Communist Party, coalition government had to come first, and integration of Communist forces into a national army second, while for the Kuomintang, integration of the Communist Eighth Route and New Fourth Armies into the national army under Chiang's command (in other words, depriving the Communist Party of its independent military force) would be the necessary condition for coalition government.[37]

Whether out of optimism, a commitment to obey orders, or sheer stubbornness, Marshall proceeded as if success was possible, engaging the Communists, the Nationalists, and independent political organizations in dialogue. From 22 December through 10 January, Marshall worked to achieve three goals: an agreement on holding a meeting of the Political Consultative Conference, a plan for the integration of the Communist Eighth Route and New Fourth Armies into the National

Armyunder Chiang Kai-shek's command, and a cessation-of-hostilities order. Arranging a meeting of the Political Consultative Conference was relatively easy. Both sides had agreed to such a meeting during the Chongqing negotiations earlier in the year. Under Marshall's guidance, the meeting was scheduled to begin on 10 January. The question of military re-organization, although broached during this time, was put off until February. Before military reorganization could be discussed seriously, the two sides would need to stop shooting at each other. Thus the most pressing item on Marshall's agenda was to negotiate a cessation of hostilities.

The negotiations were carried out by a committee of three: Marshall represented the United States, Zhou Enlai spoke for the Communist Party, and General Zhang Qun, governor of Sichuan Province, spoke for the Nationalist Party. Working with proposals and counterproposals previously submitted, the Committee of Three met from 7–10 January to hammer out the text of the Cessation of Hostilities Order. Manchuria and the adjoining provinces of Rehe and Chahar were the main items of contention. In Manchuria, as we saw in the previous chapter, Du Yuming's Nationalist troops had driven Lin Biao's forces out of the Liaoxi Corridor and were waiting for the Soviet Red Army to withdraw, when, according to the Sino-Soviet Treaty, the Soviets would transfer control of Manchuria to Chiang Kai-shek's government and army. As Zhang Qun was negotiating with Zhou Enlai, Chiang Kai-shek continued to move more Nationalist armies to Manchuria as he prepared to take control of the area as soon as the Soviets withdrew. As George Marshall was soon to learn, his mediation efforts were most significant not for any success in achieving peace, but rather for establishing the framework within which the war would be fought.

THE NEGOTIATING TABLE AND THE BATTLEFIELD

The Communists welcomed George Marshall's mediation. They and their Soviet advisors believed that as the weaker party, the Communists could use the negotiations to buy time in which to consolidate their position in the Northeast before the eventual withdrawal of the Soviet Red Army. But on the ground in the Northeast itself, the leaders of the

Communist Party's Northeast Bureau disagreed among themselves and with the Party leadership in Yan'an as to precisely how they should proceed to consolidate a Northeast base area and put themselves into the best possible position to take full advantage of the opportunities that would arise as soon as the Soviet Red Army began its withdrawal from the region. Peng Zhen, leader of the Northeast Bureau, leaned toward a "Three Big Cities" strategy, and still held out the possibility of getting into position to capture and defend Shenyang, Changchun, and Harbin.[38] Lin Biao, as commander of the Northeast People's Autonomous Army (as the Chinese Communist forces were known at that point), was reluctant to commit his forces to battles of position. He preferred to disengage from the enemy, withdraw to the hinterland, build rural base areas, and strengthen his armies. Peng Zhen's strategy called for decisive battles. Lin Biao's approach was to wear down an over-extended enemy through protracted war.

From November 1945 through June 1946 the Communist leaders in Yan'an shifted between protracted war on the one hand, and battles to capture and/or defend key positions on the other, depending on their assessment of the national and international strategic and diplomatic situations, and particularly on their understanding of the progress of ceasefire negotiations. At Shanhaiguan and in the Liaoxi Corridor in November 1945, Mao had hoped to fight a decisive battle to assert his control over all of Manchuria. This strategy had failed. As we noted at the conclusion of the previous chapter, Liu Shaoqi had ordered Peng Zhen and the Northeast Bureau to redeploy their forces away from the main cities and railway lines. Peng Zhen, however, still clung to the idea of capturing the "Three Big Cities." In late December 1945 Liu Shaoqi, writing for the Party Center, thoroughly punctured Peng Zhen's dream when he told the Northeast Bureau:

> Your main forces are deployed around the three major cities of Shenyang, Changchun, and Harbin and in South Manchuria; it seems you are still poised to wrest control over the three major cities, while you simply do not have strong forces deployed at many strategic points in East, North, and West Manchuria and you do not have capable Party leadership organizations going out to establish base areas. Your butts are sitting near the major cities, with your backs turned toward a country-side full of local bandits. Once the enemy armies take control of the major cities and your positions near the cities become untenable,

your main forces and the entire theater will inevitably be thrown on the defensive. Today you must abandon any attempt to take control of the major cities of the Northeast.... Your central task now is to build reliable base areas, get on a stable footing, and then, as the situation permits, proceed step by step to gain the upper hand in the Northeast, which should be your task at the next stage.[39]

What Liu Shaoqi and the rest of the Party Center realized was that the Northeast People's Autonomous Army was not strong enough to capture cities from and defend them against the well-armed, seasoned Nationalist forces. As a result, when Du Yuming began a new campaign on 27 December, Lin Biao initially retreated in order to avoid battle.[40] Lin's concern was to avoid costly tactical defeat in battles that, as he (and the Party Center) saw it, would be of little or no strategic value. His decisions were made primarily with an eye to the situation on the ground in Manchuria. But in Yan'an, the members of the Party leadership were asking not only which battles to avoid; they were also asking themselves where the Communist forces in the Northeast would need to stand and fight in order to gain maximum leverage in the peace talks at Chongqing and to preserve the Communists' long-term strategic advantage in North China and Manchuria. The answer was that the Communists could not afford to lose the border provinces of Rehe and Chahar.

Du Yuming's Rehe-Liaoning border campaign, launched on 27 December, was designed to secure land and sea access from China Proper to Manchuria so that the Nationalists would be able to pour troops into the area in time to take control when the Soviet Red Army withdrew. Du's Fifty-second and Thirteenth Armies moved out in multiple directions from Jinzhou: south toward the port of Yingkou, east to consolidate control of the Liaoxi Corridor and the railway to Shanhaiguan, and north/northeast toward Rehe and Chahar. With the loss of the Liaoxi Corridor, Rehe and Chahar represented the sole remaining Communist-controlled land routes into Manchuria. As long as they held these border provinces, the Communists had the hope of building a contiguous base area from Yan'an in northwestern China, across Inner Mongolia, Rehe, Chahar, and Manchuria. On the contrary, if the Nationalists could capture Rehe and Chahar, they could separate the Communist forces in North China from those in the Northeast and deal with each one separately. It was in order to cut this crucial link between Yan'an and

Manchuria that Du Yuming's Thirteenth Army advanced toward Rehe and Chahar in January 1946, putting Chengde, Chifeng, and Duolun at risk.

This was where the Communist Party leadership in Yan'an felt that it had to order Lin Biao to stand and fight. It was also where the interplay between the negotiating table and the battlefield came into play. Understanding the Communists' fundamental weakness in Manchuria, the Party Center had nixed Peng Zhen's "Three Big Cities" strategy and ordered the Northeast Bureau to redeploy its troops to the smaller towns and cities and the rural areas.[41] But at the same time, also at the end of December, Mao Zedong articulated his strategic vision for the Northeast. Mao's vision was composed of four main points: (1) an emphasis on building base areas over a period of three to four years; (2) an assumption that although Chiang Kai-shek would take the major cities and main rail lines, the Communists would continue to control small and medium-sized cities and branch railway lines; (3) that while the KMT remained stronger than the CCP, the Communists should focus on rooting out traitors, reducing rural rents, increasing agricultural production, and creating mass organizations; (4) that Communist cadres must stop complaining about not living in the cities and that they should not underestimate Nationalist strength.[42]

But while laying out a strategy for base-building and protracted warfare in Manchuria, Mao Zedong also believed that it was essential to control the border provinces of Rehe and Chahar. A few key units had been assigned to slow the KMT Thirteenth Army's advance toward Rehe and Chahar.[43] To underline the importance of this operation, the Party Center employed the same rhetoric that it had used in November when Mao Zedong had been seeking that last, decisive battle in the Liaoxi Corridor: "The battle for the defense of Rehe is a decisive factor for the hopes for peace in China Proper. At the present stage this may be the last battle."[44] In language that would be repeated three months later when directing the defense of Siping, the Party Center told Lin Biao, "If you can only hold on for a few weeks' time, it will be of tremendous significance for the Chongqing talks, [so we] hope that you will exert your utmost strength to carry out the mission: this is absolutely worth the sacrifice of thousands of men's lives."[45]

Lin Biao, who had reservations about the chances for a ceasefire, questioned the wisdom of seeking a decisive "last battle" over Rehe and Chahar. On 5 January he asked the Party Center's leaders if they were sure that peace was in the offing. If not, he suggested, it would be better to avoid battle, disperse his forces widely across the rear areas of the Northeast, and prepare to deal with an expected spring offensive from the Kuomintang. The Party Center responded that there would be a peace deal and that the defense of Rehe and Chahar was crucial. Whether he liked it or not, Lin Biao carried out his orders. On 10 January, he began moving units into position for the expected showdown.

While Lin Biao's forces conducted a fighting retreat to slow the Thirteenth Army and prepared for the "last battle" to defend Rehe and Chahar, Zhou Enlai was fighting a diplomatic battle in Chongqing. The success of the ceasefire talks clearly hinged on the related questions of Rehe/Chahar and Manchuria. Zhang Qun argued that the Kuomintang must be allowed to send troops to assert Chinese sovereignty over the key cities of Chifeng and Duolun (in Rehe and Chahar, respectively). Zhou Enlai countered that the Chinese Communist Party, by stationing its own troops there, had already asserted Chinese sovereignty over these formerly Japanese-occupied territories. Zhou also pointed out that if he accepted Zhang Qun's logic, then the assertion of Chinese national sovereignty would require the dispatch of Nationalist troops to every part of China currently under Communist control.[46] This, of course, was completely unacceptable to the Communist Party. The Nationalists certainly understood that they could only establish political control of an area if they had achieved military control on the ground. Consequently, they wanted to send troops to Rehe and Chahar, and they wanted to send more troops into the Northeast in order to accept the transfer of sovereignty from the Soviet Union when the Red Army withdrew.

As mediator, George Marshall managed to resolve the Chifeng/Duolun (i.e., Rehe/Chahar) and Manchurian issues by striking a bargain that left both sides dissatisfied. Finding that neither Zhang Qun nor Zhou Enlai would budge on the Chifeng/Duolun issue, Marshall appealed directly to Chiang Kai-shek. Chiang agreed to issue the cessation-of-hostilities order without any reference to the two contested cities. When the ceasefire went into effect at midnight on 13 January, the Thirteenth Army ended its campaign against Rehe and Chahar. In retrospect, both the Nationalist commanders and Chiang Kai-shek argued that they could have captured these two border provinces if there had been no ceasefire.[47] In essence, the Central Committee had been correct. By taking a hard line on Rehe and Chahar and preparing to defend their positions in these two border provinces, the Communists had gained traction in the negotiations. The Communist leadership also believed that their victory in the Handan Campaign in North China (where they had wiped out two Nationalist armies and in which a third Nationalist army had switched sides) had helped to strengthen Zhou Enlai's negotiating position in Chongqing.[48] As a result of these strong actions, the Communists were able to hold their positions in Rehe and Chahar without having to actually fight the "last battle" that Lin Biao had begun to prepare for.

When it came to Manchuria, the Communists were in a weaker negotiating position. The Soviet Union had a treaty obligation to transfer control to the Nationalists. The Soviets, then, pressured the Communist Party to agree to continued transfer of Nationalist troops into Manchuria in order to effect the agreed-upon transfer of sovereignty.[49] The Communist Party was also already on record as having (at least in principle) no objection to Chiang Kai-shek's government resuming sovereignty over China's long-lost Northeastern provinces.[50] On this issue, it was Zhou Enlai who had to yield. When the order for cessation of hostilities was issued on 10 January, it stated that as of midnight on 13 January, all hostilities, all movement of forces, and destruction of lines of communication by Nationalist and Communist troops must cease. But it also contained a stipulation stating that the provision for the cessation of movement of military forces "does not prejudice military movements of forces of the National Army into or within Manchuria which are for the purpose of restoring Chinese sovereignty."[51] Zhou Enlai and the Communist Party Center had traded concessions in Manchuria for peace in China Proper and the security of Rehe and Chahar.

BETWEEN PEACE AND WAR

George Marshall maintained that the ceasefire order applied to the Northeast just as it applied to China Proper. He could do so by drawing a clear distinction between the transfer of Nationalist troops into and within Manchuria for the purpose of asserting sovereignty on the one hand, and the use of those troops to displace Communist units from their positions on the other hand. In the abstract, this was a perfectly logical point of view. But on the ground the theoretical difference between troop movements and battle was meaningless. In the short term, the January ceasefire agreement and its provisions with regard to Manchuria set off a flurry of maneuvers and clashes as each side tried to consolidate its position in the run-up to the ceasefire deadline of midnight on 13 January. In the long run, the lack of clarity built into the ceasefire order created a situation in which, although relative peace reigned in China Proper, each side found justification for its own violations of the ceasefire in Manchuria. This led to the series of encounters that culminated in April with the Second Battle of Siping.

In its announcement of the ceasefire agreement, the Communist Party Central Committee optimistically declared, "China is about to enter a new period of peace and democracy."[52] The Party Center also noted that in order to welcome this new period, Lin Biao would need to fight to defend every inch of territory in the days remaining before the ceasefire went into effect.[53] Liu Shaoqi ordered Peng Zhen to be particularly sure that the Nationalists did not capture areas contiguous with North Korea, the Soviet Union, or Mongolia.[54] The Nationalists, for their part, did their best to take control of transportation routes, ports, and resources. In their advance from late December through early January, Du Yuming's armies captured military supplies, key strategic points, and an important mining center from the Communist forces.[55] On 10 January, the very day that the ceasefire agreement was announced, the Nationalist Fifty-second Army's Twenty-fifth Division captured the port of Yingkou.[56] In the spirit of not giving up an inch of territory in the run-up to 13 January, Lin Biao laid plans to recover this key Manchuria port city.

Yingkou was (and still is) the port city closest to Shenyang. Any army landing at Yingkou could strike east to threaten Dalian and Lüshun, west to take control of the Beiping–Shenyang railway, or north to Shenyang itself.[57] It was in order to prevent the Nationalists from using Yingkou to advance into Manchuria that the Communists took control of the city in the autumn of 1945. When the Nationalist Fifty-second Army's Twenty-fifth Division captured Yingkou on 10 January 1946, Lin Biao's forces looked for an opportunity to recover the city. The chance came on 13 January, when the Twenty-fifth Division transferred its main force to the suburbs of Shenyang (in preparation for the expected transfer of sovereignty from the Soviet Union on 13 January), leaving only a single battalion to guard Yingkou.[58] In line with the Party Center's command to capture as many key points as possible before midnight, the Communists attacked with five regiments (a total of ten thousand men), using their numerical advantage to overwhelm the defending Nationalist brigade's superior firepower. By midnight, when the cease-fire officially went into effect, the Communists had still not recovered Yingkou. Although the Party Center had issued strict orders that all offensive military operations should cease promptly at midnight, the local commander took it upon himself to continue the assault on Yingkou, ultimately driving the defending Nationalists out.

The fight for Yingkou was one of a number of small operations in which both the Communist and Nationalist forces tried to capture key points in the days before the ceasefire deadline. When these operations concluded and the ceasefire went into effect, the fighting should, in theory, have come to an end. The Communist Party Center, at least, does seem to have been seriously committed to making the ceasefire work in the Northeast.[59] Central Committee documents issued in January and February 1946 state that "we should have no doubt at all that that there is a possibility that we and the Kuomintang can peacefully resolve the issue of the Northeast and carry out peaceful cooperation."[60] and that China had "entered a new stage of development of peaceful and democratic reconstruction" in which "the main form of Chinese revolution has changed from armed struggle to non-armed parliamentary struggle of the masses."[61]

In their attempts to make the ceasefire work, the Party leadership was anxious to use American influence in order to restrain the Kuomintang. Zhou Enlai instructed Communist members of the mediation team in Beiping to be low-key and cooperative in their relations with the American team members.[62] Mao Zedong himself wrote to Marshall to say that China was not ready for socialism, but should instead follow the American path of democracy.[63] Zhou urged Marshall to work for peace in Manchuria, not just in China Proper, and when George Marshall asked Chiang Kai-shek and Zhou Enlai to agree to send three-man truce teams (each to consist of one Communist, one Nationalist, and one American representative), Zhou quickly agreed. Chiang refused, on the grounds that the Soviets might demand to be involved.[64]

The Party Center's determination to make the ceasefire work required a new military deployment in the Northeast. This put the Party Center at odds with its men on the ground in Manchuria. On 14 January, Lin posed a series of angry questions to the Party Center. If the Nationalists were allowed to move troops into Communist-held areas and set up governments, and if his forces were not allowed to mount offensive operations, wouldn't that leave the Communists unable to mobilize the masses and pose tremendous difficulties for building base areas? And if the Communist party had no political power and no fiscal authority, how would it feed and equip its armies?[65] Observing the extent to which Du Yuming's armies had become dispersed across southern Manchuria, Lin suggested that "if we coordinate with the Rehe forces and pursue a strategy of defeating them piecemeal, we have every chance of annihilating Du Yuming's entire army and capturing Jinzhou."[66]

The Party Center insisted that Lin and Peng Zhen respect the ceasefire. As had previously been the case, the Party Center's strategy differed from that of Peng Zhen and the Northeast Bureau. Peng Zhen suggested that troops be put in position to challenge the Nationalists for control of the cities of Harbin, Jilin, Qiqihaer, Changchun, Siping, Fushun, and even Shenyang. The Party Center once again countered that Peng could try to capture small and medium cities, but that any attempt to take Changchun or Shenyang would be too dangerous and would displease the Soviet Union.[67] At this point, the Party Center's main concern in Manchuria was to take advantage of the ceasefire and the continued presence of the Soviet Red Army to disperse its forces broadly across the Northeast. There were two purposes to this dispersal of troops. One was to establish Communist military and political presence in as many places as possible before the Soviet army's withdrawal later in the year. A second purpose was to build strength by widening the Party's base areas, carry out recruitment, and carry out military re-organization. As a part of the re-organization, on 14 January, the Northeast People's Autonomous Army was given a new name: the Northeast Democratic United Army (NDUA).[68]

While committed to making the ceasefire work in Manchuria (since a ceasefire was clearly in its own interest), the Party Center still expected further clashes with the Kuomintang. But by committing itself openly to the ceasefire process and presenting a cooperative face to the Americans, the Party consistently cast these clashes as defensive operations, so that the Kuomintang would bear the onus of having violated the ceasefire. In Liu Shaoqi's words to the Northeast Bureau:

> If the Kuomintang won't negotiate with us and mounts an offensive against our forces, then as long as our friend [the Soviet army] does not strongly object and we are completely justified in defending ourselves (having first tried to avoid conflict), give the advancing enemy a firm, thorough, fatal blow. To do this you must raise morale and make careful preparations: don't look for many battles, you have to gain a major victory in one battle in order to squelch the enemy's power and prestige in the Northeast. This will be the last battle of this new historical era, it will determine the overall status of the Northeast from now on out: [we] hope you will explain this thoroughly to the cadres [that we] should not hesitate to make a great sacrifice to achieve complete victory in this one battle in order to make this final contribution to the war. To this end, Lin Biao should find a way to go to the main front to direct the action.[69]

If Lin's Northeast Democratic United Army was obliged to wait to be attacked before fighting, Chiang Kai-shek was more than willing to give them the opportunity. Chiang had little faith in the Marshall Mission, which he feared would become a repeat of the Stilwell affair.[70] He had agreed to the January ceasefire only reluctantly, and had interpreted it in a way that, at least from his point of view, justified further action in the Northeast. That action came in early February. With Nationalist forces now in the city of Shenyang, Chiang ordered Du Yuming to begin a campaign to sweep the Communists out of positions in the vicinity of the city. In many areas, Lin Biao simply withdrew. But when the Nationalist Thirteenth Army's 89th Division sent its 266th Regiment deep to the north of Shenyang toward Faku, Lin Biao saw the chance to fight the battle of annihilation that Yan'an had been urging on him. As before, the Communists expected a short war. In Liu Shaoqi's words, "There is a possibility of fighting in the Northeast, but the fighting will not last long; after ten days to half a month [they will] be forced into a ceasefire. You lost the opportunity for battle at Jinzhou, Fuxin and Rehe, you must absolutely not lose this last chance for battle."[71]

At first, the Kuomintang's 266th regiment (four infantry battalions and an artillery battalion) advanced smoothly from Shenyang north toward Faku, where Lin Biao's forces posed a threat to key transportation lines.[72] What the commander of the 266th did not realize was that Lin Biao, whose forces retreated stage by stage, was leading him into a carefully planned trap. On 11 February, the men of the 266th reached Xiushuihezi, a small town of five hundred families sitting astride the north–south Xiushui river and the main east–west road to Faku, where they joined up with a battalion which was already in place. Although they prepared defensive works (pillboxes and trenches), the Nationalists had no idea of what was in store for them. On 13–14 February Lin Biao (who directed this operation himself) put his "one point, two flanks" (*yidian, liangmian*) tactic into action. Employing overwhelming force—ten regiments—Lin's men attacked the 266th from two sides. After a few hours of intense fighting and heavy casualties on the Communist side, the lone Nationalist regiment was completely surrounded. A relief force sent out hurriedly from Shenyang was unable to fight its way to Xiushuihezi, where nearly the entire 266th was wiped out.

At Xiushuihezi, Lin Biao's effective use of enticement and entrapment, combined with an overwhelming superiority in numbers, enabled him to thoroughly defeat units from the American-equipped Nationalist forces. The Party Center was well pleased with Lin Biao's performance. Lin, they said, should fight two or three more such battles. But at the same time, Yan'an also warned him that "at this time, it is still not good for our army to advance toward the Bei-Ning line on its own initiative."[73] The fact was that at Xiushuihezi, Lin Biao had correctly identified an opportunity that gave him optimal conditions for victory. In other than optimal conditions, his forces were still not a match for the Nationalists. This was soon demonstrated in the second battle, this one in southern Manchuria.

As part of Nationalist operations in southern Manchuria, Du Yuming's New Sixth Army, Twenty-second Division was working to clear Communist forces out of strategic areas and transportation routes crucial to the defense of Shenyang. As they moved forward, the Nationalists occupied Shaling, a village near the city of Liaoyang.

The Communist commander in this operation, Wu Kehua, had gathered five regiments to attack the single Nationalist regiment at Shaling. A sixth regiment stood by to cut off Nationalist reinforcements, if they should be sent, and to serve as a backup force. In classical Maoist terms, this battle should have gone well: the Communists had concentrated superior numbers against a single Nationalist unit. The results, however, were far from ideal. Due to poor reconnaissance and intelligence, the Fourth Column were not aware that their enemy was one of the Nationalist army's strongest and most experienced combat units, and that it both was well-armed and had constructed a system of strong defensive works at Shaling. Having severely underestimated the enemy, Wu Kehua and his cadre used the slogan "earn merit in this final battle" to mobilize the Communist troops, who marched into battle in high spirits, expecting an easy victory.[74]

The battle began at five o'clock in the afternoon of 16 February.[75] The plan was to capture the Nationalists' peripheral defenses, and then roll straight on to Shaling itself, taking advantage of the Communists' skill at night combat to capture the position and wrap everything up by dawn the next day. Things began to go wrong immediately when the Communists' opening artillery salvo largely missed its target. Incompetent cadres, hastily promoted during the Fourth Column's recent, rapid expansion, did not understand how to use their weapons. Two hours of artillery bombardment had little effect on the enemy—some of the poorly aimed shells even landed on Communist positions. By the time the infantry were ready to charge the enemy, the artillery was out of ammunition and unable to give covering fire. Uncoordinated and poorly led infantry charges failed again and again. As a result, despite their superior numbers, the Communists made very little progress in a night of fierce fighting.

Wu Kehua, acting on the assumption that night-fighting would always give him an edge, ordered his men to rest the next day. This gave the Nationalists a chance to repair their defensive works and prepare for the inevitable next round of combat. In all, the Communist spent three nights and one day trying to capture Shaling, throwing small numbers of forces against the enemy at multiple points rather than concentrating superior force at any one point in order to achieve a breakthrough. Repeated, chaotic attempts to capture enemy positions were accompanied in some cases by failure of command when officers in the field either pulled their units out of combat without warning or were unable to make quick decisions under pressure. A veteran of the battle recalled an instance when a brigade was failing to make any headway against an enemy position: "The brigade commander lost his temper: if you don't fight your way in I'll kill you! Just as he was blowing his top, from behind there came a great 'kaboom!' and nearly an entire company was wiped out."[76]

After three days of fighting, Wu Kehua withdrew from Shaling. He had lost 2,159 men to the Nationalists' 700.[77] Lin Biao (who had not been present at Shaling) could not have been pleased. Taken together, Xiushuihezi and Shaling showed that the NDUA could defeat Nationalist units, but only when all the stars were lined up just right. In general, Lin Biao's armies were still better off retreating than fighting. In February and early March of 1946, retreat still worked well for Lin Biao. Manchuria was a big place, and the January ceasefire exerted some (though clearly not much) restraint on Chiang Kai-shek's Northeast Command. More to the point, the Soviet Red Army was still in occupation of points and lines across the Northeast, creating a framework in which the Communist Party's Northeast Bureau could create "facts on the ground" as they prepared for the next stage of the Manchurian conflict.

A FRAMEWORK FOR CONFLICT

The Soviet Red Army's occupation of the Northeast and the way in which the Red Army managed its withdrawal had a far greater effect on the outbreak of full-scale war in March 1946 than Marshall's negotiations possibly could have. The Nationalists and the Communists used, interpreted, and violated the January ceasefire and its language about the Northeast as it suited them. But the Soviet occupation and withdrawal had a direct effect on the patterns of distribution of Communist and Nationalist troops on the ground in the Northeast. Thus the Soviet Union contributed substantially to the creation of the spatial framework that helped to determine how and where Communist and Nationalist troops were deployed, and which made war inevitable once the restraining presence of the Red Army was removed from the scene.

Before the Red Army's withdrawal in March and April, concern about the Soviet Union's reaction prevented both the Nationalists and the Communists from going all-out to control Manchuria. Neither the Nationalists nor their sponsor, the United States, wanted to do anything that would inspire direct Soviet military involvement in the brewing Chinese Civil War. The Soviets, for their part, helped the Communist Party at key moments both because it feared that the Communists would lose an outright civil war with Chiang Kai-shek and because they were concerned that a civil war could bring direct American involvement in North China and Manchuria.

Although they sometimes complained about the Soviet Union, it was the Chinese Communists who benefited the most from the Red Army's extended presence in the Northeast. Stalin had originally promised Chiang Kai-shek that the Soviet forces would be out of Manchuria by 15 November 1945. At Chiang's request the Soviets delayed the date to 3 December in order to give the Nationalists time to move their troops into position—Chiang feared that a precipitous Soviet withdrawal would have left a vacuum for the Communists to fill.[78] The Soviet Union subsequently pushed the date of the Red Army's withdrawal back to 1 February, and then to March. In both cases, the Soviets were motivated by their own self-interest and their interest in providing the Communist Party with further opportunities for growth.

As we have seen above, the Soviets played a key role in helping the Chinese Communist Party to establish a presence in the Northeast in the weeks and months immediately following the Japanese surrender. The Soviets tolerated, turned a blind eye to, and sometimes actively assisted the Eighth Route and New Fourth Army units as they entered Manchuria, established a military and political presence in key cities (including Soviet-occupied Shenyang), and expanded their numbers. The Soviet presence also placed limits on Communist activities in the Northeast. At times, as in September 1945, or again in November as Lin

Biao was losing the Liaoxi Corridor, the Soviets held the Chinese Communist Party back. On 10 November, just as Du Yuming was poised to attack the Communists at Shanhaiguan, the Soviets told Peng Zhen that Nationalist troops would be airlifted into the major cities then under Soviet control, and that the Chinese Communists must not clash with them. When the Chinese objected, their Soviet comrades told them, "Moscow's interests ought to be the highest interests of the Communists of the entire world."[79]

Communists on the ground in Manchuria complained about the Soviets' attitude both at the time and in retrospect in their memoirs. But at the same time, the leaders in Yan'an understood the Soviet Union's international position very well, and, though they may have preferred otherwise, they were willing to consider the big picture and to accommodate the Soviet Union, confident that, in the final analysis, they did have the support of "the big brother" to the north. They were also confident that they could work within the framework established by the Soviet occupation, and even expand their presence on the ground. In January, as the ceasefire order went into effect, the Party Center directed the Northeast Bureau, "Each place garrisoned by the [Soviet] Red Army will be turned over to the Kuomintang, therefore you should strive to get the Red Army to shrink the areas that it defends, making it so that the Red Army withdraws from some of the secondary areas and turns them over to us. . . . You must control all the key areas adjacent to the Soviet Union and Mongolia: do not allow the Kuomintang to control [them] and cut the contacts between us and the Soviet Union and Mongolia."[80]

On 13 March, the Soviet withdrawal began as the Red Army pulled its remaining troops out of Shenyang and other cities, including Siping. The withdrawal continued by stages, proceeding roughly from south to north, until the last Soviet troops left Manchuria at the end of April. As they withdrew, the Russian soldiers took advantage of the last opportunity to loot, driving off with trucks loaded with furniture and even with stolen doors and windows. Chinese citizens, too, got in their last licks at the now thoroughly despised occupation army: Chinese defended their homes from looters, and Russian soldiers caught out alone occasionally disappeared.[81]

Both the Kuomintang and the Communist Party did their best to move into and secure the positions being abandoned by the Soviets. Their international agreements obliged the Soviets to transfer sovereignty to the Kuomintang, and at times, the Soviets did fulfill those obligations. In Shenyang, where the Kuomintang already had many troops stationed and ready to move into place, the transfer of sovereignty was accomplished with little difficulty. There, Nationalist forces moved in quickly to secure the city. Communist forces and political leaders left in a hurriedly organized retreat (having been strictly ordered to do so by the Soviets), leaving underground agents behind.[82] Farther to the north, the situation was different. Already in early March, the Soviets had warned the Northeast Bureau that they would begin to withdraw on 11 March and that the Communists should act boldly to move into key positions as the Russian soldiers departed.[83] The Soviets purposely gave the Nationalists little advance warning. Instead, they pulled out of one city after another, deliberately leaving a vacuum that Du Yuming's Nationalist forces could not move fast enough to fill. As they did so, the Soviets intentionally slowed the Nationalist advance by withholding train engines and rolling stock. As a result, Du Yuming was often only able to send token occupation forces by air to take over key cities including Changchun, Harbin, Qiqihaer, and Jilin.

With the regular Nationalist troops spread thin on the ground, Du also made use of former "puppet" units that had been created under Japanese occupation and now had pledged their loyalty to the Nationalist government. One of these units, known as the "Ironstone Brigade" (*Tieshidui*), was airlifted to Siping. The Ironstone Brigade was a special force of Chinese soldiers originally organized and trained by the Japanese army.[84] Flown up to Changchun, they supplied a part of the garrison force of that city. In addition, around three thousand men from the Ironstone Brigade were sent to act as the Nationalist garrison force at Siping, which (due to an administrative reorganization of the three large northeastern provinces into nine smaller provinces) was now designated as the provincial capital of the newly created Liaobei Province.

It was precisely at this point, with the Soviet Red Army withdrawing and the Communist and Nationalist forces jockeying for position in the Northeast, that George Marshall chose to return to Washington to report on the progress of his mission thus far. With the January ceasefire (imperfect as it was) in effect, and with solid progress (at least on paper) on the National Political Consultative Conference and a plan for military reorganization, Marshall felt confident enough to take the time to go to Washington, discuss the China situation with President Truman, and work with the administration and Congress on a financial assistance and loan package for Chiang Kai-shek's government.

In the two weeks before he left China, Marshall spoke with both Chiang Kai-shek and Zhou Enlai, and also made a visit to the Communist Party's headquarters in Yan'an. In early March, Marshall, Zhou Enlai, and the Nationalist chief negotiator Zhang Zhizhong inspected areas in North China where the three-man ceasefire teams were mediating between Nationalist and Communist forces. Their tour culminated with a visit to Yan'an on 4 March. Mao Zedong greeted Marshall with great enthusiasm and declared that he would like to see ceasefire teams in Manchuria, but he also made it very clear that the Communist Party would not give up its military power until all of the outstanding political disagreements with the Nationalists were resolved.[85] Marshall left without having made any significant progress. The next day Mao Zedong called his Russian physician into his bedroom. The Russian was surprised at Mao's informality. Mao, however, soon made his meaning clear: "Yesterday we held a grand welcome ceremony and banquet for Marshall. You know this, right? The atmosphere was quite enthusiastic. But Marshall can only be a guest in a ceremonial hall; he cannot sit here in my bedroom and chat with me as you are doing today."[86]

As a representative of the United States, Marshall could never have a close personal relationship with Mao Zedong or other Chinese Communist leaders. Nonetheless, he agreed with them that the ceasefire teams should be sent to the Northeast. He continued to try to get Chiang's agreement on this, but Chiang rejected Marshall's proposals, believing that American mediation in the Northeast would elicit a strong Soviet reaction. Concerned that Marshall did not understand the significance of Soviet interests and the Soviet role in the Northeast, Chiang suggested that the United States and China should forge a common policy toward the Northeast—a policy that would be characterized by a more aggressive stance toward the Chinese Communist Party.[87]

If Chiang anticipated a coming storm in the Northeast, so too did Zhou Enlai. And like Chiang, Zhou sensed a contradiction between Chiang and the Americans. Reporting back to the Party Center on 10 March, Zhou wrote, "We estimate that the current crisis will come in the Northeast. Chiang is trying to use this to stir up a Soviet-American conflict, [and so] is not willing to resolve the Northeast problem now, but the American and Marshall's emphasis is on the quick realization of a ceasefire in the Northeast."[88] Believing that Marshall held the key to a deal, Zhou urged Marshall not to return to Washington until the Manchurian ceasefire issue was resolved.

Marshall, who had already postponed his trip, would brook no further delay. But before he left, he made remarks which Zhou interpreted to mean that Marshall was "going back to resolve the Northeast problem with Truman."[89] If, as Zhou apparently believed, Marshall was determined to do his utmost to achieve a ceasefire and a political solution to the Manchurian problem, and if he was going to return from Washington, perhaps with proposals that would give him more leverage over Chiang Kai-shek, then it was in the Communists' best interest to hold onto their current positions in the Northeast and to acquire new positions as the Soviets continued their withdrawal. Marshall left Chongqing on 13 March. With Chiang intent on a more aggressive posture toward the Communists and with Zhou convinced that Marshall would soon force Chiang into a real ceasefire, Manchuria stood on the eve of yet another battle.

5

The Second Battle of Siping

*Phase One—From Outer Defense to Stalemate,
March–April 1946*

It was the continued presence of the Soviet Red Army, and not Marshall's 10 January ceasefire, that prevented a renewed outbreak of civil war in Manchuria in the first two months of 1946. Just by being there, the Soviet forces had kept the two sides apart, forming a screen behind which the Communists could build their strength, deploy their forces to control small and medium towns and cities, and begin working to establish a presence in the rural areas and to win the support of the masses.[1] This constraint was removed in mid-March when the Soviets began to withdraw from the Chinese Northeast. As they withdrew their forces, the Soviets were once again (as they had back in October 1945) urging their Chinese Communist comrades to take a more aggressive stance toward the Kuomintang in Manchuria.

That message played well among the leaders of the Northeast Bureau, who had always had a strong interest in capturing the "Three Big Cities" of Shenyang, Changchun, and Harbin.[2] After some debate, and Mao Zedong's return to the leadership after months of illness, the Party leadership in Yan'an, too, came to support a more aggressive strategy in the Northeast.[3] As the Soviets withdrew, Communist forces moved into strategic areas from which they would be able to attack key cities, railway junctions, and mining and industrial centers. At the same time, Chiang Kai-shek was airlifting troops and officials to set up provincial and municipal governments and to garrison the major cities as the Soviets pulled out. Chiang was also ordering his armies in Shenyang to begin a major offensive against the Communists in order to consolidate his government's control over the Northeast. The heightened aggressiveness of both sides ultimately led to the First and then the Second Battle of Siping.

THE COMMUNIST PARTY CENTER AND THE NORTHEAST BUREAU

Peng Zhen and the other leaders of the Northeast Bureau had been increasingly frustrated by the Party Center's policy of accommodation and negotiation with Chiang Kai-shek and George Marshall. The disagreement over this issue was so deep that it threatened to cause a serious rift within the Party.[4] But the Party Center, under Liu Shaoqi's leadership in Yan'an and with Zhou Enlai negotiating in Chongqing, remained committed to its moderate position until the middle of March. Even the still-convalescing Mao Zedong reflected the Center's position in February and early March when he praised Marshall for his efforts and made optimistic remarks about the prospects for peace.[5]

The Party Center's moderation was based partly on the fact that the Soviet Union had been urging caution. But we cannot rule out the possibility that it was also rooted in Liu Shaoqi and Zhou Enlai's assessment of the military and diplomatic situation. At this point, the Soviets' attitude had already undergone a fundamental change. The continued American transfer of Nationalist troops to the region, American and British complaints that the Soviets' economic deals in the area violated the "Open Door Policy," and perhaps even events in the Middle East, where Turkey and Iran had fallen into the American sphere of influence, made Joseph Stalin change his mind about strategy in Manchuria.[6] Now, instead of pushing the Chinese Communists to make peace, the Soviets criticized them for having been too weak.[7] As described in chapter 4, the Soviets began pulling out of Manchuria in early March, managing their withdrawal in such a way as to facilitate a Communist takeover of key places like Fushun, Tieling, Anshan, and Benxi—all small and medium industrial and mining cities in the vicinity of Shenyang. On 9 March, the Soviets told Peng Zhen that they would leave Shenyang on the thirteenth and advised him to capture the city from the Nationalists immediately afterward.[8]

This was exactly what Peng Zhen wanted to hear. On 12 March, he and Lin Biao jointly proposed an attack on Shenyang. The next day Liu Shaoqi, writing for the Party Center, told them that their plan was militarily risky and politically disadvantageous: "Not only should we not attack Shenyang, when the Soviets withdraw from the rail line from Shenyang to Harbin, we should not occupy any of it—let the Kuomintang take it. Only if the Nationalist Army attacks our army should we organize a counter-attack from a defensive posture."[9] At this point, the Communist leadership was willing for Zhou Enlai to take a tough line in the negotiations with the Nationalists and Marshall, but this was for bargaining purposes. In the end, they acknowledged, "when the Nationalist Party negotiates with us with sincerity and acknowledges our position in the Northeast, we will have to make concessions in order to reach a compromise."[10]

This cautious approach changed abruptly a few days later when Mao Zedong returned to work at the Party Center. Both Peng Zhen and the Soviets were pushing hard for a more forward military posture in the Northeast. In a telegram to the Center, Peng Zhen quoted the Soviets as asking why the Party Center was being so polite to the Americans, urging him to fight hard for control of cities like Fushun, Shenyang, and Siping, and certainly not to let the Nationalists control any place north of Changchun.[11] Presumably it was some combination of the Soviet Union's advice, Mao's analysis of the situation, and Mao's own character which led him to steer the Party's strategy for Manchuria in precisely the direction that Peng Zhen wanted. On 15 and 16 March the Party Center told Zhou Enlai that he need not listen to the relatively soft-line Soviet diplomats in Chongqing when the Soviet military in Manchuria was in favor of a more aggressive strategy.[12] Rather than talk about giving up everything from Shenyang to Harbin, the Party Center now told Zhou, "Without simultaneous resolution of reciprocal deals on political affairs, military affairs, and territory, we must absolutely not give up any positions."[13] On 17 March, the Party Center told Lin Biao in Manchuria and Zhou Enlai in Chongqing, "Let our troops occupy the entire China Eastern railway (including Harbin) and stay there indefinitely, don't let the Kuomintang send a single soldier. . . . Let Lin Biao arrange everything to create a situation of superiority for the benefit of the negotiations."[14]

THE FIRST BATTLE OF SIPING

The Party Center's new determination to fight for its positions in Manchuria and to take control of the area from Changchun northward led straight to the battle for Siping. As described in the introduction, Siping lay at the junction of three railway lines: the China–Changchun railway, running from Shenyang through Siping and on to Changchun and Harbin, and branch lines running from Siping east to Meihekou and west toward Liaoyuan and Tongliao. Its position at the junction of three railways in the middle of the Manchurian Plain made Siping a center for warehousing and trade in agricultural commodities including soybeans and vegetable oils. In strategic terms, Siping was the gateway to northern Manchuria. If Du Yuming hoped to get his armies to Changchun and Harbin, he would have to go through Siping. If the Chinese Communists wanted to hold Changchun and Harbin for themselves and to make Changchun the capital of a base area extending from Yan'an through Rehe and Chahar and all the way across North Manchuria to the Soviet and Korean borders, they would need to stand firm at Siping. The Soviets clearly understood this: even as they made arrangements to withdraw their troops from Siping and turn it over to Chiang Kai-shek's representatives, the Soviets were telling Peng Zhen to get ready to capture the city.

The First Battle of Siping was a relatively simple affair. Before the Soviet withdrawal, Chiang Kai-shek had designated Siping as the capital of Liaobei Province (one of the nine provinces into which he had subdivided the original three provinces of Manchuria). A provincial governor, Liu Handong, had moved into the city, along with a weak garrison force of six thousand men, most of them former "puppet" forces which had been hastily incorporated into the Nationalist army and flown to Siping. The Soviet Red Army withdrew from Siping on 13 March. At the same time, on 12 and 13 March, Lin Biao deployed a single brigade in the vicinity of Siping and prepared to capture the city. The Soviets assisted by providing trains to bring Lin's troops south from Changchun. At their staging area west of Siping, the Communist commanders on the ground debriefed an underground Communist Party member who had just made his way out of Siping, bringing with him a map indicating the locations and nature of the Nationalist garrison's defenses.

Xiong Shihui, the commander of the Nationalists' Northeast Bandit Suppression Headquarters, was concerned about Siping. On 15 March, he warned Chiang Kai-shek that the Siping garrison was in danger and that "if they are hit by an attack from the 'communist army' they will not last long."[15] The assault on Siping began the same day with an attack on the airport. Here, as in many later encounters in the Northeast, the Communist forces acted quickly to control air access in and out of the cities that they intended to attack in order to prevent the Nationalists from re-supplying and reinforcing their positions by air. On 16 March, the NDUA men surrounded the city and broke through the Nationalists' hastily prepared defenses.

Once the Communists had entered the city, the Nationalist garrison rapidly collapsed, just as Xiong Shihui had predicted. Canadian Catholic missionaries in the city described the Nationalists as having put up, on the whole, a "sham resistance" which involved only a few hours of fighting. At the same time, some of the missionary sources suggest that for those few hours, there was intense fighting in at least some places.[16] One of those places may have been the provincial government compound, where Governor Liu Handong and his strongest two companies found themselves surrounded. Liu ordered his men to hold their positions while he called to the nearest Nationalist forces—in this case, the garrison at Changchun—for reinforcements. But by the time Liu made his frantic plea for assistance, it was too late. Seeing that the situation was hopeless, he tried to escape in an armored car, only to be captured when his driver mistakenly drove straight into a street controlled by Communist soldiers.[17] By 17 March, Lin Biao had captured Siping. Only two hundred of Liu's men escaped. Liu himself was later sent back to the Nationalists, as an example of the Communist Party's policy of lenient treatment of prisoners.

By this time, the Party Center had adopted its hard-line strategy. Behind the scenes, Mao Zedong and the Soviets had agreed that the Communists would have to give up South Manchuria, but that they would hold firm to their positions in the north.[18] Mao and the Party leadership understood that to make this work, they would need to fight and negotiate at the same time. The fighting was Lin Biao's affair. The negotiating would require Zhou Enlai to get Marshall to put pressure on Chiang Kai-shek. Both Zhou and Mao Zedong were confident that Marshall would indeed force Chiang to accept a ceasefire that would divide Manchuria into a Communist north and a Nationalist south.[19] As Zhou told the Party Center on 19 March:

> America needs China to be peaceful and stable before it makes any big loans, this is the crux of the contradiction between America and Chiang, and in the end, Chiang has no choice other than to do what the Americans want. . . . [I] estimate that while Marshall is in America working on a loan, Chiang will not dare to cause a break [in negotiations], and that he will be fearful of internationalizing the crisis; thus it is very advantageous for us to counter-attack, naturally we also need to be aware of the big picture and of the plusses and minuses, and make it clear that we did not start the fight.[20]

Mao and Zhou were sure that the Americans wanted a ceasefire, and that Chiang was so beholden to the Americans that he would have to agree to Marshall's demands. As Mao told Lin Biao on 25 March, "Chiang will be forced and unable to avoid a ceasefire."[21] In the meantime, the Northeast Bureau would "fight for every inch of land."[22] Plans were already laid to capture Harbin, Qiqihaer, and Changchun as soon as the Soviets withdrew from those cities.[23] In order to guarantee their control over the these "Three Big Cities" of northern Manchuria, the Communists would need to hold on to Siping. On 23 March, the Party Center instructed Lin Biao to sabotage the north–south China Changchun railway line south of Siping and to act boldly to wipe out advancing enemy units whenever possible—and not to fear casualties.[24] On 24 March, the Party Center told Lin Biao:

> Our Party's policy is to use our entire strength to control the two cities of Changchun and Harbin and the entire China Eastern Railway, not to spare any sacrifice to prevent Chiang's armies from capturing Changchun, Harbin, and the China Eastern Railway, and to take Southern and Western Manchuria as secondary theaters. . . . Resolutely control the Siping area, if the enemy advances north thoroughly annihilate them, absolutely do not allow them to advance to Changchun.[25]

CHIANG KAI-SHEK SEIZES THE INITIATIVE

When Mao Zedong ordered Lin Biao to defend Siping, Chiang Kai-shek's armies had already begun a major operation intended both to consolidate the Kuomintang's hold on South Manchuria and to strike north toward

Changchun and Harbin. As we have seen earlier, Chiang had been reluctant to send troops too deeply into Manchuria: he had hoped to acquire control over the territory through negotiations with the Soviet Union. But now the Soviet army was pulling out and the Communists were moving into the vacuum. Diplomacy had failed, and Chiang faced intense criticism from within his own party, with members of the Kuomintang leadership arguing that "bandit extermination is a struggle to overthrow imperialism," which no country had the right to interfere with, and castigating the government for giving too much up to the Soviet Union and for letting its hands be tied by a severe case of "Soviet-phobia."[26]

At the same time as Chiang was moving toward a more aggressive posture, the Nationalist forces in Manchuria were going through a temporary change in command. In February Du Yuming, Chiang's commander in the Northeast, had been diagnosed with severe kidney stones and had gone to Beiping to have his left kidney removed. As he left the Northeast, Du was terribly worried that Chiang would take this opportunity to replace him. Unwilling to lose his command, Du appointed his old friend, Whampoa classmate, and loyal subordinate Zheng Dongguo as his temporary replacement.

As Zheng Dongguo tells the story in his memoirs, Chiang Kai-shek gave the orders for this spring offensive to him and to Xiong Shihui shortly after 13 March, when the Soviets had finally turned Shenyang over to Nationalist troops. Chiang's orders were to capture Siping by 2 April. In an all-night meeting, Zheng and his fellow commanders in Shenyang agreed that Benxi was in fact the Communists' most important stronghold at the time: the terrain made Benxi easy to defend and difficult to attack, and its position made it a danger to the safety of the Nationalist forces in Shenyang. Zheng and his colleagues would have preferred to focus their attention on Benxi, but there was the unequivocal order from Chiang Kai-shek: strike north and capture Siping by 2 April. As a result, the generals decided to split the difference. They would attack both Siping and Benxi.[27]

The Nationalists' spring offensive began on 19 March 1946. The campaign involved three directions of advance. Elements of the New Sixth Army pushed southward and eastward out of Shenyang to sweep the Communists out of towns in those areas and to lay the groundwork for an attack on Benxi. The New First Army advanced north toward Siping, moving along the east and west flanks of the main railway line. The Seventy-first Army, landing at Qinhuangdao, was to proceed north via Xinmin and Faku to attack Siping from the west. Once the Nationalists had captured Siping, they were to move on to Changchun and on up to the Songhua River.[28]

Nationalist operations in the cities immediately surrounding Shenyang proceeded smoothly. Nationalist forces quickly pushed the Communists out of Fushun, Liaoyang, and other towns. Zhou Enlai protested to Caughey, the American negotiator then visiting Yan'an, and reiterated the Communist Party's desire to send truce teams to Manchuria.[29] Benxi, as we shall see in the next chapter, was a more difficult nut to crack. The march north toward Siping went more slowly than expected. The spring thaws were just beginning. Melting snow and ice turned roads into mud and small streams into roaring torrents. Communist saboteurs had destroyed or damaged bridges and railways. Nonetheless, the Kuomintang armies pressed onward. By 24 March the New First Army had only gotten as far as Tieling.

Chiang Kai-shek, concerned about the lack of progress, sent General Fan Hanjie to Manchuria to find out why it was taking so long to capture Siping. Both Du Yuming, still in his hospital bed in Beiping, and his officers in Manchuria feared that Fan was about to replace Du, and that he would carry out an all-around purge of top officers in the Northeast. But Fan simply made his inspection, re-emphasized that Siping must be captured by 2 April, and returned to Nanjing. The Nationalists continued their slow progress north. By the end of the month, they had occupied Kaiyuan, about seventy-two kilometers south of Siping.[30] The Seventy-first Army's Eighty-seventh and Ninety-first Divisions, west of the main railway line, worked their way north through Faku, which they occupied on 4 April, and thence to Tongjiangkou in an attempt to attack the right (west) flank of the Communists at Siping.[31] By early April, it was clear that Siping would be the focal point of the battle for the control of Changchun and all points north, while the fighting in the south would center on Benxi.

Chiang Kai-shek had two goals for the north Manchuria campaign: to control Changchun and to annihilate Lin Biao's army. Chiang's diary entries for March and April 1946 show how he gained confidence as the campaign progressed. Contrary to Zheng Dongguo's account of Chiang's impatient demand to capture Siping by 2 April, Chiang, at least in his diaries, initially expressed a degree of caution, remarking on 21 March that the best approach would be to recover sovereignty over as much territory as his limited forces would allow.[32] By 6 April, however, he was envisioning an aggressive push toward Changchun and a decisive battle somewhere along the way. South Manchuria was of less concern to Chiang, who hoped that Xiong Shihui and Zheng Dongguo would recover Benxi but otherwise focus on the north.[33] Chiang was not entirely confident that his generals in Manchuria were up to the task—he wanted to fly to Shenyang and direct the battle himself, but was afraid that his personal involvement would complicate relations with both the Americans and the Soviets.[34] On 13 April, Chiang made it clear that he wanted Siping captured by the twentieth. His commanders assured him that this could easily be done.[35] Chiang, reassured, wrote in his diary, "Of all the issues I have been confronted with this week, in each case danger can be transformed into safety, and my heart and spirit feel comfortable and at peace. This is the result of the accumulation of virtue through self-cultivation."[36]

LIN BIAO DENOUNCES PENG ZHEN

As their position in the Northeast deteriorated from November 1945 and on into 1946, the Communist Party leadership in the region disagreed on how to move forward. The way that this disagreement was eventually resolved would have a deep and lasting effect on Communist strategy in Manchuria. The heart of the matter lay in a conflict between two powerful and ambitious men: Peng Zhen, then secretary of the Northeast Bureau, and Lin Biao, commander of the NDUA. Looking back at the matter over sixty years later and without the benefit of firsthand access to archival sources or even objective secondary accounts, it is difficult to understand exactly what happened and why. Nonetheless, if we hope to gain even a tentative understanding of the development of Communist strategy in the Northeast and to assess the significance of the Second Battle of Siping, we need to do our best to try to understand the Peng Zhen-Lin Biao rivalry as it is revealed in the sources that we do have.[37]

When they established the Northeast Bureau to exercise overall leadership over Communist social, political, and military action in Manchuria, Liu Shaoqi and the Central Committee had put Peng Zhen in charge. Peng's background was in labor organization and underground work in occupied areas—he had little or no experience in military affairs, and certainly no experience of military command. As leader of the Northeast Bureau, Peng did what he knew and did best. He worked to establish local governments and local Party organizations and he bent the ears of the Soviets in meeting after meeting, asking them for more support. In terms of military strategy, Peng advocated fighting to take and keep control over the "Three Big Cities" of Shenyang, Changchun, and Harbin and, when this became impossible, the "Three Big Cities" of northern Manchuria: Changchun, Harbin, and Qiqihaer.[38]

Lin Biao had professional military training, had been in combat, and had commanded troops. However, he ranked lower than Peng Zhen in the Party hierarchy. As mentioned in chapter 3, in October 1945 the Party Center had sent Lin Biao to Shenyang to "assist Peng Zhen" in military affairs. Lin obeyed orders, but he was clearly not happy playing second fiddle to the civilian-oriented Peng Zhen in a theater of operations increasingly dominated by military, rather than political, struggle. Lin seems to have dealt with the contradiction by staying in the field with his army, directing operations, and meeting with Peng Zhen and the rest of the Northeast Bureau (of which he was not actually a member) as little as possible. This created a distance, or even a disconnect, between the Communist Party's civilian and military leadership in the Northeast and, perhaps, contributed to the development of disagreements between Lin and Peng.

Whatever the reason, there is no doubt that serious disagreements were developing, and that there was no institutional mechanism to resolve them. In the first week of March 1946, at a meeting of the Northeast Bureau, Lin Biao put his cards on the table. The Northeast Bureau, he said, "lacked a clearly defined starting point for all of its work," was guilty of "rightist tendencies" because it did not recognize the importance of or go far enough in mobilizing the masses, did not have "a unified opinion on the question of urban versus rural areas," and lacked any "concept of war."[39] Lin also held Peng Zhen responsible for the NDUA's disastrous performance and losses at the battle of Shaling.[40] An authoritative secondary source—but one frankly taking Peng Zhen's side in this matter—says that Peng Zhen addressed all the issues that Lin raised and that Lin, finding no support among the others in attendance, performed a reluctant self-criticism (which is to say that he recanted and apologized for his remarks).[41]

Whether Lin performed a self-criticism or not, he certainly had not changed his mind about what he saw as fundamental problems with the leadership of the Northeast Committee. On 13 March, Lin discussed his concerns with Gao Gang (1905–1954), a member of the Northeast Bureau. Finding Gao sympathetic, Lin also put his criticisms in a telegram addressed directly to Mao Zedong and Liu Shaoqi. In this telegram, Lin outlined what he saw as a fundamental split within the Northeast Bureau. On the one hand, Lin said, he himself and a majority including Luo Ronghuan and Chen Yun advocated a strategy based on working in the countryside to build base areas in preparation for a long-term military struggle—precisely, said Lin, what the Party Center itself wanted. On the other side were Peng Zhen and his supporters, who, in Lin's words, advocated "military adventurism or blind hopes for the rapid arrival of peace, illusions about and attachments to the cities, [and] lack of planning for an extended period of bitter struggle."[42]

Lin followed with a series of recriminations against Peng Zhen. In the aftermath of the withdrawal from Jinzhou, Peng's strategy of fighting for control of sections of the Shanhaiguan–Shenyang and Shenyang–Changchun railway lines had resulted in substantial losses of newly recruited troops and the unnecessary death of over one hundred Party cadres. Peng's unrealistic expectations of peace and his flawed understanding of the extent to which control of the cities would bring domination of the countryside were driving him to deploy troops in order to stage a rapid takeover of Shenyang and other major cities at the expense of establishing a presence in the countryside itself. He was stalling on the amalgamation of new and old units to the detriment of older units, whose losses of personnel and weapons could only be made up by combining them with some of the units established with new recruits and equipped with newly acquired weapons.

Lin's criticisms extended to Peng's leadership style. Peng had failed to control waste, corruption, and extravagance among Party cadres, had not done the research needed to design and implement effective policies on issues like the handling of Japanese nationals or the management of the Northeast Bureau's finances, and had made a mess of logistics. Finally, Peng's management style was undemocratic (meaning that he failed to consult with older, more experienced cadres), he spent most of his time meeting with a variety of individuals, telling each one whatever they wanted to hear, and dealing with issues on an ad hoc, reactive basis rather than taking the initiative to identify, focus on, and resolve major problems.

Lin Biao's denunciation of Peng Zhen may very well have been politically motivated, but his criticisms made a certain amount of sense. Peng did have a different leadership style from Lin Biao, and he did lack military experience—surely a disadvantage in a theater in which the competition between the Nationalists and the Communists was clearly going to be resolved through battle, not through negotiations. And when it came to battle, Peng Zhen did have a different strategic vision than Lin Biao. As Peng saw it, the industrial and transportation resources that the Communists would need in order to win a military struggle against the Nationalists were concentrated in the cities and along the railway lines. As we saw above, when the Soviets began their withdrawal from Manchuria and urged Peng Zhen to take a more aggressive stance, Peng used this to present the Party Center with an argument in favor of returning to the "Three Big Cities" strategy. The Party Center first rejected the idea, but then in mid-March, with Mao back in control, shifted to support of a revised "Three Big Cities" strategy involving Changchun, Harbin, and Qiqihaer, all in Northern Manchuria.

Peng Zhen and his supporters, writing in the late twentieth and early twenty-first centuries, argue that while he was leading the Northeast Bureau in the first nine months of the Communist struggle in Manchuria (September 1945–May 1946), Peng Zhen consistently implemented policies defined at the Party Center in Yan'an. Peng's camp has a valid point here. As we have seen, the Party Center's strategy for Manchuria shifted several times between September 1945 and March 1946, often in response to the desires and attitudes of the Soviet Union as well as in response to the Center's assessment of conditions on the ground. Sometimes the Center had instructed the Northeast Bureau to disperse its forces broadly and build rural base areas; at other times, it had ordered them to hold onto the major cities, railway lines, and industrial and mining centers.

When it came to responding to Lin's accusations that Peng Zhen was naive about the prospects for peace and therefore inclined toward "military adventurism," Peng and his supporters vigorously deny that Peng had any illusions about an imminent peace. But as we have also seen, in February and March 1946 Mao himself, although ill and not bearing a full workload, was expressing optimism about the chances for peace. If Lin was critical of Peng Zhen on this point, he should also have been criticizing Mao. Apparently, he did just that. Back in mid-February, around the time of the battle at Xiushuihezi, Lin reportedly telegraphed Yan'an and questioned Mao's confidence in the peace talks, asking, "Chairman, please think this over with a clear head."[43] Some of Lin's comrades in the Northeast certainly shared his concerns. Luo Ronghuan, for example, warned the Party Center in mid-March, "Do not be hasty in estimates for peace. . . . Don't develop a psychology of recklessness."[44]

Lin and Luo's lack of faith in the Marshall Mission led them to question the idea of fighting that one final battle to secure an advantageous deal in the peace negotiations. Indeed, Lin is said to have questioned the whole idea of defending Siping at the Northeast Bureau's meeting in Fushun in early March (the same meeting at which Lin is said to have criticized Peng Zhen so harshly).[45] Lin and Luo favored a long-term struggle in which base-building, guerrilla operations, and mobile warfare would slowly wear down an over-extended enemy.[46] Moreover, while disagreeing with Peng Zhen and Mao Zedong on strategy and on the likelihood of a ceasefire, Lin also disagreed with Mao about the main thrust of the Nationalist offensive. Lin believed that Zheng Dongguo would focus first on capturing Benxi, and that the advance toward Siping was of secondary importance to the Nationalists. Mao, on the other hand, was convinced that Zheng's first priority was to capture Siping in order to be able to move onward to Changchun and Harbin.[47]

THE OUTER DEFENSE OF SIPING

By late March, Lin's opinions about the direction of the main Nationalist advance, the chances for peace, and the advantages of mobile and guerrilla warfare as opposed to positional defense of cities were immaterial. Mao Zedong had decided to defend Siping long enough to allow Zhou Enlai, Marshall, and Chiang Kai-shek to negotiate a ceasefire that would leave the Communists in firm control of North Manchuria. On 26 March the Northeast Bureau issued its "Deployment for the Decisive Campaign in the Northeast," suggesting that the impending battle to defend Siping would "be the final battle to decide our Party's status in the Northeast."[48] Lin Biao's orders were to use his main forces to halt the Nationalist advance while using militia to consolidate the rear areas.[49]

Since he was obliged to defend Siping, Lin's first choice was to use guerrilla and mobile warfare tactics to sabotage transportation infrastructure and to conduct a peripheral defense. On 5 April, Lin told the Party Center that his plan was to annihilate K M T units in mobile operations south of Siping. If that should fail, his fallback position would be to defend the city itself.[50] Mao Zedong responded the next day:

> To concentrate six brigades in the Siping area to annihilate the enemy is absolutely correct. If there are any feelings of vacillation within the Party, even in the slightest, they must be thoroughly overcome. [I] hope that in the Siping area, you are able, through repeated bitter combat, to annihilate all or most of the enemy's northward-advancing forces, even if it requires our forces to sacrifice several thousand dead and wounded.[51]

Lin's strategy was based on two assumptions about the enemy. First, Communist intelligence assessments showed that the Nationalists were highly dependent on roads and railways both in conducting their advance north and for continued logistical support.[52] As a result, the N D U A forces were instructed to place special emphasis on the destruction of bridges and railways.[53] Second, Lin was confident that he could, in fact, inflict significant casualties by conducting mobile operations designed to cut off and annihilate individual enemy units while they were in motion.[54]

Lin Biao's plans were essentially an attempt to do the best that he could with the limited resources at his command. Robert Rigg, then serving an American military attaché in China, believed that Lin did, in fact, have at least a chance of defeating the Nationalist troops piecemeal as they advanced to the north.[55] Mao Zedong and the Party Center approved Lin's plans. In doing so, the Center held up the recent Handan Campaign as an example for Lin Biao to consider as he planned and carried out the defense of Siping.[56] In the Handan Campaign sixty thousand regular troops and one hundred thousand militia-men, all under the command of Liu Bocheng and Deng Xiaoping, successfully defended a chunk of territory, including a section of the Beiping–Hankou (Wuhan) railway line, centering on the city of Handan. In that campaign, the Liu/Deng armies had drawn enemy troops into Communist territory, cut them off, and then attacked them. These maneuvers, aided by the defection of the Nationalist New Eighth Army, resulted in a major victory for the Communist side.[57]

The Handan Campaign was a worthwhile reference point for Lin Biao, but his circumstances were quite different from those of Liu Bocheng and Deng Xiaoping. Lin's position at Siping lacked the geographical advantages of the Handan area, nor did he have a strong base area or mass support from which to draw militia forces. In addition, where Liu Bocheng and Deng Xiaoping had been able to take advantage of the alienation of the Nationalist New Eighth Army, none of the Nationalist troops advancing toward Siping were likely to switch sides. Nonetheless, Lin did initially conceive of the defense of Siping in terms similar to the operations that the Liu/Deng army had carried out in the Handan campaign. Lin would send his strongest units south of Siping, hoping to draw in, cut off, and ambush advancing Guomindang units.

Lin's peripheral defense of Siping lasted from 3 to 14 April. His forces were occasionally able to inflict significant casualties on KMT units and certainly slowed their advance, but ultimately he was unable to stop the Nationalists south of Siping. The peripheral defense began on 3 April when NDUA units attacked the Nationalist Seventy-first Army's Eighty-eighth Division at Jingjiatun, sixty-four kilometers southwest of Siping. Nine thousand Nationalist soldiers were killed or captured, along with their equipment. The Communist units pressed their attack against the Nationalist Thirty-eighth Division for another two days, but then withdrew, having lost 2,500 men in fruitless human wave assaults.[58] In another encounter on 8 April, Lin's forces attacked advance units of the New First Army, capturing high ground near the town of Xinglongquan, north of Changtu. This operation was only partially successful because Communist units that were supposed to swing around and cut off the enemy's route of retreat lost their way and wound up in a firefight with their fellow Communist soldiers. As a result of this error, the KMT units under attack were able to escape, although at the cost of some twelve hundred casualties.[59]

In a more successful operation, Lin's forces employed their classic "pocket" ambush technique against an unwary advance unit of the Nationalist Seventy-first Army. On 15 April, the Seventy-first Army's Eighty-seventh Division approached the area of the villages of Dawa and Jinshanbao. At this point, they were separated from the closest New First Army units by a distance of some twenty-five kilometers, about a day's march. An advance regiment of the Eighty-seventh, moving through the countryside, entered a bustling local marketplace to ask the villagers whether any Communist units were in the vicinity. Assured that the Communists had withdrawn, the soldiers fell out to rest and to buy food and drink. At that point, Communist soldiers burst into the marketplace—indeed some of the "villagers" were in fact Communist soldiers in civilian clothing. The entire regiment was captured. In the meantime, Communist units attacked other nearby Nationalist regiments in fighting that continued through the next morning.[60] This operation is said to have cost the Nationalists over four thousand casualties.[61]

Operations like those that Lin carried out at Xinglongquan and Dawa were possible because the Nationalists were advancing confidently along a broad front, with many of their units widely dispersed. Experience soon taught them that this left them vulnerable to Lin Biao's favorite tactical maneuvers—attacking isolated units with overwhelming force and cutting off and attacking relief forces sent out to rescue the units under attack. The Nationalist commanders were not unaware of Lin Biao's methods. Their response, after the fighting at Xinglongquan and Dawa, was to draw their forces more closely together, the Seventy-first Army joining the New Sixth Army in making an advance straight on toward Siping. In this way, the two armies would be able to coordinate with and support each other, and avoid falling into Lin's traps.[62]

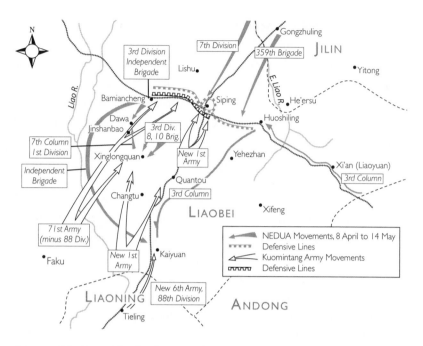

MAP 5.1. The Second Battle of Siping, Phase One:
8 April–14 May 1946. *Map by Tracy Ellen Smith.*

PREPARING THE DEFENSE OF SIPING

As the Kuomintang's New Sixth and Seventy-first Armies pressed slowly but surely northward, Lin Biao became less confident about the wisdom of occupying and defending major cities. On 11 April he told the Party Center, "The chances of our defending Siping and capturing Changchun and the chances of a quick achievement of peace in the Northeast are both unlikely. Therefore it seems that our army's main strategy should be to annihilate enemy forces, and not to defend cities, in order that we not be forced into battle."[63] Mao and the Party Center initially agreed, but later the same day Zhou Enlai, still in Chongqing, sent a pressing message stating that Nationalist officials were ready for a ceasefire in the Northeast: "I estimate that [the Nationalists] may not be able to get past Siping [and] will not reach Changchun before the fifteenth.... Recommend sending troops into Changchun within two days."[64] This convinced Mao to instruct Lin Biao to take advantage of the opportunity to capture Changchun.

When the Soviet Red Army pulled out of Changchun on 13 April 1946, it left the city in the hands of a Nationalist government and a hodge-podge of some twenty thousand Nationalist forces (as in Siping, most of them former "puppet" and local forces—not units of the regular National Army). Lin Biao, now under orders to take the city, moved his troops into position, the Soviets providing engines and passenger cars to transport some of the Communist soldiers down from Soviet-occupied Harbin.[65]

To defeat the isolated, poorly trained, and disjointed Changchun garrison would not be particularly difficult, nor would it require the Communists to achieve overwhelming numerical superiority. Dividing Changchun into three sectors, three Communist units attacked at dawn on 14 April, quickly capturing the airport and breaking into the city itself. Once they were in the city, the Communist soldiers met the real challenge. The Nationalists, though weak and divided, made use of defensive works as well as the city's many steel-and-concrete buildings to resist the Communists. The NDUA soldiers, having little experience in urban warfare, failed to divide the enemy into smaller pieces that could be dealt with one at a time. Instead, they pressed stubbornly forward from all sides, so that "in the end most of the enemy retreated to the center of the city, which somewhat increased the difficulties and the casualties of the final assault."[66]

The fact that the Communist troops prevailed despite their lack of experience in urban warfare was largely due to the fact that in Chang-chun, they were fighting a poorly integrated collection of irregular troops rather than the real Nationalist Army. Compared to their foes at Changchun, the Communists were well-trained, well-armed, and in high spirits. Indeed, some of the Communists attacking Changchun had been inspired by the claim, made by their officers, that *this* was the "last battle" for the Northeast. It was a slogan that they remembered bitterly when, not long afterward, they were sent south to help to defend Sip-ing.[67] But that disillusionment lay in the future. In mid-April, what Mao and the Party Center had in mind was that Changchun would become the capital of a large Communist base area extending from Yan'an across Inner Mongolia, Rehe, Chahar, and northern Manchuria to the borders of the Soviet Union and North Korea. Mao ordered the Northeast Bureau to "preserve all of the defensive works in Changchun, prepare to make Changchun another Madrid."[68] But still, Siping remained the key to the defense of Changchun. If Lin Biao's attempt to use mobile warfare to stop the Nationalists south of Siping failed, he would need to be prepared to defend the city itself.

Siping was not an easy place to defend. As a new railway city, Siping had no traditional city walls. The north–south railway divided the city into two parts: Tiexi (west of the rails) and Tiedong (east of the rails). The railway station itself faced west, and Tiexi was the location of the city's government buildings and major hotels, businesses, and shopping districts. From the point of view of the defense, Tiexi's main attraction was its multi-story Japanese-constructed government office buildings. Tiedong was (and still is) a more working-class area, characterized by low-slung family dwellings and a large Catholic church. Siping has little in the way of natural defenses. Gentle hills of around two hundred meters lie to the south and to the north-northeast. Southeast and about twelve kilometers from the city is the high ground of Tazishan, rising to 390 meters. Roughly north of the city at a distance of around ten kilometers is the gently sloping ground of Sandaolinzi, a not very impressive, but, given its position, still important 190 meters in height. There were a number of streams crisscrossing the plain south of the city, and some small groves of trees, but no heavy forest to provide cover to either defenders or attackers.

Lin Biao's initial reluctance to mount a positional defense of Siping at all, and his preference, if he must defend the city, for a mobile defense south of it, meant that preparations for the positional defense started rather late in the game. One high-ranking leader at the time recalled that there had been no discussion of or planning for a static defense of Siping either in the meetings of the Northeast Bureau or at Lin Biao's headquarters before 6 April.[69] An officer whose unit was transferred into the city on 14 April—only five days before the Nationalist assault—later recalled four days and nights spent throwing together pillboxes, bunkers, and other defenses, using steel rails scavenged from the railway line.[70]

Lin's preparations were predicated on his knowledge (gained through experience, observation of the Nationalist deployment, and intelligence

FIGURE 5.1. Lin Biao's former headquarters at Lishu. *Photograph by the author.*

reports) that the Nationalists were likely to attempt a flanking movement, and that they relied heavily on their artillery but were reluctant
to engage in hand-to-hand combat. His plans called for defensive lines
to be laid out with plenty of open space in front of them.[71] In terms of
deployment, Lin Biao chose to station a light garrison for the city itself:
two units totaling six thousand men under the command of Ma Renxing (?–1947). One regiment would defend Siping's Tiexi district, while
a second would be stationed in Tiedong.[72] Lin's main force was stationed
north-northwest of Siping in the area between Lishu and Bamiancheng,

from which it would be deployed to trouble spots as required. Lin himself established his headquarters in a small landlord's compound in Lishu, just fifteen kilometers north of Siping.[73] At this point Lin had around sixty thousand to seventy thousand men from various backgrounds: experienced units from the Eighth Route Army and from Zhou Baozhong's Soviet-trained Northeast People's Self-Defense Army, men from Zhang Xueliang's old Northeast Army under the command of Zhang's younger brother (and Communist Party member) Zhang Xuesi, and a large number of soldiers who had been recruited in Manchuria itself.[74]

As they took their places in and around the city in early to mid-April, the Communists began to prepare their defenses. For veterans accustomed to guerrilla warfare and for new recruits alike, digging trenches and building pillboxes, bunkers, and other defensive works was a new and not necessarily welcome task.[75] They often did not know exactly what it was that they were to do or how to do it. One unit, for example, used Japanese gun emplacements as a model when they were told to construct pillboxes. The result was structures with such a high profile that they made easy targets for Nationalist artillery.[76] The Communists also requisitioned strong multi-story buildings that they incorporated into their defenses. In Tiedong, this included parts of the French-Canadian Catholic mission. Machine guns were placed in the windows of the bishop's residence, which was apparently a solid edifice in the southern part of the Tiedong district, precisely in the line of the expected Nationalist advance.[77] Soldiers dammed up the streams south of Siping, creating a massive swamp to serve as a barrier to the advancing Nationalists.[78] A military telephone system was set up entirely separate from the civilian telephone lines. All telephone lines to Shenyang were cut in order to prevent telephonic communication to Nationalist-held territory.[79]

In retrospect, some observers blame Lin Biao for not having paid sufficient attention to preparing for the positional defense of Siping. Xing Cheng, then a regimental commander, recalls that when Lin visited Siping sometime in April to inspect Ma Renxing's work, he told Ma to be ready to defend the city for ten days. Xing Cheng relates this last-minute preparation to Lin's initial unwillingness to defend Siping at all and even to the underlying disagreements between Lin and Peng Zhen, saying that "if [Lin] had followed the Party Center's telegram of December 12,

FIGURE 5.2. Ma Renxing (first from left), Lin Biao (fourth from left), and others at Siping, March or April 1946. *Courtesy of the Liao-Shen Campaign Memorial Hall.*

1945 and the Northeast Bureau's deployment order, then the battle to defend Siping could have been fought very well."[80]

PEOPLE AND PROPAGANDA

As Lin Biao's NDUA prepared for the Second Battle of Siping, so too did the ordinary people whose city was, for the second (but not the last) time, about to become a scene of battle. There are few sources from which we can learn how the residents of Siping prepared for the coming storm, or how they lived through it. Official histories and museum displays tend to portray "the people" in one-dimensional, stereotyped terms as enthusiastic supporters of the Communists, volunteering to help dig trenches, carry stretchers, bring food and drink to the troops, and transport grain and other supplies in their humble ox-carts. There is no need to deny that there probably was some degree of popular support for the Communist Party or that citizens volunteered to support the Communist troops in various ways, and for various reasons. But a close reading of the available sources, supplemented by conversations with elderly residents of Siping, gives us a more complicated picture.

At first, the people of the Northeast were deeply affected by what the Communists referred to as "orthodox thinking," meaning that they regarded Chiang Kai-shek's government and its National Army as the real Chinese government and army, coming to restore order and national self-respect after fourteen years of Japanese occupation. Elderly residents of Siping and other cities in northeastern China, too, remember that many people supported the Kuomintang, whose regular army had American equipment and nice uniforms. At the same time, they say that it was difficult sometimes to tell one group of armed men from another.[81] One man recalls that everyone was scared of the Communist troops when they first entered Siping. All they knew about the Communists was what they had learned from the Nationalist government media: that the Communists were bandits.

In fact, some of the Communist soldiers who first entered Siping were very likely to have been bandits: the NDUA had been carrying out aggressive recruitment campaigns in Manchuria, with little regard as to the newcomers' former identities or class backgrounds. In 2010 one elderly man, seven years old at the time, remembered that some of the Communist soldiers still behaved like bandits: "My father had a fine pair of dogskin boots. A Communist soldier came into the house and when he saw them, he just said, 'Hand them over.'"[82] Another man recalled that ordinary people feared the Communists in particular, because the Communists would draft citizens to serve as stretcher-bearers.[83] Others, however, remembered the Communist soldiers as having been friendly, helpful, and well-disciplined. Even the man whose father's dogskin boots had been taken noted that the Communists soon imposed better discipline on their men.

The people of Siping needed to prepare for the worst, whether they supported the Communists or not. Some families sent women and children away to live with relatives in nearby—and hopefully safer—towns and villages.[84] Others remained behind. Members of the Canadian Catholic missionary community in Siping laid in supplies of food and prepared to take shelter in the large cellars of the bishop's residence. As it turned out, the Catholic sisters of the M.I.C. and other refugees, three hundred in all, would spend a month in the cellars, praying, conducting their religious ceremonies, and fearing for their lives as they listening to incoming artillery fire from the Kuomindang forces exploding above them.[85]

As garrison commander, Ma Renxing, too, had to prepare to manage the civilian population as well as his troops. He would need to maintain social stability, root out spies and saboteurs, and ensure that the civilian population had adequate supplies of food, fuel, and water. A basic administrative infrastructure for the city was already in place. It was standard procedure in 1946 for the Communist Party to establish Party-dominated local governments in the towns and cities that it controlled and to institute military control over the markets in food, coal, and charcoal and over key services like electricity.[86] In Siping, each city district organized a collective to address the problem of supply of vegetables. The people used soybeans (which were in plentiful supply) to grow soybean sprouts and to make tofu. District cadres took inventory of all the shops in the city to see what goods they had stored up. The city government then sold the goods at set prices and reimbursed the merchants.[87]

In managing the economy, the Party had to walk a fine line between controlling prices, winning the support of the common people through socioeconomic reform, and maintaining production. The Party Center ordered Lin Biao and Peng Zhen to carry out land reform and reforms in the economic status of the working class. But at the same time, they warned Lin and Peng to proceed with caution, not to raise wages too much, and not to demand too much improvement in the working conditions in industry. The point of mobilization was to get as broad a base of support as possible and to get workers and capitalists to cooperate in raising production—not to conduct violent class struggle.[88]

Propaganda was another aspect of Ma Renxing's preparation for the defense of Siping. The Party needed to be able to explain and justify to the people what was happening, and to show that the responsibility for war lay firmly with the Nationalists and that the Communists were simply defending themselves against aggression. In order to communicate both with Party members and with ordinary citizens, the Party published two newspapers in Siping. One, a mimeographed broadsheet called *Zhandou Siping* (Fighting Siping), was published for limited circulation among Communist Party members. The second, *Xinwen Jianxun* (News Digest) came out in a regular newspaper format with a circulation of some three thousand for distribution to the general public.[89] As would be expected, the propaganda effort portrayed the Guomindang as having sent rapacious officials supported by "bandit" forces to take control of Siping in the aftermath of the Soviet withdrawal.

Another way of preparing the city psychologically for war, and of fixing the blame for the war on the Nationalists, was for the Communist Party to organize a rally to demonstrate for peace and democracy.[90] The demonstration took place with much fanfare on 6 April on the plaza in front of the railway station. A public telegram sent on behalf of the reported twenty thousand demonstrators denounced the Nationalist forces as bandits.[91]

DU YUMING TAKES CHARGE

While the people of Siping demonstrated and the Nationalist armies fought Lin Biao and the spring mud of Manchuria, Du Yuming had been in the hospital in Beiping for treatment of his kidney disease. Du's absence had created concerns both in his own mind and in the minds of Zheng Dongguo and the other commanders on the ground in the Northeast.[92] When Chiang Kai-shek, who was traveling at the time asked Du to meet with him in Guizhou to discuss the situation in the Northeast, Du feared that he was about to be fired. Telling Chiang that he had not fully recovered from the operation and could not take the long flight southwest, Du hastened to Shenyang, where he resumed his command of the Nationalist forces in Manchuria.

Back in Shenyang, Du Yuming asked himself why Zheng Dongguo had been unable to capture Siping. Discussing the situation with Xiong Shihui, Du concluded that the reason for the failures and the consequent low morale was that the KMT had been making a mistake in trying to capture cities and control territory. They hadn't been able to concentrate sufficient force to defeat the Communist main force in battle and thus resolve the Communist problem in the Northeast once and for all.

Du's approach to the problem was to devote some ten days to gathering and analyzing intelligence in order to better understand the situation. He realized that he needed to attain a good understanding of what was happening on the ground both in South Manchuria, where the Nationalists had failed to capture Benxi, and in the north, where the New First and Seventy-first Armies had been making such slow progress toward Siping. At the end of that time, Du concluded that although the CCP armies in Benxi and in the Siping area each had around one hundred thousand men, the firepower and the combat effectiveness of the CCP troops in Siping were superior to those in Benxi. In addition, Lin Biao was in command personally at Siping. Accordingly Du realized that Siping, not Benxi, must be the Communists' focal point, and as such, Du would focus on the south, where the Communists were weaker. He would capture Benxi, and then turn to resolve the problem at Siping.[93]

ZHENG DONGGUO FAILS TO CAPTURE SIPING

On the evening of 19 April, Chiang Kai-shek held yet another banquet for General Marshall. Over dinner, Chiang tried to convince the American that temporary avoidance of war should not be the sole measure of the success of mediation.[94] Chiang's choice of conversation topic was far from coincidental. Earlier in the day, in Manchuria, General Zheng Dongguo had thrown the New First and Seventy-first Armies into what became a failed nine-day assault on Communist positions in and around the city of Siping.

Chiang's statements about the strategic goals of the operations in Manchuria often seem contradictory and probably reflect his ongoing assessment of a constantly changing situation. On 15 April he evinced impatience when he asked the Northeast command, "So by what day will our armies be able to reach Sipingjie and Changchun?"[95] Five days later, he struck a more cautious note when he told Xiong Shihui to first capture Siping, and then to pause to consider the overall situation. If there was an opportunity to capture some of the nearby smaller cities (Gongzhuling and Liaoyuan), Xiong should proceed to do so. But if not, then for the time being Xiong should "temporarily adopt a defensive posture at Sipingjie, and pull a part of your troops out to . . . recapture Benxihu."[96]

Chiang was also conscious of the need to wipe out Communist armies, not just to acquire more territory. He wanted Xiong Shihui to make sure that Nationalist forces did not get drawn into battle until all the troops were concentrated and in their places. But when all was ready, Chiang expected a decisive engagement: "Decisive battle is the issue of major significance, to which you must devote everything; whether you lose Changchun and recover it sooner or later is not that important."[97] If all went well, the battle at Siping would be a decisive one, in which the KMT would "defeat the Communists' main force in one blow." In the meantime, Chiang would continue to try to convince Marshall that compromise was hopeless.[98]

As the Nationalist onslaught began, Lin Biao assured the Party Center in Yan'an that his forces at Siping would "fight to the last man" to defend the city. Lin Biao personally took command of the defense of Siping from his headquarters in Lishu. In directing operations, Lin tried to walk the fine line between defending the city itself and carrying out mobile operations to isolate and wipe out enemy units. Lin still strongly preferred mobile operations to the static defense of a city. However, his orders to defend Siping were clear and unequivocal. Furthermore, as Lin himself observed, the New First and Seventy-first Armies were wise to his game: they were advancing on Siping in close formation so that they would not present Lin with any opportunity to cut off and attack individual units.

Lin's response was, in his words, "Our army will first use Siping to wear down the enemy and give him a setback, and then concentrate our main force and use the technique of defeating the enemy piecemeal in order to wipe out the New First Army."[99] Lin's plan would require a very strong defense of the city combined with mobile operations around the city designed to force the Nationalists to attempt a flanking movement, and thus to disperse their forces to the point where Lin could once again employ his preferred mobile operations.

Lin's plan worked, but only to a degree. The Nationalists opened the attack with their strong suit: days of artillery barrage, supplemented by air support and tanks.[100] With the New First Army attacking Communist positions on the southern edge of the city and the Seventy-first pushing from the west, Siping was under attack from two sides. The defenders fought by day and repaired their increasingly battered defensive works by night. Although the city and its defenses were hit hard by artillery bombardment and the enemy made small inroads, the defenders successfully fended off multiple assaults over a period of nine days. On 27 April, the Nationalist armies at Siping suspended their assault. Peace—of a sort—descended on the city.

From the Communist point of view, 27 April was an occasion for rejoicing. Chiang Kai-shek's vaunted American-trained armies had been stopped in their tracks! The Party Center sent a telegram offering praise for the bravery of the defenders of Siping and adding, "Please consider adding to the defending forces (for instance, one to two regiments), make Siping into a Madrid."[101] Lin Biao, too, extended his congratulations to the troops: "Although the enemy bombarded you with airpower and artillery, [he] was not able to shake you even an inch."[102]

Behind the morale-boosting congratulations, Lin Biao had a sober assessment of the performance of his troops and of the challenges that they would soon face. Although they had fended off the New First and Seventy-first Armies, Lin's NDUA men were still unaccustomed to the tactical techniques of standard warfare. For example, the Communist officers and men did not understand how to use cross-fire to support their fellow units to the left and the right; instead, they steadfastly fired on the enemy straight in front of them, each individual firing as he saw fit, and without any coordination between different ranks of soldiers or between machine gunners and riflemen. In addition, many of the NDUA soldiers had not yet been taught how to maintain their weapons. As a result, overheated and poorly cleaned machine guns and other automatic weapons jammed up. There were also problems when one team relieved another at a defensive position—as when neither team took responsibility for repairing defensive works, or when they got in the habit of changing shifts so regularly that the enemy figured out the schedule and took advantage of it to attack precisely when the transfer of responsibilities was taking place.[103]

Nine days of battle at Siping had stretched Lin Biao's men to the limits of their endurance and their abilities. But, for all their American training and American equipment, the Nationalist forces, too, were testing the limits of their endurance. The New First and Seventy-first Armies had still not had an opportunity to recover and reorganize from the casualties they had incurred as they fought their way up to Siping. The Nationalist Armies were also plagued by a logistics nightmare which had delayed the arrival of key weapons (like 37 mm antitank guns and 105 mm howitzers) and left them unable to replenish their stocks of ammunition.[104] As the weather warmed, mud and floods were replaced by spring winds blowing in with dust, making it difficult for the Nationalist gunners to aim their artillery.[105] Finally, the Nationalist troops were strained by the need to fight the Communists both at Siping in the north and at Benxi in the south. With the fighting at Siping having reached a stalemate, both Lin Biao and Du Yuming, and their leaders, Mao Zedong and Chiang Kai-shek, would need to consider their next moves.

6

The Second Battle of Siping

Phase Two—From Defense to Retreat,
April–May 1946

From the beginning, the Nationalist assault on Siping had been accompanied at the same time by an attack on the Communists at Benxi, an industrial city south of Shenyang. As we noted in chapter 5, both General Du Yuming and his subordinate, General Zheng Dongguo, suggest (in their memoirs, written well after the fact) that Chiang Kai-shek and Xiong Shihui were responsible for the decision to fight the Communists on two fronts. When he returned to Manchuria in mid-April following his kidney surgery, Du Yuming had come to the conclusion that the Communist forces at Benxi were more vulnerable than those at Siping. Du then decided to set Siping to one side and to focus first on defeating—and ideally destroying—the Communist forces at Benxi so that he would then be able to transfer more troops north to capture Siping and press onward toward Changchun.

The Communist leaders, for their part, realized full well that the fighting in the Northeast was not over. The public declarations of a great victory at Siping were accompanied by continued planning on the part of the Communist Party Center, the Northeast Bureau, and Lin Biao, still commanding the Communists' Northeast Democratic United Army from his headquarters at Lishu, north of Siping. Mao Zedong, now fully recovered from his own health problems and back in control of day-to-day business at the Party Center in Yan'an, told Lin Biao on 1 May that since Chiang Kai-shek still refused to accept proposals for a ceasefire agreement in the Northeast, "[the Nationalists] will continue to advance toward Changchun. Therefore, we must continue to fight at Siping and Benxi, to exhaust the enemy forces at these two places, to attrite their troop strength, to destroy their will to fight, and to cause them to greatly deplete the men, weapons, and ammunition that they have transferred over the past six months so that they don't have time to replenish them, while, by taking Changchun and Harbin, we gain ample sources of men and materiel, and then we may be able to pursue peace on terms that are beneficial to us."[1]

In short, Mao Zedong wanted Lin Biao to fight on both at Siping and Benxi, in hopes that further military setbacks would strengthen Zhou Enlai's negotiating position at Chongqing and force Chiang Kai-shek, finally, to agree to a ceasefire that would leave the Communists in control of northern Manchuria. Mao and the Party Center were still searching for that decisive "last battle" that would resolve the situation in the Northeast, at least for a substantial period of time during which they could prepare for the next phase of the struggle. Chiang Kai-shek, too, was pursuing the "decisive battle" that would knock the Communists out of the equation—a battle that he still expected would take place at Siping. Du Yuming had decided that the road to victory at Siping lay through Benxi. And so we too must turn our attention southward, to the mountainous terrain in which the Nationalist troops had already tried twice, and failed, to displace one hundred thousand poorly armed but determined Communist fighters from Lin Biao's Third Column and associated units.

SIDESHOW: THE BATTLE OF BENXI (1 APRIL–3 MAY 1946)

Benxi is very different from Siping. Rather than lying on a plain and at a major railway junction, Benxi is nestled amid the mountains sixty-two kilometers south of Shenyang in an area flanked by the deep and fast-running Taizi River. The plentiful iron and coal deposits in the mountains had made Benxi into a major industrial center—China's "coal and steel capital." In strategic terms, Benxi posed a significant threat to Shenyang. An unfriendly force in Benxi could either attack Shenyang directly or cut off the major transportation routes leading from Shenyang south to the coast. Both these economic and strategic factors were on the minds of Xiong Shihui when he chose in late March to attack the Communists at both Siping and Benxi, and of Du Yuming when he decided to focus first on Benxi.

Xiong Shihui tried twice to defeat the Communist forces at Benxi. In the first operation, beginning on 30 March, he threw two well-armed divisions (the Twenty-fifth and the Fourteenth) against the Communist defenders. Advancing through the mountains toward Benxi along two different vectors, both soon encountered stiff resistance from Communist fighters, who used the mountainous terrain to their advantage. The planned rendezvous of the two Nationalist divisions never happened, and the operation came to an end after two days.[2] The second attempt was launched on 7 April. This time, Xiong staged a three-pronged attack, the Twenty-fifth and Fourteenth Divisions on the right and left flanks and a single regiment in the center. Once again, the Communists were able to concentrate superior force against Nationalist units as they made their way along winding roads through the mountainous terrain around Benxi. The second attack on Benxi ended on 10 April, but fighting continued in the area.

The first two attempts to take Benxi failed not only because the terrain favored the Communists, but also because Xiong Shihui did not use enough troops to overcome the twin challenges of terrain and numbers. Both operations relied almost exclusively on a single division—the Twenty-fifth. In the first attack on Benxi, the Nationalists were stopped in their tracks and then forced to retreat because they were substantially outnumbered. In the second attempt, superior Communist forces caught the Twenty-fifth Division in an ambush from which it barely extricated itself.[3] Sheer physical exhaustion as the division attempted to fight its way through the rough territory around Benxi was also a factor in the Nationalists' defeat in these operations.[4] So too was a more fundamental problem: poor fire discipline. When they came under attack, the soldiers of the Twenty-fifth Division fired wildly, using large amounts of ammunition but with very little effect.[5]

Fortunately for the Nationalists, the solution to their problems around Benxi was simple: more men and more equipment. For the third assault, Du Yuming used overwhelming force, with five divisions advancing along three vectors.[6] In the meantime, as will be discussed in more detail below, Lin Biao had chosen to pull the Third Column out of Benxi in order to reinforce Siping, which he still believed was the main thrust of the Nationalist offensive. As a result, the reorganized Communist units defending Benxi were fewer in number than they had been during the first two Nationalist attacks on the area. Nevertheless, Xiong Shihui was worried that Du's plan would not work, and that numerically superior Communist forces would once again stymie the Nationalist armies.

On 29 April, having planned the operation against Benxi and set it into action, Du Yuming took a highly publicized visit to a location just south of Siping, where he was supposed to be taking a personal look at the situation at the front. This was intended to distract the Communists from the fact that the assault on Benxi was getting under way. It also allowed Du Yuming to keep away from Xiong Shihui in the crucial first hours of the operation. As Du later described, "If that day's preliminary battle went well and there was progress, then when I went back in the evening, Xiong wouldn't force me to change my plans; if by chance we should hit the wall, then evening would still be time enough to change the plans."[7] By the time Du had returned to Shenyang to speak with Xiong Shihui, the good reports that he had been waiting for were coming in. The Communist forces now faced an enemy with superior numbers and superior firepower. With their units spread thinly along a long line of defense and their men not trained for defensive warfare, the Communists fell into a reactive mode in which they lost the initiative and were forced into battles of attrition. As a result, the Nationalists broke through the Communist lines and headed straight for Benxi. On 1 May, the Communist commanders told the Northeast Bureau that it would be impossible to hold Benxi, and that to risk all in the attempt would not be "beneficial to the long-term struggle."[8] On 3 May, the Communists retreated from Benxi. They had held the area against three Nationalist attacks for over a month and, in the words of a U.S. Army intelligence report, "had caused a considerable number of KMT casualties, loss of equipment, and successfully had tied up the main bodies of two armies that might have decided the issue at Ssupingchieh [Sipingjie] some time previously."[9]

In the aftermath of the battle of Benxi, both the Nationalists and the Communists summarized the lessons learned. The Communists noted that they were still making the transition from guerrilla to mobile warfare, that they had no real grasp of the technique of concentrating superior force to cut off and annihilate enemy units in motion, and that instead, they tended to put their backs to the cities and disperse their forces along a long but shallow line of defense.[10] The Nationalists, for their part, noted their initial underestimation of the enemy and consequent failure to use overwhelming force. Poor use of artillery and lack of coordination between airpower and ground units had hindered Nationalist operations. And most regrettably (from their point of view), even though they had defeated the Communists at Benxi, they had failed—yet again—to envelop and annihilate the enemy. The two major prongs of the operation, advancing within twenty-five kilometers of each other, formed a narrow front as they pressed southward toward Benxi. Unfortunately for the Nationalists, the commander of a third unit that was supposed to have performed the envelopment refused to advance according to schedule, arguing that his division had been treated unfairly, was exhausted, and was not fit to be thrown into combat. As a result, although the Communist forces at Benxi retreated, they lived to fight another day.[11] Nonetheless, Du Yuming had achieved his fundamental goal: he had driven the Communist forces out of Benxi. With this threat to his rear area and to his headquarters in Shenyang eliminated, Du could now turn his attention—and transfer the New Sixth Army—to Siping.

STALEMATE AT SIPING (28 APRIL–14 MAY 1946)

At Siping, the suspension of the Nationalist attack after 27 April stretched out into eighteen days of stalemate. This did not mean that life in the city returned to normal or even that the shooting stopped. The two sides, Communist and Nationalist, took the opportunity to replenish their supplies, to repair and strengthen their defenses, and to ready themselves for the expected resumption of hostilities. Both sides made attempts at psychological warfare. Nationalist airplanes dropped propaganda pamphlets urging Communist soldiers to surrender. (Some soldiers later recalled having used these as toilet paper.) The Communists, for their part, used megaphones to shout at the Nationalist soldiers, "Chiang army brothers, don't fire! Does your conscience let you kill ordinary North-easterners? Listen to some Cantonese music!" These would be followed by gramophone recordings of Cantonese music—an attempt to make the Cantonese troops of the New First Army homesick.[12]

The shouting and the music could be heard because the National-ists dug a system of trenches that allowed them to approach within fifty meters of the Communist front lines. From these trenches, they launched rapid probing attacks by night in order to identify weak points in the Communist defenses. The Communist troops often failed to sta-tion enough sentries along their front lines and found themselves get-ting into sudden, unexpected firefights.[13] There was shooting every day, bombing, and even the occasional artillery duel as the two sides contin-ued to test each other's resolve and probe each other's weak points. In one of these actions, the Communist troops drove a Nationalist unit out of a forward position—a red building on the edge of Siping. In another one, the commander of the Communist Seventh Division decided, on his own accord and without even notifying the units adjacent to his, that he would wipe out a newly arrived Nationalist division which had just taken a position on a nearby hilltop. As they tried to maneuver their way up to the enemy position through the gullies by night, the Communist soldiers lost their way. When dawn broke, they were fully exposed to enemy fire and had soon taken over one thousand casualties. Lin Biao was furious. His verdict: "This is the way small-time guerrillas attack the enemy."[14]

In the context of this ongoing low-grade warfare, Liu Baiyu, a re-porter for the Communist Party's mouthpiece the *People's Daily* newspa-per, made a visit to Siping and the surrounding area. Liu's report is cer-tainly biased and strikes an optimistic note (from the Communist point of view), but it is perhaps the only extended description of the situation in Siping at the time to make it into the public record. In his account, Liu Baiyu described the intense fighting that the city had endured over the course of the first fifteen days of battle—artillery fire at up to 3,500 shells in two hours, civilians killed and injured and houses destroyed. But he also notes with pride that "up to today, Siping's electricity and water have not been stopped even once." He describes the sacrifices of the soldiers, the optimism and support of the people, people spending their days in makeshift bomb shelters, streets with piles of sandbags, and the slogans on the walls of machine-gun emplacements: "Gunners, take accurate aim" and "Do not fear blood or sacrifice."[15]

Liu Baiyu also visited some of the rear areas that were supporting the battle at Siping. Until the very end of the battle in mid-May, the Communist forces at Siping did not suffer from any significant problems in logistical support. Siping was connected to the rear areas by three working railway lines. When they captured Changchun in mid-April, the Communists had acquired a large warehouse full of Japanese weapons and ammunition. A regimental commander at the time recalled that his three thousand men were all issued with new 38-style rifles, straight out of the boxes in which they had been stored, along with some light and heavy machine guns.[16] Throughout their battle to defend Siping, the Communist forces relied largely on Japanese weapons and ammunition recovered from Kwantung Army warehouses.[17]

In order to gain access to these stockpiles of Japanese arms and other resources, Lin Biao and the Northeast Bureau had to establish and maintain control over an extensive base area behind the front line at Siping. Changchun, as we have seen, was captured from a small Nationalist garrison on 14 April. On 28 April, Communist forces similarly defeated the token Nationalist force that had been installed in Harbin when the Soviet Red Army withdrew on 25 April. This gave the Communists possession of two of Manchuria's "Three Big Cities"—only Shenyang remained in Nationalist hands. But there were also medium and small cities which, when brought under Communist control, contributed to the overall strength of the Communist position—places whose names simply don't make it into the history books, or even onto the maps: Qiqihaer, Angangxi, Mudanjiang, Jilin City, Gongzhuling, and Meihekou, to name but a few.

While they were fighting against Chiang Kai-shek's government, the Communist forces in the Northeast were also conducting what we might call "counterinsurgency operations" in their own rear base areas. The collapse of the Japanese Manchukuo regime had created a security vacuum in much of Manchuria. Soviet troops, stationed only in some of the major urban areas and controlling strategic points, were unable to fill that vacuum. The result was a proliferation of groups of armed men—former Manchukuo "puppet" army soldiers, local militia, and other armed groups. In the eyes of the Communist Party, these were all "bandits" (the same term that the Nationalists applied to the Communists). In fact, many of these groups did have a degree of political coloring to them: some were associated with local landholding elites. Others either had, or hoped to have, a connection to the Nationalist Party and were angling for legitimacy and local power when the Nationalists came to assert sovereignty over northern Manchuria.

The Communists regarded these groups as competitors for power. Before, during, and after the Second Battle of Siping, Communist units were deployed to key areas of northern Manchuria to conduct "bandit elimination" operations, which turned the stereotypical picture of Communist strategy on its head. Mao Zedong's approach to warfare is often summed up as "surround the cities from the countryside." But in the case of North Manchuria, it was the cities that the Communists first acquired. Using the cities as their base areas, units from the Northeast Democratic Army were sent out to wrest control of vast areas of the countryside from these local "bandit" forces. In the winter of 1945–1946, for example, most of the rural counties around Harbin were under the control of local bandits, and the population in general was supportive of the Kuomintang.[18] Although some of them were well-armed, the bandits of north Manchuria were not a serious match for the better-trained and more experienced Communist combat troops, but there were so many bandits that it took time to eliminate them. Although some areas were cleared in the winter and spring of 1945–1946, it was not until after 1 June that Lin Biao's forces would be able to undertake a systematic effort to bring the countryside under control. Nonetheless, in the months before and during the Second Battle of Siping, Lin and the Northeast Bureau had built a substantial base area comprising both rural districts and major cities, including Harbin. These were essential both for the support of the front and as a possible refuge if Lin should be forced to retreat.

Retreat was, in fact, an option that Lin Biao was seriously considering in early May. Despite the Communist Party's public cries of victory at having halted the Nationalist advance at Siping on 27 April, Lin Biao realized that he was still in a vulnerable position. Just as in the planning stages of the Communists' decision to defend Siping, Lin Biao's views differed from those of Mao Zedong. Once again, Communist strategy in the Northeast would be forged in the context of a debate between the two men. Mao's position changed even as he and Lin Biao exchanged points of view on the strategic situation, but he remained steadfast on one fundamental point: Lin must continue to defend Siping. On 27 April Mao had told Lin to "make Siping into a Madrid."[19] Mao expressed his strategic analysis and goals at greater length in a telegram the next day:

> Please consider whether it is beneficial to continue to fight, or if it is [more] beneficial to come quickly to a cease-fire agreement. If we are to fight on, you must prepare for the enemy side to increase its forces by an army (the Ninety-third Army has already begun to ship out on 20 April, estimate the entire army will arrive in the Northeast by mid- or late May). If we are able to annihilate or defeat the New First Army which is now attacking Siping by the middle of May, then it will be to our benefit to fight one more battle and then have a ceasefire, if not, then it would seem that an early ceasefire is [more] to our benefit.[20]

Mao was clearly concerned about the safety of Lin's main force and was aware of the risks involved. He wanted Lin to proceed with due caution and not to incur any disastrous losses. But the context of his remarks makes it clear that he was still determined to hold Siping and that he wanted Lin to fight that "last battle" to wipe out all or part of the New First Army before the negotiators in Chongqing agreed to a ceasefire. This put Mao at odds with Lin Biao. As military historian Victor Cheng puts it, "While Mao believed that the war could be won by a heroic battle orchestrated on positional warfare principles, his field commander Lin Biao was engaged in an attempt to salvage his troops from the siege."[21]

Lin Biao laid out his thinking in a diplomatically worded response to Mao's telegram quoted above:

> In the next ten days there will be no moonlight, so conditions are not favorable for our main force to conduct night offensives; in addition, because the terrain is flat, and the New First Army has built defensive works, and also because the 71st Army and one division each from the 52nd and 60th armies have taken positions close by the New First, there is little chance that we will be able to annihilate or defeat the New First in ten days. The enemy units entering the Northeast are the Nationalists' crack troops. The New First Army is the strongest of them, and so although our army has fought hard and bravely, casualties have been heavy and much of our ammunition has been depleted. But we have only been able to annihilate or defeat a portion of the enemy, and it is difficult

to annihilate or defeat him entirely. Siping remains in our hands, the enemy's advance has been dealt a setback, but he is redeploying, preparing to launch a new offensive against us. I offer the situation as described above for your study and consideration.[22]

Mao's study and consideration depended largely on his assessment of the chances for peace. Mao's views on this changed from optimism to pessimism over the next two days. On 30 April, Mao told Lin Biao that "the situation is changing, a ceasefire agreement may be signed tomorrow or the next day; expect you to defend Siping, fight for every inch of land."[23] The imminent prospect of a ceasefire certainly suited Lin and the Northeast Bureau. Lin's troops were exhausted from three months of combat, supplies were low, and the Party's rear areas in north Manchuria were still far from secure.[24] But with a ceasefire on the horizon, Lin would still have to defend Siping from any last-minute Nationalist offensive. The next day, 1 May, Mao told Lin that the situation had changed yet again, and that now "the slim hope for a peaceful settlement has evaporated altogether."[25] For Mao, this simply made it even more imperative that Lin Biao continue to hold out at Siping, and (as we saw above) at Benxi as well: "We must continue the fight at both Siping and Benxi, fighting until the enemy army at each place is exhausted, attrite their troop strength, break their spirit, force them to deplete as much as possible of the soldiers, weapons, and ammunition that they have shipped to the Northeast over the course of six months so they haven't time to resupply, while we, because we have taken Changchun and Harbin, have ample sources from which to replenish troops and materiel, and then it will be possible to gain peace on terms beneficial to us."[26]

With the Chairman determined not to allow the Nationalists to capture Siping, Lin Biao's challenge was to find a way to defend the city while at the same time avoiding another round of the sort of grinding positional warfare that put his troops at a disadvantage. Lin was a man who preferred movement and flexibility. He wanted to regain the initiative. In order to do that, he suggested, also on 1 May, a bold new plan: he would send two brigades around the New First Army to open up a second front in the enemy's weakly defended rear area, threatening Du Yuming's supply lines and forcing Du to transfer troops away from the front lines at Siping. At the same time Lin, who assumed that Du was still focusing on Siping, would (as we saw above) transfer some of his forces from Benxi north to strengthen the defense of Siping.

Over the next few days, Mao Zedong and Lin Biao refined the idea of a second front. Despite their differences, Lin Biao respected Mao's authority, and Mao placed a great deal of trust in Lin Biao. Mao's trust in Lin was underlined on the first of May when he told Lin, "All military and political command at the front lines is invested in you: it should not be dispersed."[27] Mao's decision suggests that he saw a need for a greater level of centralization of authority over operations in the Northeast, and that he was not confident that Peng Zhen, the secretary of the Northeast Bureau and ostensibly in charge of political affairs even at the front, was the man for the job. As we saw above, Lin Biao had already, in March, criticized Peng Zhen in extremely harsh terms. On 28 April an incident occurred which may have contributed to Mao Zedong's disillusionment with Peng Zhen: a Nationalist airstrike on the railway station at Communist-held Meihekou destroyed 260 freight cars loaded with arms and ammunition from the Soviet Union. Luo Ronghuan, ill with kidney disease and resting in Dalian, had arranged for this important shipment of war materiel. The reason that the train had been sitting at the platform at Meihekou, a prime target for the Nationalist airplanes, was that Peng Zhen's Northeast Bureau was moving its headquarters and personnel from Meihekou to the newly acquired cities of Changchun and Jilin. As Lin Biao described it to the Party Center some days later:

> This loss occurred because at the time, the Northeast Bureau was busy moving house to Changchun and Jilin, taking everything from sofas to bed-frames so that a big shipment of munitions was stuck at the platform without locomotives to move it. It is evident that problems in leadership are bound to be exposed to the light of day in large and small affairs and will lead to all kinds of disastrous consequences.[28]

The loss of supplies at Meihekou was regrettable (and professionally embarrassing for Peng Zhen), but certainly not so damaging that it would stand in the way of Lin Biao and Mao Zedong's planning for the continued defense of Siping and the opening of the second front. The second front operation commenced on 5 May.[29] On Mao's recommendation, Lin doubled the number of units involved from two to four brigades. In the meantime, Mao had ordered new attacks against the

FIGURE 6.1. Communist machine-gun unit on the front lines at Siping, April or May 1946. *Courtesy of the Liao-Shen Campaign Memorial Hall.*

Nationalists in Rehe and along the railway from Chengde to Jinzhou in order to prevent Chiang Kai-shek from transferring reinforcements from Rehe to Siping. At the same time, Peng Zhen ordered the local Communist Party leadership in north, west, and east Manchuria to recruit a total of seventeen thousand new soldiers to reinforce the troops at Siping.[30] Lin, as mentioned earlier, had already transferred troops away from Benxi up to the Siping area shortly before Du Yuming's successful offensive against Benxi.

Unfortunately for Lin Biao, the fall of Benxi on 4 May allowed Du Yuming to transfer the New Sixth Army up toward Siping precisely at the same time as Lin was opening up the "second front." The well-trained, well-equipped, and high-spirited professionals of the New Sixth gave Du Yuming, for the first time, numerical superiority in the Siping area.[31] They and other Nationalist units quickly defeated Lin's four brigades as they tried to harass the New First Army from the rear and to cut the main north–south railway line. The second front operation was over within a few days. By 12 May, the New Sixth Army was sweeping north to outflank Siping from the right (east). The Seventy-first Army moved forward from Bamiancheng to threaten Lin Biao's left (western) flank. The New First Army continued to press up the middle, straight on toward Siping itself.

To deal with this triple threat, Lin Biao had to string out his limited forces over a defensive line extending some fifty-sixty kilometers from east to west.[32] In Changchun, ordinary people and even the Communist Party rank-and-file continued to believe that the Communists had the upper hand in Manchuria and that even in the unlikely event that Siping should fall, Lin Biao would fall back to Changchun and turn that city into "another Madrid."[33] In fact, it was the turn of Du Yuming and the Nationalist command in Shenyang to feel confident. Nonetheless, Du Yuming's actions, like those of Lin Biao, were tied more closely than he might like to the status of the ongoing three-way negotiations among Chiang and his representatives, George Marshall, and Zhou Enlai.

BACK AT THE NEGOTIATING TABLE

When George Marshall flew back to Washington on 11 March 1946, it appeared that he had made some real first steps toward the Truman administration's goals in China. He had negotiated a ceasefire and he had begun to build the foundations of a democratic system in which the Nationalists and the Communists would, it was hoped, work together peacefully. When he returned to China on 18 April, everything that he had been working for seemed to be falling apart. By the end of the first week of May, with the fighting still simmering away in Manchuria, Marshall was visibly depressed. What had gone wrong and why?

In the previous chapter we have seen what went wrong (from Marshall's point of view) on the ground in Manchuria: a Nationalist offensive that captured a number of Communist-controlled towns and cities and the Communist seizure of cities that the Soviets had turned over to small, isolated Nationalist garrisons—Siping and, spectacularly coinciding with Marshall's return to China, Changchun. We have also suggested that the spark which set off this new conflagration was not Marshall's departure. It was the Soviet withdrawal which removed the only effective buffer between the National Army and Lin Biao's NDUA.

As they withdrew, the Soviets encouraged the Communists to take a strong stand against the Nationalists, and they purposely conducted their withdrawal in ways that would help the Communists to move into new positions and to capture cities including Siping and Changchun. At the same time, Chiang Kai-shek steadfastly refused to recognize any legitimate role for the Communists in the Northeast and sought to achieve a military solution to the Communist bandit problem. With both sides determined to achieve military advantage and to occupy as much territory as possible, and with the Soviets removing the only barrier that stood between them, a new round of clashes was inevitable.

George Marshall did, of course, anticipate that the January ceasefire would be interrupted by sporadic outbreaks of violence. To prevent such incidents from occurring, and to resolve them quickly if they did occur, Marshall devised a system of field teams as a part of the January ceasefire agreement. These field teams were run out of an Executive Headquarters that was responsible for implementing and overseeing the terms of the ceasefire. The Executive Headquarters—located in Beiping, just east of the Forbidden City—and its field teams each consisted of three members: one Nationalist, one Communist, and an American, who acted as chairman. Each of the three members had one vote, but all action had to be by unanimous agreement. Marshall recognized that the Executive Committee and the field teams were based on the most fragile of foundations: a "spirit of cooperation between the National Government and the Chinese Communist Party." Nevertheless, this was what Marshall had to work with. He could only hope for the best.[34]

The Executive Headquarters had sent field teams to some of the hot spots in Rehe and in Inner Mongolia in January and February, but none to Manchuria. Chiang Kai-shek argued that the presence of field teams with American personnel would provoke the Soviets, who might very well demand that they be represented in any field teams working in the Northeast. Marshall, however, came to believe that Chiang's real reason was that he feared that the field teams would force him to recognize a legitimate role for the Communists in the Northeast and prevent him from using military force against them.[35] Nonetheless, Marshall continued to try to find a way to bring the field teams into the Northeast. On the eve of his departure for Washington, Marshall presented the Communists and the Nationalists with a draft proposal for the terms under which field teams might enter Manchuria. The proposal stipulated that the mission of the teams be limited to military matters, that they keep clear of areas still under Soviet occupation, and that they proceed to points of conflict or of close contact between Government and Communist troops in order to bring about a cessation of fighting or in order to avoid future trouble.

Marshall's draft also included two points regarding the transfer of sovereignty over Manchuria to Chiang's national government. The first of these two points authorized the government to "reestablish the sovereignty of China in Manchuria" and specifically to control the territory thirty kilometers on either side of the main railway lines. The second stated that

> Communist troops will be required to evacuate such places as are necessary for the occupation of government troops in reestablishing the sovereignty, including coal mines. Communist troops will not be permitted to move in and occupy places evacuated by Russian troops.[36]

These last two points were utterly unacceptable to the Chinese Communist Party. Zhou Enlai also argued that the field teams should take up political as well as military issues—a position completely unacceptable to the Nationalist side.

The negotiations over when and under what conditions to send ceasefire field teams to Manchuria dragged on in Marshall's absence. While Marshall was in Washington, General Alvan C. Gillem was left in charge of the negotiations. Gillem, in the words of the American diplomat John Melby, was "a very nice guy and from all reports an exceedingly competent military man, but politically he is limited and is the first to say it." On the morning of 11 March, the day before he was scheduled to take over the negotiations, Gillem was heard to ask what "this Kuomintang thing" was.[37]

Gillem was soon to hear a lot about the Kuomintang, not only from its own representatives, but also from Zhou Enlai. With Marshall pushing from Washington, Gillem tried to arrive at some formula under which the Nationalists and Communists could agree to the dispatch of the field teams to Manchuria. Finally, on 27 March, Zhou, Gillem, and Nationalist negotiator Zhang Zhizhong signed an "Agreement on Ceasefire Mediation in the Northeast."[38] By the first week of April, field teams were on the ground in Shenyang, but they were not able to leave the city. The Nationalist team members claimed that they had not received authorization to act, and were purposely rude to the Communist team members. Nationalist agents organized demonstrations against the field teams in Shenyang. When the teams finally went out to problem areas around Shenyang the next week, they still accomplished nothing: neither the Nationalist nor the Communist team members would divulge their sides' troop positions to each other, because they regarded each other (probably with good reason) as spies.[39] In the absence of any feelings of trust between the Nationalist and Communist team members, and with Chiang Kai-shek and his generals more interested in pursuing a military solution than in agreeing to a ceasefire, the field teams were not able to prevent war in the Northeast.

The failure of the field teams, however, did not mean that the ceasefire negotiations were not relevant to the development of the situation in Manchuria. We have already seen that the ways in which Mao Zedong, Zhou Enlai, and Lin Biao viewed the status and direction of the ceasefire negotiations had a direct effect on their views of what should be done on the battlefield. It is important to note here that there was not unanimity of opinion within the Communist leadership. Lin Biao's point of view, expressed both in his criticisms of Peng Zhen and in his messages to the Party Center, was that there was little hope of peace. Lin argued that if peace was not imminent, then the NDUA should avoid positional defense and major set-piece battles; instead, it should focus on guerrilla and mobile operations in order to wipe out enemy units when the opportunity presented itself, and on base-building in preparation for a protracted war. At one point—in early April—Zhou Enlai, too, argued that the Communist forces in the Northeast should put their emphasis on annihilating enemy units, rather than on positional defense of cities. Zhou's concern was that it looked as if Lin Biao would lose Siping and Benxi. If that happened, these losses would have weakened Zhou's position in the ceasefire negotiations, whereas victories in mobile operations against carefully chosen targets would work to Zhou's advantage. At this point, Zhou was pessimistic about the chances for peace and believed that Lin Biao would need to find and win a major battle in order to force the Nationalists to reach a compromise.[40]

Such was Zhou's view in early April. But Zhou's advice at any given time on what sort of military action would be most beneficial depended on his assessment of the current state of the negotiations—and his assessment changed often in response to new proposals, initiatives, and even public statements made by Marshall and by his Nationalist negotiating partners. As we have already noted, in mid-March Zhou was optimistic about the chances for peace: his optimism was based on the assumption that the United States wanted peace, and that Chiang Kai-shek would have no choice other than to give in to American demands. In early April, Zhou thought that the Americans were conniving with Chiang Kai-shek, that there was no hope for compromise, that the Communists would lose Siping, Benxi, and other cities, that the Communists had no choice other than to defend themselves, and that the only hope for the future was if Lin Biao could fight and win a battle along positional warfare lines. On 11 April, remarks made by high-ranking Nationalist leaders reignited the flames of optimism in Zhou's heart: convinced that peace was now possible, he called on Lin Biao to capture Changchun.

Whatever Zhou Enlai and Lin Biao thought and reported to him, Mao Zedong maintained a single, consistent focus: defend Siping and Benxi. Mao shared Zhou's optimism about the chances of peace in mid- to late March. This optimism led Mao to order Zhou to take a hard line in the negotiations. On the battlefield, he ordered Lin Biao to prepare for a major battle, but on the assumption that it would be a short war, not a protracted struggle.[41] By 18 April, when Marshall had returned to China, the Communists had taken Changchun, and with the Nationalist armies just beginning their first assault on Lin Biao's positions at and around Siping, Mao was more optimistic than Zhou about the chances for peace.

Here again, Mao's optimism led him to believe that with the end of the fighting drawing near, Lin Biao must defend Siping (and Changchun) at all costs. As for the negotiations, Zhou Enlai, who was less optimistic than Mao, argued that the only way to force Chiang Kai-shek to compromise on Manchuria was for the Communists to reach an impasse with George Marshall—that, in turn, would force Marshall to put some real pressure on Chiang. Mao disagreed. He believed that there were still important differences between Marshall and Chiang, and that Zhou Enlai could play on those differences in order to use Marshall to put pressure on Chiang.[42] Mao, then, ordered Zhou Enlai, "Do not prepare to come to an impasse simultaneously with both the Nationalists and the Americans. We firmly oppose the Nationalists' policies of civil war and dictatorship and strive for peace and democracy; to that end, do not fear reaching an impasse with the Nationalists. But with regard to the Americans, we should not reach an impasse unless they resurrect the Hurley policies and offer open and across-the-board support for the Nationalist Party's pursuit of civil war and dictatorship."[43] Mao apparently feared that if the Communist Party destroyed its relationship with Marshall, this would bring Marshall and Chiang Kai-shek closer together, rather than (as Zhou Enlai argued) forcing Marshall to strong-arm Chiang into making concessions.

While instructing Zhou not to cause a breakdown in relations with Marshall, Mao was also, on 21 April, telling Lin Biao to continue to defend Siping and Changchun and that "everything is decided by victory on the battlefield[;] do not put any hope in negotiations."[44] As time went on, the Communist Party leaders became more pessimistic about the chances for peace, and more convinced than ever that Marshall, far from being a neutral mediator, was in fact actively supporting the Nationalist effort to eliminate the Communists in Manchuria. On 22 April, Zhou reported to Mao Zedong that "Chiang is still not willing to have a ceasefire in the Northeast, and is currently waiting for reinforcements. Marshall may allow Chiang to fight, and therefore is not anxious to see me. In the next ten days we should prepare to sabotage the railways in the Northeast and to fight a major battle."[45] Nonetheless, the negotiations continued, with Zhou complaining regularly to Marshall about Nationalist and American actions. The Nationalist capture of Communist-controlled cities was a violation of the ceasefire, he said, while Communist occupation of Changchun was simply a defensive measure undertaken in response to Nationalist aggression; the Communists had no desire to occupy the Northeast single-handedly and wished, more than anything, for a ceasefire; Chiang Kai-shek was stubborn, preferred to settle issues by force if possible, and was impossible to negotiate with.[46]

While Zhou Enlai and Mao Zedong's reading of Marshall and their level of optimism about the chances of using Marshall to force Chiang to agree to a ceasefire changed from week to week, Chiang's attitude toward Marshall had the virtue of consistency: from start to finish, Chiang was convinced that Marshall was naive, unfair, self-centered, and utterly biased in favor of the Communist Party. With his troops fighting at Siping and the field teams effectively neutered, Chiang had little interest in agreeing to a ceasefire. In meetings with Marshall, he offered ceasefire terms that had already proved to be unacceptable to Zhou Enlai: for instance, Nationalist control of the territory forty-eight kilometers on either side of the main railway lines, troop deployments that would have given the Nationalists an overwhelming advantage, discussion of only those political issues related to the presence of Communist forces in the Northeast, and an insistence that the Communists return Changchun to Nationalist political and military control.[47]

In his diary, Chiang continued to vent his anger and frustration. To compromise with the Communists as Marshall demanded would be the same as surrendering to the Soviets; Marshall's request that the Nationalists recognize Communist-dominated local governments was "unreasonable"; and Marshall's pressure on the Nationalists was one-sided because the Communists, knowing that the American policy was to seek peace, had no incentive to cave in to American pressure.[48] At the same time as Zhou Enlai was coming to the conclusion that the Americans were conniving with Chiang to push the Communist Party out of the Northeast, Chiang deeply regretted that the Americans were not giving him the kind of military support that he felt he needed and deserved. He lamented the fact that Marshall was decreasing the level of American naval support for moving Nationalist troops and equipment to Manchuria—this reduction in logistical support, he complained, would leave the supply lines of his troops in Manchuria vulnerable, while the Communists enjoyed Soviet support and a secure rear area in Harbin and beyond.[49]

But most of all, Chiang believed that Marshall did not know what he was doing, and that the Truman administration's China policy was utterly wrongheaded. "If the United States does not change its previous passive policies and actively support our government," Chiang warned (in his diary), "then it will be absolutely unable to carry out its policy of coordinating with us for peaceful reunification and recovery of the Northeast, and furthermore, America's reputation in East Asia will be thoroughly and irretrievably destroyed because of this."[50] Marshall, Chiang thought, should understand the need to rethink American policy, to no longer "kneel down to" the Soviet Union, and to give Chiang's government more support: "This is basic common knowledge of the international situation—how could Marshall not know it?"[51] On 28 April, after a fruitless five-hour meeting with Marshall, Chiang suggested an answer to his earlier rhetorical question: Marshall's "spirit is already completely controlled by the Communists."[52]

Marshall and his negotiating team, for their part, were increasingly frustrated and depressed by the way things were going. In mid-May, as they observed the failure of the ceasefire field teams and the early stages of the battle for Siping, the Americans at the ceasefire Executive Headquarters in Beiping came to "feel that neither the Nationalists nor the Communists are willing to make any real concessions for the sake of peace, and that both sides have been attempting to deceive the Americans by a mere show of conciliation and compromise."[53] Marshall regarded the Communist takeover of Changchun as a major blow to his negotiating efforts. In his view, the Communist capture of Changchun both contributed to the Communists taking a hard line in the negotiations and undermined his credibility with the Nationalists.[54] Faced with unwillingness to compromise on both sides, Marshall announced, on 29 April, that he would no longer attempt to mediate the Manchurian issue. Pointedly blaming the impasse on the Communist capture of Changchun, he told Zhou Enlai, "I have done the best I can in an effort to negotiate this critical situation. The matter, with this statement, virtually passes out of my hands. I do not see anything more I can do in the way of mediation."[55]

Marshall's withdrawal from the attempt to mediate a ceasefire in the Northeast was an attempt to force both sides to rethink their positions. But it was also a recognition of the fact that Marshall was powerless to prevent the course of events in Manchuria from playing out. By this time (late April–early May), Marshall's relations with Chiang Kai-shek were distinctly cool and he was visibly depressed.[56] On 6 May he reported to Truman, "The outlook is not promising and the only alternative to a compromise agreement is, in my opinion, utter chaos in North China to which the fighting will inevitably spread."[57] Nonetheless, Marshall continued to present Chiang Kai-shek with advice and to offer draft ceasefire proposals to both Chiang and to Zhou Enlai.

Speaking to Chiang, Marshall warned of the danger of extending his troops too far north into Manchuria. Although he blamed the Communists for having violated the ceasefire when they took Changchun, he also blamed Chiang for having garrisoned the city in the first place and thus presenting the Communists with an easy target. Marshall warned Chiang, "In the present situation, I am of the opinion that should a northern advance of the Nationalist army in Changchun be carried out before a possible basis of agreement is reached regarding the cessation of hostilities there would remain small prospect of reaching any agreement, except by the destruction of the Communist military forces in Manchuria, which I do not think is within the power of the government."[58] Marshall further advised Chiang that any future Nationalist troop deployment in Manchuria should focus on southern Manchuria, both because the Nationalists could not offer logistical support to large numbers of troops in the north and because of the "uncertainty as to the future actions of the Communist Party and the possible reactions of the Soviet Government in connection therewith."[59]

Although he had ostentatiously removed himself from the effort to mediate a ceasefire in Manchuria, Marshall did make another attempt. The new plan would still require the Communists to withdraw from Changchun, but instead of turning the city over to the Nationalists directly, a field team from the Executive Headquarters would move in to establish order, and Nationalist troops would follow within six months. The troop ratio in Manchuria would be five Nationalist units to one Communist, and Marshall would undertake to talk Chiang Kai-shek out of trying to occupy any cities north of Changchun. To placate Chiang Kai-shek, the procedures of the three-man field teams would be revised so that the American member had final decision authority. Both sides rejected the proposal, Chiang on the grounds that the presence of Americans in Changchun would cause the Soviets to demand that they be included, and Zhou Enlai because giving decision authority to the

Americans was a violation of the original spirit of unanimity on which the field teams had been founded.[60]

Marshall's advice to Chiang Kai-shek—that he should not deploy substantial troops in North Manchuria—and Chiang's constant complaints about Marshall clearly indicate that there were substantial differences between the two. But from Zhou Enlai's perspective, the continued American logistical support for Chiang's troops (even if at levels that failed to satisfy Chiang) and Marshall's attempt to give the Americans decision-making power in the three-man field teams simply proved that "on the Northeast question, there is now little difference between the opinions of Marshall and Chiang."[61]

Marshall, for his part, had completely failed to understand Zhou Enlai. In Marshall's view, it was the "hard-line generals in the field" who had taken the initiative to capture Changchun and who were pushing for Zhou to take a tough stance in the negotiations. In fact, it was Zhou Enlai who had recommended the capture of Changchun, and Lin Biao who had been reluctant. It was Zhou Enlai, not Lin Biao or Mao Zedong, who had suggested that the only way to squeeze a compromise out of Chiang was to reach an impasse with Marshall. And it was Zhou Enlai who, on 13 May, reported to the Party Center that "a fundamental improvement in the situation is completely impossible, Chiang still has reservations about causing an all-around breakdown, but the danger has increased; perhaps half-peace, half-fighting is the most likely, but ultimately the issue will be decided by the relative military strengths of both sides, [so] we must mobilize the masses in preparation for the decisive battle."[62]

DU YUMING'S VICTORY

If the issue was to be decided by a contest of strength and will, Du Yuming was ready to rumble. The New First and Seventy-first armies were already in position. The New Sixth was moving up from Benxi toward the right (east) flank of Siping. If all went well, Du Yuming would conduct a double envelopment of Siping, bringing his forces through Lin Biao's fragile lines to a point thirty-two kilometers north of Siping. This would enable him to cut off Lin Biao's route of retreat, and destroy the NDUA's main combat force.[63] Du Yuming had now achieved overwhelming superiority—ten divisions, with modern weapons and air support. Chiang Kai-shek was still cautious about advancing farther north: from early to mid-May, he had been ordering Du not to think about capturing Changchun and to stop making inflammatory comments to the press.[64] Du's own plan of battle, however, included the possibility that the Communists would retreat from Siping toward Changchun. In that case, Du wanted his troops to trap and annihilate the retreating Communists at Gongzhuling and to "follow up on the victory by sweeping on to Changchun and areas to the north."[65]

Communist intelligence networks had given Lin Biao and his officers a general idea of what Du Yuming was up to: they were keenly aware of, and concerned about, the possibility that they might be seriously defeated or even see their main combat force entirely wiped out. None, perhaps, was more concerned than Huang Kecheng. Huang's Third Division was responsible for defending the left (west) flank of Siping, including the route to Lin Biao's headquarters at Lishu. Huang was no coward, but he was also not willing to see lives and resources sacrificed for nothing. Convinced that he and the NDUA in general were about to fight a losing battle, Huang sent several messages to Lin Biao, suggesting that the Communists abandon the apparently futile attempt at positional defense and transition to a mobile warfare strategy. Lin did not respond. Never timid about cutting through the chain of command, Huang then sent his opinion straight to Mao Zedong.

In his telegram of 12 May, Huang Kecheng pointed out that since entering the Northeast, his Third Division had lost half its combat strength to casualties, and more than half its company, platoon, and squad officers. New soldiers had made up for some of those losses, but the division remained weak. If a ceasefire was really imminent, Huang said, then of course the Communists should do their utmost to hold on to Siping and Changchun. But if not, and if the fighting dragged on, they would both lose Siping and Changchun and suffer very heavy casualties. Instead of fighting a losing battle to hold onto Siping and Changchun, Huang Kecheng made the following recommendations: (1) give up Siping and Changchun in order to gain time in which to rest and reorganize Lin Biao's troops; (2) consolidate control over the North Manchurian base area; (3) if there was no ceasefire in the Northeast, the Communists should initiate all-out civil war in China Proper in order to prevent Chiang Kai-shek from transferring more troops to the Northeast; and (4) in the context of an all-out civil war, the Communist forces in the Northeast should "wipe out the Nationalist forces step by step in order to achieve the goal of controlling the entire Northeast."[66]

Huang's telegram was a part of a broader debate within the Communist leadership over the question of what strategy to adopt in the face of the imminent Nationalist offensive at Siping. Huang was clearly in favor of trading Siping and Changchun for time—and of expanding the war to North China. Although Lin Biao did not respond to Huang Kecheng, he may very well have agreed, at least with the idea of trading territory for time and switching from positional to mobile warfare. But Lin did not answer to Huang Kecheng—he answered to the Northeast Bureau and, beyond that, to the Party Center and to Mao Zedong.

Chairman Mao, writing on behalf of the Party Center, weighed in on 15 May. In a telegram sent only to Lin Biao and Peng Zhen, Mao asked Peng and Lin to consider whether they should continue fighting or if it would be more advantageous to trade Siping and Changchun to the Nationalists in return for concessions in other areas.[67] But on the same day, Mao sent another directive not only to Peng Zhen's Northeast Bureau (and thus indirectly to Lin Biao), but also to each of the Party Center's other regional bureaus across China, to Zhou Enlai, and to the Party representatives at Marshall's ceasefire Executive Headquarters in Beiping. In this directive, Mao laid out his analysis and recommendations for action. In framing his decisions, Mao, characteristically, took multiple factors into consideration: for him, the "Battle to Defend Siping" could only be understood in the context of the overall military situation in China, the negotiations, the dynamics of relations within the ceasefire teams, and the situation in Rehe Province. As he had revealed in his private telegram to Peng and Lin, Mao, like Huang Kecheng, was willing to trade Siping and Changchun for gains in other areas if Lin Biao was really unable to defend the two cities. But Mao also realized that he could not trade territory that he lost or gave up voluntarily. Thus he required Lin Biao to continue to defend Siping, "the longer the better," while at the same time, Zhou Enlai, at the negotiations, would talk peace and try to hammer out a ceasefire agreement.[68]

At the same time, Mao believed that although George Marshall agreed with Chiang Kai-shek that Changchun should be turned over to the Nationalists (as Marshall continued to make plain in his ongoing negotiations with Zhou), there were still differences of opinion between Chiang Kai-shek and George Marshall when it came to other issues in China and the Northeast. Although Chiang was (in Mao's view) preparing for all-out civil war, he would not dare to initiate a broader conflict because the Americans opposed it. Marshall and Chiang also did not see eye-to-eye on the balance of military forces and political and economic issues in the Northeast. All this led Mao to believe that it was still possible to use Marshall and the Americans to force Chiang to make compromises on the Northeast.[69]

For this reason, Mao instructed the Party and the army as a whole not to initiate any hostilities with Nationalist forces. They could, and should, defend their positions if attacked and even try to recover territory if it was lost, but there should be no offensive operations. The Communist representatives at the Executive Headquarters and in the field teams should stop being rude and uncooperative with the Americans; instead, they should win the Americans over. Communist troops in Rehe should sabotage the railway from Rehe to Jinzhou in order to prevent Chiang Kai-shek from transferring more troops into Manchuria by rail. In all places other than the Northeast, the Party's main task for the next six months was not to fight. Instead Party leaders should focus on training, rent reduction campaigns in the countryside, and agricultural production in order to be ready for all-out civil war when and if Chiang initiated it.[70]

Mao's directive was essentially a refutation of Huang Kecheng's arguments.[71] In Mao's view, the Communists should postpone a broadening of the civil war, not initiate it, and Lin Biao should fight on, not withdraw. Zhou Enlai seconded this the next day when he suggested to the Party Center that under the current circumstances, "the places that our army has occupied in the Northeast absolutely cannot be given up at this time."[72] Mao was apparently confident that Lin Biao could hold on at Siping.[73] Whatever Lin Biao's (or Huang Kecheng's) reservations might be, they were immaterial. The NDUA would have to continue to defend Siping to the best of its ability for as long as it could. Even as the debate

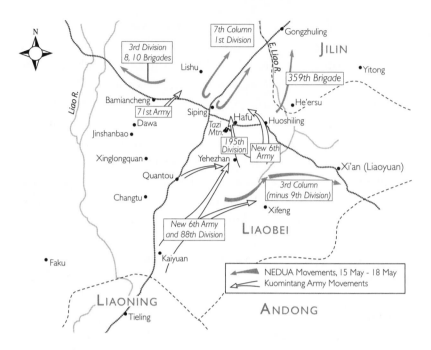

MAP 6.1. The Second Battle of Siping, Phase Two: 15–18 May 1946. *Map by Tracy Ellen Smith.*

was going on, Lin Biao had adjusted his troops to meet the anticipated Nationalist onslaught.

Du Yuming set his armies into motion on 14 May. The Seventy-first Army advanced toward Siping from the west and the New First from the south. In the west Liao Yaoxiang, a Whampoa graduate and veteran of the Burma Campaign in the Second World War, led the New Sixth Army. Liao, observing the setbacks that the New First Army had run into in its earlier attempts to take Siping straight on, ordered his forces to advance in two columns, close to each other so that Lin Biao would have no opportunity to cut off and wipe out isolated units. Local men were drafted to guide his forces through the unfamiliar territory[74]

Soon after they set out, one of Liao Yaoxiang's regiments ran into a Communist unit which had taken a position on a hilltop. The Communists' rifles and machine guns were no match for the Nationalists, who battered the Communist position with heavy artillery. The Communists quickly abandoned their position and fled to the north. After the shooting was over, the Nationalists figured out what had happened: their single regiment had just driven off Lin Biao's Third Column.[75] Neither Lin Biao nor the Third Column had been prepared for the rapidity and intensity of the New Sixth Army's advance. In this case, the New Sixth's American equipment, and particularly their mechanized transport, played a crucial role. While a single regiment fought and drove off the Third Column, Liao's main force used six hundred trucks to quickly and quietly push its way through the Communist line. When the trucks got stuck in the mud, the Nationalists laid down steel plates to drive over. The Communist soldiers of the Third Column, on the other hand, had not had a full night's sleep in seven days, were poorly armed, and were running out of ammunition.

Liao Yaoxiang's goal was to capture Tazishan. Tazishan, or "Pagoda Mountain" in English, was so named because a Buddhist pagoda had been built there during the Liao Dynasty. The pagoda was long gone, but at four hundred meters above sea level, Tazishan was the highest ground in the vicinity of Siping and thus a key to the defense of the city. Breaking through the Third Column's defenses, Liao's New Sixth Army swooped down on Tazishan, capturing nearby hilltops. On 17 May, Tazishan was surrounded on three sides. As the Nationalists closed in on Tazishan, Lin Biao remarked, "I expect that the enemy will be able to take Tazishan tomorrow; Liao Yaoxiang is sure to throw his entire force against Tazishan. If Tazishan is lost, the enemy can come around and envelop us from the rear, seal off the route of retreat for our forces defending the city, and then we will be in a completely passive position and in danger of being annihilated."[76] Lin Biao sent two urgent messages to the single regiment responsible for defending the mountaintop position. First: "Hold on to Tazishan for another day if at all possible." And then, some hours later: "Tomorrow hold on for at least half a day—do not spare any sacrifice."[77]

On the morning of 18 May, Liao Yaoxiang stood on a tank directing the assault on Tazishan. The Nationalists opened with their artillery, systematically bombarding Tazishan from bottom to top. Liao Yaoxiang, himself an artilleryman, ceremonially fired the first round. Nationalist airplanes bombed and strafed the Communist positions. The Communist Nineteenth Regiment fought bitterly to defend an exposed mountaintop position of around seventy to eighty square meters. Because Tazishan is a rock outcropping with only a shallow layer of topsoil, there was no possibility of digging in. All they could do was to arrange rocks and boulders as best they could to provide some cover. Despite the odds, the Nineteenth Regiment fought bitterly, repulsing wave after wave of Nationalist forces that sought to charge up the mountain.

When Liao Yaoxiang's attempt to dislodge the Communists with a straight-on assault failed, he swung around to the right. He now had the mountain completely surrounded. In the meantime, Lin Biao had ordered reinforcements to hasten to Tazishan. The relief force, just like Liao Yaoxiang's Nationalists, relied on local guides to show them the way through unfamiliar terrain. In general, these local guides, drafted by both the Communists and Nationalists, did as they were told. As one man who had served as a guide for the Nationalists reflected years later, "You didn't have much choice!"[78] In this case, however, the Communists had drafted a local man whose sympathies lay firmly with the Nationalists. He purposely misled the Communist reinforcements, taking them by a circuitous route in order to slow them down.[79] With no assistance in sight, the dwindling number of men on Tazishan fought on until shortly after noon, when Nationalist troops overwhelmed the last of them.

When he heard the news that Tazishan was lost, Lin Biao knew that the game was over. At nine o'clock that evening, he telegraphed the Northeast Bureau and the Party Center: "Today the enemy launched a ferocious infantry assault under cover of airpower, artillery, and tanks, key positions northeast of the city have been lost, to recover them is impossible, the forces defending the city are in danger of being cut off, [we] are now withdrawing from battle."[80] Lin was not waiting for permission to withdraw. The orders had already gone out. Some of the troops who had continued to hold off the enemy at their own positions and did not understand what had happened elsewhere were unhappy with the decision to retreat.[81] Whatever their feelings about Lin Biao, the men obeyed their orders, which were that they should be out of the city by midnight.

Lin's retreat from Siping was so carefully conducted that the Nationalists did not realize that it had taken place. All was quiet the next morn-

FIGURE 6.2. Tazishan (Pagoda Mountain). *Photograph by the author.*

ing. After some hesitation, the men of the New First Army established that the Communists had fled. When they were sure of themselves, the Nationalists staged a formal entrance into the city. The victorious soldiers looked impressive in their sharp American uniforms, holding American assault rifles, and marching smartly along with a military band.[82] The Catholic Sisters of the M.I.C. and other members of the Canadian Catholic community emerged from their month-long incarceration in the coal cellars of the bishop's residence and surveyed the damage to their cathedral and other buildings. The residents of Siping likewise began to repair and rebuild the war-torn city. In Changchun, not so far away, ordinary Communist Party members soon heard the news. Miss Luo Wei, a young reporter for the Chinese Communist Xinhua News

Agency in the Northeast, wrote in her diary on 20 May, "Got the report this afternoon, our army has already retreated from Siping. This news comes too suddenly, I simply find it hard to believe my own ears and eyes. Weren't they still reporting military gains yesterday? . . . My heart is in turmoil, I desperately want to understand the current and future situation. But we certainly can't give up Changchun!"[83]

7

The Chase and the Ceasefire

May–June 1946

Those who suggest that George Marshall's June ceasefire cost Chiang the opportunity to recover the entire Northeast base their arguments on assumptions about the aftermath of the Second Battle of Siping. In order to analyze those arguments, we too need to look at what happened in the weeks after the battle, and to answer a series of questions: How badly defeated was Lin Biao? How many casualties had the Communist forces suffered? How did Lin and the Party Center intend to deal with the situation following the defeat at Siping? Could they have survived a Nationalist advance on Harbin? On the Nationalist side, could Du Yuming's pursuit of Lin's forces have been handled differently? If they had tried, could the Nationalist forces have utterly destroyed the Communist forces and secured all of Manchuria? When and why did Chiang Kai-shek suspend the pursuit and agree to the ceasefire? In what ways did Marshall, the Soviet Union, and the situation on the ground in the Northeast and in China Proper influence Chiang's decision to agree to a ceasefire?

There are no easy answers to these questions. On the Communist side, memoirs, publicly released documents, and secondary sources written in the People's Republic generally tell a single, coherent narrative, although a few sources do present somewhat different interpretations of events. On the Nationalist side, memoirs and biographies of some of the main characters (Du Yuming, Sun Liren, Zheng Dongguo, Chiang Kai-shek) tell quite different stories. Even works attributed to Chiang himself, but written at different times (and perhaps by different ghost-writers) contradict each other. The best we can do is to look critically at all the available sources and try to put together a reasonable account of the events of May and June 1946.

DU YUMING PRESSES HIS ADVANTAGE

On 17 May, Chiang Kai-shek sent Bai Chongxi—one of his top generals—to find out why Du Yuming had still not captured Siping. Bai Chongxi, speaking for the Generalissimo, argued that since the Communist defense had been so effective, Du Yuming should pause after capturing Siping and allow time for the peace talks to go forward. In the meantime, Du could consolidate his position in Siping and South Manchuria and prepare for another offensive if the peace talks failed.[1] The position that Bai is reported to have laid out is roughly that which Chiang had expressed in his diary almost a month earlier, on 20 April: that after occupying Sipingjie, his forces should focus on consolidating their positions in South Manchuria and on securing the Bei-Ning railway rather than advancing farther north.[2]

Du Yuming disagreed. The whole purpose of the offensive against Siping, Du argued, was to wipe out the NDUA's main force and to capture Changchun and nearby cities, including the Xiaofengman hydroelectric station. If he followed Chiang's orders and ended the offensive, then the capture of Siping itself would be meaningless. If he pressed on, he could easily capture all the territory south of the Songhua River. As for using a temporary ceasefire to rebuild his strength and prepare for a second offensive, Du suggested that the Communists could recruit and incorporate new troops faster than the Nationalists could—a ceasefire would leave him at a disadvantage. Du sealed his case for continued action by telling Bai Chongxi that he had already issued orders for his armies to pursue the Communists once they had captured Siping. Retracting the orders would lead to chaos and leave his forces vulnerable to Communist attack.

Reassured by Du's expressions of confidence, Bai Chongxi supposedly said to Du, "As I see it, if you do succeed in capturing Changchun, Mr. Chiang will probably not be unhappy!" The next day, after inspecting the front with Du, Bai's confidence increased, and he told Du, "Well then, you fight according to the original plan. I will go back right away and tell the committee head [i.e., Chiang Kai-shek] to talk to the Communists about a ceasefire after we have recovered Yongji and Changchun."[3] Whatever the truth of these recollections, which were written long after the fact, Du Yuming clearly felt empowered to proceed with his plan, and he acted quickly, pursuing the NDUA northward across a broad front. Aware that Changchun was poorly defended, Du sent part of his force directly on toward the city, capturing it on 23 May.

BALANCING BETWEEN SUPERPOWERS

As Lin Biao's position in Siping deteriorated, Zhou Enlai became more and more interested in seeing Marshall succeed in negotiating a ceasefire on terms that would force Chiang Kai-shek to recognize the Communist Party's position in northern Manchuria. This would require deft management of Marshall on Zhou's part. But Zhou was finding Marshall less and less tractable. As he reported to the Central Committee on several occasions in May, Zhou felt that although Marshall and the United States were not entirely on the same page as the Nationalists, Chiang was trying to manipulate the Americans—and succeeding. Nationalist propaganda and (presumably) Chiang Kai-shek's personal charm were bringing the Americans closer and closer to the Nationalist position. The chances of the Communists using Marshall to their advantage were decreasing day by day.[4]

When Siping fell to the Nationalists, Zhou presented the Party Center with the following possible scenarios:

1. If we do not give up Changchun, then sooner or later the Americans will help Chiang to capture Changchun; we will be forced to sign a treaty under duress, in which case the terms will inevitably be harsh; or if we do not sign terms, and continue to fight, we will lose more territory in the Northeast and it will be hard to avoid nationwide civil war.

2. If we are able to defend Gongzhuling, and on the one hand, strike hard against Chiang, and on the other hand prepare to withdraw from Changchun in return for other beneficial terms, then we should make up our minds and deploy and negotiate that way. So-called other beneficial terms means sporadic fighting, which would gain a year or a year and a half of peace to rest and reorganize.[5]

Zhou continued to work with Marshall—after all, at this point, the Communists, particularly Lin Biao's forces in the Northeast, were desperately in need of a ceasefire agreement. But Zhou Enlai was under no illusions about the long-term prospects for peace: "When compromising with Chiang, we cannot again harbor illusions of real peace or real democracy, but it is possible that we just halt large-scale fighting for a period of time in order to consolidate our current positions and our own strength, win over new masses, and prepare for further development.[6] Part of Zhou's concern was that under the international conditions of the time, the Soviet Union was still unwilling to openly support the Communist Party in the Northeast while the Americans (Zhou assumed) would openly support the Nationalists.

In one sense, Zhou was right about the Americans and the Nationalists. When push came to shove, the Americans would support Chiang—that had been clearly established in Marshall's conversations with President Truman back in December. But Marshall, his staff, and the American military intelligence community in China were not exactly fans of Chiang Kai-shek (which Zhou also realized, at least to a degree).[7] In fact, they had little confidence in the military capabilities of either Chiang or his armies. From the beginning, General Wedemeyer had thought it unlikely that Chiang had the military strength to control all of North and Northeast China. Observing how long it had taken Du Yuming to capture Siping, the Americans did not think that Chiang's armies were capable of going much further. One military attaché predicted that, just on the basis of the logistical challenges involved, it would take the Nationalists at least a month to reach Changchun.[8] As the *New York Times* reported, Nationalist units advanced north from Siping at the rate of seventeen to twenty miles a day, their advanced American weapons loaded onto mule carts.[9]

It was concerns like these that had earlier (on 10 May) inspired Marshall to caution Chiang:

> In the present troop situation, I am of the opinion that should a northern advance of the National Army in Changchun be carried out before a possible basis of agreement is reached regarding the cessation of hostilities there would remain small prospect of reaching any agreement, except by the destruction of the Communist military forces in Manchuria, which I do not think is within

the power of the Government. Incidentally, if such an advance should be undertaken and repulsed, then the government's position would, in my opinion, be so seriously weakened that little could be done in the way of a compromise toward a peaceful solution without an unacceptable sacrifice on the part of the Government.[10]

Marshall's fundamental conviction that the Nationalists were not capable of successfully advancing much farther to the north was a driving force behind his attempts to end the fighting as soon as possible after the fall of Siping. Marshall's goal at this point was to get the Communists to negotiate a peaceful turnover of Changchun—a real possibility, inasmuch as Zhou Enlai and the Communist Party Center were in fact considering the possibility of bargaining Changchun away in return for recognition of their control over other areas of northern Manchuria.[11]

While Du Yuming was marching his troops northward from Siping, Chiang Kai-shek was reassuring Marshall that he had no intention of trying to recapture Changchun.[12] Chiang was, in fact, in the midst of a very complicated game of "barbarian management." On the one hand, he wanted to keep the Soviet Union at arm's length from any negotiations involving Manchuria. When Stalin invited him to Moscow for a discussion of these issues, Chiang (on 21 May) turned down the invitation. As Chiang saw it, "Since our army captured Sipingjie and the Communist bandits' main forces went down in defeat their attitude has changed once again, and we have turned down Soviet [leader] Stalin's invitation to visit Russia, so the Communist bandits have no choice other than to continue to rely on America's mediation."[13] Forcing the Communist Party to rely on American mediation was, however, only half the diplomatic battle. The other half was for Chiang to manage the pace and conduct of the negotiations with Marshall in order to achieve the best possible outcome for the Nationalists.

Chiang did not find George Marshall an easy man to manage. His diary includes consistent complaints that Marshall was concerned only about the success of his mission, that he did not care for China's interests or the fate of its people, and that he was blind to the machinations of the Soviet Union and its attempts to use the Chinese Communists to create a "second Manchukuo" in China's Northeast.[14] Marshall was, of course, not unaware that the Soviet Union was deeply interested in Manchuria or that it supported the Chinese Communist Party. At the same time, however, Marshall's low estimate of Nationalist military power made it all the more difficult for Chiang to guide the negotiations to his advantage. But he would certainly try.

On 22 May, Chiang Kai-shek—perhaps as a part of his attempt to manage his American friends—gave an American reporter named Richard Lauterbach over two hours of time with himself and his private secretary. Lauterbach was a very well-connected newsman who worked for Henry Luce's publishing empire. Ironically, Lauterbach (unlike his boss, Mr. Luce) was distinctly sympathetic to the left, had once been considered for recruitment into the KGB, and became known later as a strong critic of Chiang Kai-shek.[15] Lauterbach's access was based on the fact that Luce, the publisher of *Time* magazine, was a longtime supporter of Chiang Kai-shek. Lauterbach was also—as Chiang Kai-shek must have been aware—a confidante of George Marshall.

During the visit—which was completely off the record—Lauterbach was, in his own words, "intent on finding out from the Gimo whether or not the government would proceed further especially if Changchun fell quickly and without much of a show of resistance."[16] Lauterbach came out of the conversation convinced that the Nationalist troops would go further, possibly all the way to Harbin, although Chiang was concerned about the possible Soviet reaction.[17] On the same day, Chiang sent orders to Du Yuming authorizing him to keep his armies in their positions and await orders unless the Communists pulled out of Changchun voluntarily—in which case, Du should occupy the city in order to "protect foreign nationals."[18] The next day (23 May), Lauterbach spent three hours with Chen Lifu, who assured the American reporter that the Nationalist armies would capture Changchun but would not launch an overall offensive in the Northeast to capture Harbin or other Communist positions north of the Songhua River. The Generalissimo, said Chen, "has made up his mind and there will be a truce."[19]

THE GENERALISSIMO VISITS MANCHURIA

Lauterbach's report did not reach General Marshall until 29 May. In the meantime, on the twenty-third, Chiang and his wife Soong Meiling borrowed Marshall's personal airplane and flew to Shenyang in order (or so Marshall thought) to prevent Du Yuming from advancing rashly to capture Changchun. Given his and Chen Lifu's conversations with Richard Lauterbach and his orders to Du Yuming, it seems that Chiang was being less than forthright about his position. Du, of course, announced the capture of Changchun the very same day. Chiang saw the capture of Changchun as miraculous evidence of "the protection of God."[20] Marshall saw it as an infuriating further escalation of hostilities. Later, he described Chiang's trip to Shenyang as "starting a chain of events which were almost completely disastrous in their effects on the situation."[21]

The problem for Marshall was that the Nationalist capture of Changchun had fundamentally undermined his negotiating position, which had been based on the idea of getting Zhou Enlai to trade Changchun in return for Nationalist concessions in other areas. Chiang, however, was elated with the capture of Changchun. He knew very well that Marshall disapproved, but he bridled at the American's criticism and continued pressure, lamenting in his diary, "[I] do not know why our Republic of China must put up with this humiliation."[22]

Chiang kept the humiliation to a minimum by spending ten days in Shenyang and Changchun, and another day in Beiping, before finally returning to Nanjing on 3 June. Throughout that time, Chiang deliberately kept Marshall at arm's length, communicating with him indirectly through his prime minister (and brother-in-law) T. V. Soong. Chiang clearly wanted to stall the ceasefire negotiations until he had achieved his military goals in the Northeast. The victory at Siping and the easy capture of Changchun had given Chiang the confidence to continue to pursue Lin Biao. In Chiang's words: "As the Communist bandits' main force in the Northeast has been crushed, [we] should quickly establish a blueprint for recovering the entire territory. This is why it is best if the mediation executive headquarters does not come to the Northeast and gain freedom of movement, so as the Communist bandits will not gain another chance at recovery under [its] protection."[23] Not only Chiang, but also his generals, were concerned that if the ceasefire were extended to Manchuria, it would prevent them from continuing their pursuit of the defeated NDUA.[24]

Chiang seems to have been striving for the best possible outcome under circumstances in which he was subject to several contradictory pressures: the Soviets' concern about his advance north of the Songhua, his generals' (and perhaps his own) desire to continue the advance north, and Marshall's determination to negotiate a ceasefire. In order to ease the pressure from the American side, Chiang tried—via T. V. Soong—to convince Marshall that the situation in the Northeast had changed, and that there should be no hurry to achieve a ceasefire. Chiang instructed T. V. Soong to tell Marshall that the situation in the Northeast was not at all what it appeared to be from the perspective of Nanjing: the Communists' main force had been crushed and the Soviet Union had "repeatedly made indirect representations that it would absolutely not prop up the 'Communist side' or obstruct our unification, that they had not done so in the past, and absolutely would not in the future."[25] Contrary to Marshall's thinking, the capture of Changchun would make it easier, not more difficult, to achieve a ceasefire in the Northeast. Marshall need not go to Zhou Enlai: Zhou would come to Marshall of his own accord, because the Communists had no other choice. As to the military situation, T. V. should reassure Marshall that all was well: "If only the 'Communist army' in the Northeast is thoroughly defeated, then it will be easy to resolve the military problems within the passes [in China Proper]."[26]

Chiang's confidence about the military situation in the Northeast translated directly to a stronger stance in the ceasefire negotiations. His position was laid out in two letters, dated 24 May, from his wife, Madame Chiang, to Marshall. Chiang demanded that the January ceasefire agreement be carried out in the Northeast, that demobilization and reorganization of armies (that is, the incorporation of the Communist armies into a single national force commanded by Chiang) be accomplished, that his government be allowed to take over sovereignty of the areas formerly occupied by the Soviet Union, and that the American officers on the truce teams have absolute authority to interpret and apply the terms of the ceasefire in cases where the Nationalist and Communist team members disagreed with each other. Chiang's proposals avoided the question of when ceasefire teams would be sent to the Northeast, and returned to the principle—already rejected by the Communists—that unification of the Communist military under Chiang's command be achieved before the political issues could be addressed.[27] As Chiang saw it, "This week I have exhausted heart and soul in explaining our strategy toward the Communists to Marshall, but I do not know if I have been able to bring him to enlightenment."[28]

Marshall did not share Chiang's rosy assessment of the military situation in the Northeast—which is to say that Marshall did not share the fundamental premise of Chiang's hard-line negotiating position. As already noted above, Marshall had little faith in the strength and abilities of the Nationalist armies, their officers, or, for that matter, Chiang's own military prowess. Unconvinced by T. V. Soong's arguments that Lin Biao's forces were on their last legs and that the Communists would soon come begging for peace, Marshall relayed a message to Chiang, telling him, "I urge that you immediately issue orders terminating advances and pursuits by the National Government troops within twenty-four hours. . . . To press your present military advantage will invite a repetition of the unfortunate results of earlier Nationalist Government experiences in Manchuria."[29] Chiang, of course, had just ordered Du Yuming to capture Harbin and then to pause and plan the next stage of operations in the Northeast.[30]

Messages continued to fly back and forth between the three corners of the negotiations—letters from Madame Chiang to Marshall, discussions between Marshall and T.V. Soong, meetings between Marshall and Zhou Enlai, and radio messages from Marshall to Chiang, relayed via Premier Soong. Nobody was particularly satisfied. Zhou was not as motivated a negotiator as Chiang had expected, and Marshall, fundamentally in disagreement with Chiang's confident assumptions about the military situation in Manchuria, continued to press the Nationalist side to make concessions. Zhou believed that Chiang was manipulating Marshall in order to drag the United States into the war. Chiang's reaction to Zhou's proposals for a ceasefire, as conveyed by Marshall, is evident from his diary: "Zhou Enlai's vicious duplicity is to be expected, and Marshall is the same as ever, concerned only with achieving the goals of his mission as quickly as possible, with no concern for the life or death of our country and our people—it is a terrible shame."[31] Marshall, for his part, was losing patience with Chiang, telling him on 29 May:

> The continued advances of the Government troops in Manchuria in the absence of any action by you to terminate the fighting other than on the terms you dictated via Madame Chiang's letter of May 24 are making my services as a possible mediator extremely difficult and may soon make them virtually impossible.[32]

What bothered Marshall—and Zhou Enlai—was that Chiang seemed intent on an open-ended continuation of hostilities in the Northeast. But in fact, neither Chiang's confidence nor his goals in the Northeast were unlimited. Chiang's and Chen Lifu's conversations with Richard Lauterbach suggest that Chiang's goal was to assert control of Manchuria south of the Songhua, or perhaps as far north as Harbin, and then to pause to consolidate his position and strengthen his forces in the Northeast before beginning a new offensive against Lin Biao's NDUA.

At this point, any hint of caution was anathema to Chiang's commanders in the field, and particularly to Du Yuming. Du was anxious to advance to Harbin as fast as possible—and certainly before summer, when the corn and sorghum crops would be growing high in the fields, giving cover to the Communists. Newspapers published in Nationalist-controlled Shenyang (presumably under Du's control) reported that the Communists had been thoroughly defeated, that their main force no longer existed, and that the remnants were retreating in disarray. The Nationalists (according to these reports) were advancing rapidly toward Harbin. Unnamed "military experts" estimated that Du Yuming would recover the entire Northeast within a month.[33] The more objective *Dagongbao* (*The Impartial*), published in Shanghai, was less sanguine. While reporting that Du Yuming's forces were advancing toward Harbin, it added, "If the National Army pushed north from Harbin toward Qiqihaer, it can be expected that it will encounter strong resistance from the Communists."[34]

Wellington Koo (Gu Weijun), China's representative at the United Nations and, beginning in May 1946, ambassador to Washington D.C., shared the *Dagongbao*'s more conservative attitude. Visiting Shenyang in late May, Koo advised Du Yuming not to proceed hastily.[35] Koo's advice was based on his memory of a similarly ambitious offensive on Harbin back in 1929. The Japanese had assassinated Zhang Zuolin, the warlord of Manchuria, just the year before. His son, the dashing "Young

Marshall" Zhang Xueliang, had taken over the old man's army and had pledged his loyalty to Chiang Kai-shek and the Republic of China. Chiang and Zhang Xueliang wanted to assert Chinese sovereignty over the Soviet-controlled Chinese Eastern Railway and had peremptorily evicted Russian railway managers from their offices in Harbin (in violation of a treaty agreed to by the Soviet Union and Zhang Zuolin back in 1924). When the Soviet Union responded with an invasion, it fell to Zhang Xueliang to defend China's sovereignty. His army, advancing from Shenyang to Harbin, was easily defeated.[36] The Soviet Union reasserted its control over the railways of northern Manchuria, Zhang Xueliang and Chiang Kai-shek himself were humiliated, and thirty-nine Chinese generals in Beiping signed a circular telegram denouncing Chiang Kai-shek as incompetent.[37]

Chiang Kai-shek, who had certainly not forgotten the Sino-Soviet war of 1929, was deeply aware of the continued strong Soviet interest in China's Northeast. While he told Marshall that the Soviet Union's attitude had changed and that they would not intervene directly on behalf of the Communists, Chiang still had legitimate concerns about how the Soviets would react if his armies advanced from Changchun to Harbin and beyond. Back in March, Chiang's diplomats, reporting on their discussions about transfer of sovereignty with the Soviets, concluded that the KMT army would only be able to advance as far as Harbin: "As to gaining control over the five northern provinces [i.e., the territory north of Harbin], [we will] encounter resistance."[38] Chiang's own concern is clear as well. On 25 May, while he was stonewalling Marshall, Chiang confessed in his diary that "the status of the Northeast is related to delicate foreign policy factors concerning relations with the United States and Russia," and that any error could lead to serious consequences.[39]

All this suggests that, despite the bluster that he showed to Marshall during his eleven days of absence from Nanjing, Chiang was in fact prepared to pursue a more cautious strategy in Manchuria, but that he would not announce this publicly until he had gained as much advantage as possible. Also on 25 May, Chiang noted, "Order commander Du Yuming's forces to advance toward Harbin on the double; we must first capture that strategic point. Only then can military operations in the Northeast come to a halt, and then we can plan the second stage."[40]

TAKING REFUGE NORTH OF THE SONGHUA

Lin Biao had originally laid plans for an orderly retreat from Siping. Fallback defensive positions had been prepared north of Siping in the hope that the fall of Siping would not lead inevitably to the fall of Changchun. On 19 May, Mao Zedong himself ordered Lin Biao to prepare to defend Changchun. As Mao saw it, one of the main reasons for the loss of Siping had been Lin's failure to thoroughly sabotage the north–south railway line from Shenyang to Siping. Mao now instructed Lin Biao to destroy the railway from Siping to Changchun—to remove the rails and cart them away, blow up bridges, water tanks, and stations, and dig up large sections of rail bed. The garrison forces in Changchun should prepare to defend the city itself for at least a month while Lin's main forces conducted operations on the enemy's flanks and rear areas. Mao's assessment of the situation was that the enemy's troops were now spread thin and his supply lines long, and that this presented the Communist forces with opportunities to harass him and slow or halt his advance.[41]

Any defense of fallback positions north of Siping, including Changchun itself, could only be attempted if the retreat from Siping went according to plan. Unfortunately for Lin Biao, that did not happen. The initial withdrawal from the city itself was carried out masterfully, but things quickly began to fall apart. The New Sixth Army, with its mechanized transport, was soon on the NDUA's heels. The retreat became a rout. As the New Sixth pushed forward, some Communist units wound up behind enemy lines, and others fell out of contact. Demoralized NDUA soldiers, particularly the new recruits, abandoned their units and faded into the countryside.

Most vexing to Lin Biao, his chief of staff, Wang Jifang, suddenly went missing. Wang had been stationed with Lin at the campaign headquarters in Lishu, just north of Siping. While there, Wang had apparently fallen for a local girl and was unwilling to leave her behind when the army retreated.[42] He disappeared on the night of 18 May, as the Communist positions in and around Siping were falling apart. In his debriefing by Nationalist officers, Wang revealed that the NDUA units retreating from Siping were suffering from low morale and included a large number of conscripts.[43] Wang also brought along with him a number of documents, including the plans for the retreat and the defense of Changchun.[44] All these proved quite valuable to the Nationalist forces as they conducted their pursuit of the defeated NDUA. Two days after Wang had gone missing, Lin Biao, frustrated by the way in which the New Sixth Army seemed to be anticipating his every move, put two and two together. As for Wang Jifang, he married his sweetheart from Lishu and was given a commission in the Nationalist army. His new career ended badly in the fall of 1949, when he was captured by Communist forces, tried, and executed for his act of betrayal.

With their positions north of Siping collapsing, their retreat falling apart, and soldiers deserting in droves, the men of the Communist Party's Northeast Bureau called a hasty meeting on 20 May to decide their next moves. The Party Center and a number of the members of the Northeast Bureau itself were still determined to defend Changchun and the nearby cities of Gongzhuling and Jilin—to make Changchun the symbolic "Madrid" of the Northeast. Lin Biao, joined by an ailing Luo Ronghuan, who had dragged himself up to North Manchuria from Dalian, disagreed. Lin, Luo, and the commanders in Changchun itself argued that there was no way that the bedraggled NDUA forces, short on weapons, ammunition, and supplies, could defend Changchun—a large city sitting out on the Manchurian plain with no natural defenses to speak of. A failed attempt to defend Changchun would not only result in the loss of the city, but could force the NDUA to retreat to the deserts of western Manchuria and eastern Mongolia.[45]

The vote was very close, but Luo and Lin won the day. The NDUA would abandon Changchun and Jilin and withdraw its main force north of the Songhua River to the city of Harbin. In their haste to retreat, Lin Biao's forces had no time to sabotage the railway lines from Changchun to the south bank of the Songhua. Even the main railway bridge across the Songhua was left intact. Nationalist forces crossed the bridge in early June to establish advance positions on the north bank of the river. There, they posed a threat to the new Communist position in Harbin. Would Lin Biao defend this position? Or, if pushed, would he retreat even farther into the rural areas of the far north, or even to the Soviet Union?

By this time, Lin had built something of a reputation for retreating. In fact, some of his detractors in the NDUA had given him a nickname: "General Retreat" (*chetui jiangjun*).[46] In retreating so often, Lin had frustrated both Mao Zedong and the Party Center, on the one hand, and Chiang Kai-shek and Du Yuming on the other. Ever since the beginning of the fighting in Manchuria back in November 1945, both Mao and Chiang had been searching for the decisive battle. Chiang wanted to use his technically and (at first) numerically superior troops to pin down and thoroughly annihilate Lin's main force in the Northeast. Mao had been looking for the battle which, in his mind, would deal the Nationalist forces a setback, stopping them in their tracks long enough to force Chiang to agree to a ceasefire that would, for at least a while, leave the Communists in control of a substantial swath of territory in North China and Manchuria.

By retreating from Shanhaiguan and refusing to engage in a showdown at Jinzhou in November 1945, Lin had avoided the "decisive battle" that both Mao and Chiang had been seeking. In April, Mao had forced the issue by ordering Lin to stand, fight, and make Siping "another Madrid," but when he faced the possibility of having his army cut off from the rear, Lin chose to withdraw from Siping as well. In Lin's eyes, retreat was a better choice than to be forced into a decisive—and for him, potentially disastrous—encounter on Du Yuming's terms. Now ensconced in Harbin, Lin Biao prepared to retreat once more if push came to shove. Lin himself—apparently deeply depressed—told Western journalists that he would not fight another battle of positional defense until his forces were much stronger.[47]

As he withdrew north of the Songhua, just how badly damaged were Lin Biao's forces? What level of capability was he left with? What could he reasonably have accomplished with the resources at hand in June 1946? The evidence and different historians' choice and interpretation of the evidence are unclear and sometimes contradictory. But if we are to understand and assess the judgments and decisions that Lin Biao, Du Yuming, Chiang Kai-shek, Mao Zedong, and George Marshall made at the time, we need to do our best to answer those questions.

Clearly, Lin Biao's forces at Siping were badly defeated, their retreat to Harbin was chaotic, and they lost a significant number of men, not only to casualties, but also to desertions. In addition, the Communist troops were seriously low on ammunition.[48] But just how significant was the damage and what did it mean, operationally? This is a difficult question to answer. One problem is that different sources give widely divergent figures for casualties and numbers of men lost to desertion. Standard military histories published in China give the number of eight thousand casualties at Siping. In a telegram of 24 May 1946, Huang Kecheng gives a figure of fifteen thousand casualties incurred in North Manchuria from late March through the retreat from Changchun.[49] Historian Yang Kuisong cites evidence suggesting that Lin's NDUA forces suffered a total of "nearly 20,000 dead and injured" in the defense of Siping.[50] Lin Biao's former chief of staff told Du Yuming that the Communist forces at Siping had lost half their troop strength (a statement that makes no distinction between casualties and desertions).[51] John Beal, a reporter working (at Marshall's request) as a consultant to Chiang's government wrote in his diary that "Communist casualties at Ssupingkai [Sipingjie] were 40,000 plus the desertion of thousands of untrained factory workers.[52] Chiang Kai-shek stated forty thousand casualties (dead and wounded), a figure that also appears in the English-language translation of a Nationalist account of the war.[53] Donald Gillin, Ramon Myers, and Arthur Waldron, all of whom follow Chiang Kai-shek in blaming Marshall and the June ceasefire for the loss of Manchuria, and even of China, use the same number, but change it from "casualties" or "dead and injured" (*shangwang*) to "nearly 40,000 . . . dead" or, in Waldron's case, a simple, straightforward "40,000 dead."[54]

With widely ranging estimates of NDUA casualties and desertions at and following the Second Battle of Siping, Marshall's critics tend to choose the higher numbers in order to give credence to the argument that Lin's army was on its last legs. But was it? George Marshall clearly did not think so. U.S. embassy reports from Nanjing on 4 and 8 June express skepticism of Nationalist claims. As the Americans saw it, "Withdrawal before Kmt [*sic*] forces advancing north . . . hardly means that a Kmt victory in Manchuria is assured" and "Evidence thus far indicates Communist strength Manchuria did not receive Ssuping-Changchun sector crushing blow reported by Kmt sources."[55] An American intelligence report dated 30 May 1946 stated, "The 80,000 men whom the

Communists originally committed to the defense of Ssupingchieh were organized in 24 brigades. The effective strength of this CCP force is now believed to be about 40,000. Despite the loss of 40,000 Communists (captured or left behind) in a few days of fighting, the actual number killed and wounded was light."[56]

Lin Biao and the Northeast Bureau, deeply aware of the dire straits that they were in, had already decided not to defend Harbin. On 1 June, Lin told the Party Center that if threatened, he was prepared to "retreat from Harbin and fight guerrilla war."[57] Lin's approach—which gained the approval of Mao Zedong—was to prepare for guerrilla and mobile operations in eastern Manchuria. At the same time, Lin was concerned with the task of re-building the strength and morale of his main forces. In doing so, Lin is said to have drawn inspiration from the Russia's defeat of Napoleon in the Great Patriotic War of 1812.[58]

Like Lin Biao, the Russian generals (first Michael Andreas Barclay de Tolley and then Mikhail Kutuzof) had retreated time and again in the face of the seemingly unstoppable advance of the enemy—in their case, Napoleon's Grande Armée.[59] After he failed to stop Napoleon at the Battle of Borodino on 8 September 1812 (just as Lin failed to stop Du Yuming at Siping), Kutuzov declared victory but withdrew from the field—much to the anger of many of his men and officers, who believed that they could have gone on fighting. After careful consideration, Kutuzov then decided to pull out of Moscow. The French believed that they had won. But by retreating to a new position, Kutuzov had both secured the southern provinces, with their abundant resources and industrial base, and retained forces that threatened Napoleon's rear areas and lines of communication.[60] As winter drew near, Kutuzov reorganized his troops and prepared to force the French out of Moscow. With Kutuzov on the move and winter closing in, Napoleon's forces began their disastrous retreat. Kutuzov gave chase, using partisan tactics to strike weak points in the French train.

Lin, too, had to explain a series of retreats to his dispirited troops and to give them hope that in the end, they could and would turn the situation around. He explicitly referred to Kutuzov's retreat from Moscow when talking with his men, and even screened a Soviet film on Kutuzov and the War of 1812. For Lin, the withdrawal from Siping presumably corresponded to Kutuzov's abandonment of the field at Borodino. The expected withdrawal from Harbin would have been his Moscow—the last stage of a Kutuzov-like strategy of retreat.

While he contemplated the loss of Harbin and showed his men films of Kutuzov's ultimate victory, Lin Biao had yet another trick up his sleeve. His main forces had fled north of the Songhua, but there remained several NDUA units in South and West Manchuria. It was to these units that Lin would turn, both in the immediate aftermath of Siping and again in the autumn of 1946, in a bid to divide the attention of the Nationalist forces and so relieve the pressure on the battered NDUA forces in Harbin.

ATTACKING BEHIND NATIONALIST LINES

As the Nationalist armies moved triumphantly into Siping and Changchun, Communist-dominated local governments toppled, and the people greeted the Nationalists enthusiastically. The warm welcome was, in part, a function of the ordinary people's desire for peace, no matter which army brought it. In 2008, when asked who the people supported back in 1946, an elderly resident of Siping laughingly replied, "The people supported whoever was in power!"[61] The fact that the Communists had drafted people for labor and requisitioned supplies, often without compensation, may have contributed to a warm welcome for the Nationalists. Nationalist propaganda at the time celebrated the triumph of Du Yuming, the brilliance of his generalship, and the close relationship that his armies forged with the people. Just as in Communist Party propaganda, photographs were taken to illustrate ordinary people's warm welcome of the victorious army: schoolchildren waving flags, the people taking to the streets, and soldiers exchanging greetings with grateful peasants.[62]

Behind the propaganda and the victory parades, there were some serious problems in Du's army. Even when his forces began the drive north toward Changchun, Chiang Kai-shek had realized that this would leave the rear areas in South Manchuria only lightly defended. The Nationalist Sixtieth Army's 184th Division was responsible for the defense of the railway lines and towns from Anshan to Yingkou. Now, with Siping and

Changchun lost, Lin Biao moved to take advantage of that weakness. His first target was Anshan.

Anshan was a major center of coal, iron, and steel production. Despite its importance, it was lightly defended by two battalions.[63] The defenders had established positions and strong defensive works outside of the city, but the defenses in the city itself were relatively weak. At dawn on 24 May, the N D U A's Third Column, under the command of Wu Kehua, attacked Anshan with two brigades and an artillery regiment.[64] Their first objective was to sweep aside the Nationalists' outer defenses. This was accomplished in one day of fighting, in which the Communists used artillery fire to destroy Nationalist fortifications. The next morning, the Communist Twenty-ninth Regiment, advancing under the protection of artillery fire, captured high points of Shenshe Mountain and Duilu Mountain on the outskirts of the city. Two other regiments cut off and defeated a Nationalist relief force that had been sent out from Haicheng. Communist units then pushed their way into the city itself, engaging the Nationalists in street fighting, which was accompanied by a propaganda blitz that convinced a large number of the defending forces to put down their weapons and surrender.

The Communist Party Center was very pleased with the capture of Anshan, and with the surrender of so many Nationalist soldiers. In a directive issued on 29 May, the Center gave explicit instructions on how to proceed, and how to use the prisoners:

> The battle of Anshan was well-fought. [We] hope that you will completely destroy that section of railway, blow up the bridges and water towers, remove the rails and sleepers, and pay particular attention to destroying the rail bed so that it will not be easy to repair for a long time. As to the captured officers and soldiers of the Sixtieth Army, give them especially good treatment, make a detailed investigation of the internal situation [of their units], take the anti-Chiang feeling of the enemy forces, transform it into opposition to civil war. . . . Enthusiastic mass welcome meetings should be held for these prisoners, assign people to be responsible for talking to them individually, create a strong anti–civil war feeling in the Sixtieth Army, and then send some of the more advanced elements among them back to their units by different routes, ten-some to each unit, and give them a generous sum of money for the road.[65]

The Communist attempt to undermine the Sixtieth Army's loyalty to Chiang Kai-shek was based on a very clear understanding of the army's characteristics. The Sixtieth Army had been organized from local troops in Yunnan Province, in the deep southwest, during the war against Japan. These units had been part of the army of the Yunnanese warlord Long Yun, whom Chiang Kai-shek regarded as a threat. In August, they had been sent to Vietnam, ostensibly to accept the surrender of Japanese troops, but in fact in order to weaken Long Yun. In October 1945, Du Yuming, acting on Chiang's behalf, had attacked Long Yun's remaining forces in Yunnan in a plot to push Long out of power. Afterward, the American Seventh Fleet brought the Sixtieth Army from Vietnam to Manchuria, where it was put under Du Yuming's command.[66] Du and Chiang's distrust of the Sixtieth Army was evident in the way in which the army was deployed in the Northeast. In order to weaken the Sixtieth Army even further, several of its divisions were removed from the army command: The 182nd Division was put under the command of the New First Army and assigned to the area from Tieling to Changtu. The Temporary Twenty-first Division was under the Northeast Peace Preservation command in Shenyang. The 184th Division was under the New Sixth Army, which, as we have seen, had assigned it to defend the line from Anshan to Yingkou, which split up its forces among four different cities (Haicheng, Anshan, Dashiqiao, and Yingkou) in a linear formation. The divisional command did not have the authority to change or even adjust this deployment. This left the individual units of the 184th vulnerable to attack and unable to respond quickly and flexibly.[67]

The disaffection within the Sixtieth Army would play a key role in the NDUA's next operation: an attack on the city of Haicheng, a key transportation chokepoint. Rail and road traffic from Anshan and Shenyang to the ports of Yingkou and Dalian had to pass through Haicheng. Defending Haicheng was the Nationalist Sixtieth Army, 184th Division's 552nd Regiment. An outer defense line incorporated high ground around the city, while the urban center itself was surrounded by a traditional wall. In their attack on Haicheng, the Communist Fourth Column combined military with psychological (or what they would call political) operations. Thirty captured Nationalist soldiers were sent to 184th Division units at Haicheng and nearby Dashiqiao, bringing Communist propaganda and spreading word of the NDUA's generous policies toward those who surrendered. On 28 May, while the turned Nationalist soldiers were conducting their propaganda, the Fourth Column attacked high ground along the outer perimeter of Haicheng. In this case, however, the attackers did not have the benefit of artillery support. As a result, the Nationalists were able to hold the attackers off.[68] The next day, artillery was brought in. The Communists took the high ground, and put Haicheng under siege.

In command of the defense at Haicheng was Pan Niduan—commander of the 184th Division. Pan was a complicated man. He had just recently been put in command of the 184th, in the wake of a purge of Communist agents. He was said to have been an avid listener of the Voice of America, whose accurate reports of Lin Biao's capture of Changchun back in April had convinced him that Kuomintang news broadcasts were worthless, and that the only way to really understand the enemy was to listen not only to the Voice of America, but to Yan'an's broadcasts as well.[69]

Whatever his doubts about Chiang Kai-shek and Du Yuming, Pan was initially determined to defend his position. Realizing that he was outnumbered, Pan sent an urgent message to Du Yuming in Shenyang, asking for reinforcements. Here, we see another wrinkle in the complex internal politics of Chiang Kai-shek's armies. Observing the loss of Anshan and the siege of Haicheng, Du Yuming ordered Sun Liren's New First Army to move south to assist the 184th Division. Chiang Kai-shek, who was on the ground in Shenyang at the time, intervened, telling Du Yuming that Sun Liren's New First Army needed to rest for three days. Du was reportedly outraged, but had no other choice than to order Pan Niduan to resist to the death and await reinforcements.

The concept of fighting to the death to hold a position was an important component of the sense of dedication and discipline that Chiang Kai-shek had tried to inculcate in the officers whom he had trained back in the 1920s at the Nationalist Party's Whampoa Military Academy. Fighting to the death was a part of the "Whampoa spirit." This expectation may have been in Chiang Kai-shek's mind when he told Du Yuming that the 184th Division would need to hold its position against all odds while waiting for the New First Army. But Pan Niduan and his officers were not willing to fight to the death for Chiang Kai-shek. They had reached the breaking point—and they knew that they had another, more attractive option. On the night of 29 May, Pan negotiated his surrender with the Communists, who had initiated contact with him that evening. On the thirtieth, the Communist forces entered Haicheng. Pan Niduan and 2,700 soldiers from the 184th Division were sent to the rear to be reorganized and incorporated into the NDUA.[70]

Not all of Pan's 184th Division obeyed his orders to go over to the Communist side. The officer in command at Dashiqiao, a town south of Haicheng, was determined to defend his position, perhaps because Du Yuming had promised him that if he held out, he would succeed Pan Niduan as division commander. As they had at Anshan, units from the NDUA's Fourth Column employed artillery and infantry to capture high ground outside the city, break through the defensive perimeter, and defeat the Nationalists. This victory marked the end of the "An-Hai Campaign." With the New First Army approaching Haicheng, the commanders of the Fourth Column realized that they stood no chance either of capturing Yingkou (which would have been their next target) or even of defending Haicheng and Dashiqiao.

Although it did not result in the permanent acquisition of territory, the An-Hai Campaign indicated that the Communist forces had learned a lesson from their loss at Shaling.[71] In that battle, the Communists had attempted to overpower a better-armed enemy with repeated but poorly organized assaults, taking massive casualties and failing to achieve their goal. In the An-Hai Campaign, the Fourth Column made a point of concentrating superior numbers against first one, then another target, moving from Anshan to Haicheng to Dashiqiao. In all three encounters, the Communists successfully employed artillery to soften up enemy positions and then sent infantry in under artillery cover. The successful use of these techniques represented a move from simple guerrilla warfare toward mobile warfare, in which different branches—artillery, armor, and infantry—would need to coordinate with each other in more complex operations.

Both the development of mobile warfare capability and the Communists' ability to identify contradictions within the Nationalist ranks and use propaganda techniques to bring over disaffected Nationalist units would play an increasingly important role in the fighting in the

Northeast over the next two years. But for the moment, Du Yuming had barely enough troops to react to the Fourth Column's threat to his rear areas in South Manchuria while continuing his drive toward the Songhua River in the north. Some historians in China argue that with his mechanized armies already in Changchun, Du Yuming could very well have continued to advance to and beyond Harbin in the summer of 1946 and still have had enough troops to maintain control over the rear areas of South Manchuria.[72] Most, however, agree that the Nationalist forces were spread thin in the Northeast. We must also remember that Chiang's armies faced significant challenges beyond Manchuria. There were large Communist base areas in North China, including Shandong, where, according to Chiang Kai-shek, 90 percent of the province was under Communist control.[73] American intelligence also observed Nationalist weakness in the areas adjacent to Manchuria:

> The Nationalist situation in southern Jehol (Rehe) remains unfavorable.... The situation in Jehol does not jibe with that around Changchun. The Nationalists are on the defensive in Jehol and are in danger of losing their outlying garrisons. The CCP units in that province are acting aggressively, although their situation is far less favorable than was that of their compatriots around Changchun. They show no indication of imminent collapse. Their situation is much the same as that of the Manchurian CCP prior to Ssupingchieh [Sipingjie], but it does not follow that they will share a similar history. It is argued that the CCP units are successful in only two types of warfare which they are now carrying on in Jehol; that when they attempt position defense, they are unable to stand against the KMT. The earlier effectiveness of the CCP in such fighting in Manchuria does not confirm this opinion. Nor does the fact that the CCP units in Jehol have confined their operations to sporadic raids against the railroads mean that they are incapable of larger-scale and more sustained operations. Rather, they are carrying out the tactics most suited to the situation in which they find themselves, and their refusal to adopt any other kind of warfare is a tribute to their sagacity rather than an adverse commentary on their lack of training for other than guerrilla action.[74]

These threats in Rehe, as well as Communist operations in Shandong, meant that Chiang could not afford to send more armies to increase Du's strength. All of this very likely played some role in Chiang's thinking as he considered how to respond to Marshall's persistent attempts to hammer out a ceasefire agreement.

THE CEASEFIRE

By this time (30 May), George Marshall's persistence was combined with liberal doses of anger and frustration. As discussed above, on 29 May, Marshall had sent a message to Chiang, stating that Chiang's continued advance in the Northeast was making his (Marshall's) position as negotiator impossible. This message crossed paths with a message from Chiang to Marshall, dated 28 May and received on 30 May, in which Chiang reiterated his willingness to halt the advance in the Northeast if the Communists would immediately put the military reorganization plan into effect and allow Nationalist administrators and police to take over the areas of the Northeast not yet taken over by the Nationalist government as well as areas that had been briefly under Nationalist control but were now occupied by the Communists (such as Harbin). These conditions were, of course, unacceptable to the Communist Party. Marshall, having received no response to his harsh message of 29 May, sent another strongly worded communication on 31 May, again telling Chiang that "under the circumstances of the continued advance of the Government troops in Manchuria my services in mediation are becoming not only increasingly difficult but a point is being reached where the integrity of my position is open to serious question."[75]

The uncooperative positions of both Chinese parties were also reflected in the press. The Nationalist and Communist propaganda machines were cranking out strong denunciations of each other. The Communist press was also attacking Marshall and the United States in articles with headlines like "America and Chiang cooperate closely to butcher the Chinese people."[76] Marshall found the negative propaganda (especially Communist attacks on himself and the United States) to be particularly unhelpful. The propaganda war was also being waged in Washington. According to a report sent to Marshall in late May, Patrick Hurley's supporters, the notable anti-Communist congressman Walter Judd, and possibly people from the Chinese embassy were involved in a "serious undercover rumor campaign in Washington to effect that you have been working with the Chinese Communists against Chiang and that this is the reason for present state of affairs."[77]

As bad as things looked on the surface, behind the scenes there were significant factors that ultimately pushed both the Communist Party leaders and Chiang Kai-shek to agree to a ceasefire. The Communists were suspicious of Marshall and were fast losing their faith in his sincerity as a negotiator, but, in Zhou Enlai's words, "We want him to succeed, not to fail."[78] The fact was that Lin Biao's forces in the Northeast needed time to rebuild their strength after the losses they had incurred in their retreat from South Manchuria, and especially at Benxi and Siping. Lin's NDUA was still capable of small-scale operations like the An-Hai Campaign, but nothing more. Even in central China and Shandong, the loss of Siping had inspired the Party Center to avoid launching any operation that would give Chiang Kai-shek an excuse to widen the scope of hostilities.[79]

For all his apparent foot-dragging, Chiang Kai-shek, too, was prepared to halt Du Yuming's advance north and agree to a ceasefire. As we have seen above, Chiang and Chen Lifu had both left Richard Lauterbach with the distinct impression that there would be a ceasefire, either when Chiang had captured Harbin or possibly under circumstances that would leave the Nationalists and the Communists facing off across the Songhua River. On 30 May, Chiang flew to Changchun to review the troops there and to meet with his generals. Rather than enter the city, Chiang addressed a group of men and officers gathered in an airport hangar. Officers recognized for their bravery on the field were rewarded by having a photograph taken with the Generalissimo, who sat stiffly in a chair as one man after another posed by his side.

When the formal speech-making and photography were done, Chiang met with his generals. As Zheng Dongguo recalled in his memoirs, Chiang told them that the ceasefire negotiations were already under way, and that if there were no change in the situation, the ceasefire order would be issued within a few days.[80] Around the same time, in early June, Mao Zedong and his comrades in Yan'an learned that Chiang was on the verge of agreeing to a ceasefire. Mao urgently ordered Lin to prepare to defend Harbin for at least ten days.[81]

George Marshall was not privy to the internal considerations of the Communist Party Central Committee or Chiang's conversations with his generals in Manchuria. Nonetheless, Marshall, who had been getting quite irritated and short-tempered about the negotiations, became more optimistic in early June.[82] On 1 June (a day after he had finally received Richard Lauterbach's account of his conversations with Chiang and Chen Lifu), Marshall wrote to Albert Wedemeyer, "I had hoped to have fighting terminated several weeks ago but matter still drags with government military now pressing their temporary advantage to the limit," but adding, "I have a hope to precipitate initiation of settlement within next forty eight hours."[83]

Marshall's hopes were well-founded, though it would take a bit more than forty-eight hours. On 2 June, Foreign Minister Wang Shijie telegraphed Chiang in Beiping to tell him that Marshall's attitude was "very serious" and asking him to return to Nanjing as soon as possible. Chiang spent the evening thinking about what approach to take toward Marshall. It should be a carefully measured approach, he thought, neither arrogant nor humble, and making sure not to hurt Marshall's personal feelings.[84] Chiang returned to Nanjing on 3 June, when Wang Shijie again told him that Marshall was pushing hard for an immediate ceasefire. Chiang felt, in his words, "extremely aggrieved and humiliated," but he also felt that he had no choice.[85] Chiang met with General Marshall for an hour the next morning.[86] He was visibly annoyed but, as his biographer Jay Taylor describes it, with "little or no pressure from Marshall," he agreed to a ten-day ceasefire in the Northeast, which was changed, at Zhou Enlai's insistence, to fifteen days.[87] In his diary, Chiang explained that he had agreed to the ceasefire because his and Marshall's opinions of the Communist Party had begun to draw relatively closer to each other.[88] The ceasefire order was issued on 6 June, to take effect at noon on Friday, 7 June. This marked the definitive end of Du Yuming's advance north toward Harbin and the beginning of a period of rest and reorganization for both the Nationalist and Communist troops in the Northeast.

Marshall knew well that the ceasefire would be fragile. Even as he gave his agreement, Chiang Kai-shek had told Marshall that this would be his last attempt at dealing with the Communists. From Chiang's point of view, continued Communist ability to cut rail transport routes from Manchuria to China Proper—which meant interruptions to the supply of coal to Chinese cities—created unbearable economic stress.[89] To maintain their transportation lines, the Nationalists reserved the right to recover Haicheng, Yingkou, and Dashiqiao even after the ceasefire order took effect. The Communist Party's Central Committee had decided that "without jeopardizing any of our basic interests, pursue peace; a long period of war is not in our interest."[90] However, ceasefire or not, the Communist forces in the Northeast were slated to carry out two small operations to consolidate their position. These engagements took place at Lafa and Xinzhan.

Lafa sits astride a key railway junction. Both Lafa and nearby Xinzhan would be natural staging areas for a future Nationalist advance north of the Songhua.[91] Chiang himself is said to have ordered Du Yuming to capture Lafa as his armies pursued the NDUA north toward the Songhua River. Du obeyed the Generalissimo's orders, sending one of Liao Yaoxiang's regiments out to capture Lafa and the nearby town of Xinzhan in early June. Du was obedient, but he may have had his doubts about the wisdom of the Generalissimo's orders. Lafa and Xinzhan lay at the periphery of the Nationalists' newly acquired territory. Lafa itself was in an exposed position, on flat land with no natural defenses.

Although the NDUA was now in full retreat and suffering from losses and desertions, its intact units were not tied down by the need to defend any positions. On 7 June, Liang Xingchu's First Division conducted the kind of operation that the Communists were already famous for. Advancing by night, Liang's men moved out from Jiaohe, enveloped the Nationalists at Lafa, and attacked at three o'clock in the morning. The embattled Nationalist regimental commander, caught unawares, contacted his divisional commander to ask for reinforcements. The divisional commander relayed the request to Du Yuming, who ordered the men at Lafa to defend their positions and wait for help. Help did not arrive, and within a few hours, Liang Xingchu's Communist soldiers had broken into and captured the city and its defenders. Having gained the initiative, Liang Xingchu's forces now moved to attack the Nationalists at the nearby city of Xinzhan. Once again, Liang staged a night attack, capturing the city and killing or capturing Nationalist forces. The battles of Lafa and Xinzhan were small but vivid demonstrations that the NDUA was still not to be taken too lightly. But these encounters also underlined one of the Communists' continued weaknesses: lack of airpower. During the battle for Xinzhan, a Nationalist air strike hit Lafa and a Communist troop train, inflicting over a hundred casualties.

The battles of Lafa and Xinzhan marked the end of hostilities in the Northeast (until October). The ceasefire was fragile, and minor clashes continued to occur. In mid-June, Du Yuming, clearly exasperated, declared that "if [the Communists] show no sign of good faith and keep attacking government troops under my command then it is my intention to resume attack and pursuit tomorrow." Marshall noted, "I have been told that careful instructions have been given to General Tu Li-ming [Du Yuming] to restrain him, but this fresh indication from Peiping disturbs me greatly." Chiang had indeed ordered Du to stop talking to the press (not for the first time), telling him that his loose tongue was causing diplomatic problems.[92] Around the same time, on 17 June, Marshall telegraphed President Truman that "the situation is extremely critical."[93]

Nonetheless, on 20 June, Chiang accepted Marshall's request to extend the ceasefire to the end of the month, when Chiang issued new orders instructing his troops not to engage in offensive action.[94] The combination of circumstances on the ground in the Northeast and in his talks with Marshall in Nanjing had convinced Chiang Kai-shek to adopt a new strategy for the Northeast: "At this time," he wrote on 26 June, "we should temporarily adopt a defensive posture in the Northeast, rather than advance, because the military goal of our original policy was to recover Changchun and the China-Changchun and Bei-Ning railway lines to the south [of Changchun], and to use political means to seek resolution of [the question of] other areas, on the one hand, so that the Soviet Union does not intervene directly, and on the other hand, for the ease of deployment of our troops, so that they do not become too widely dispersed and thus create opportunities for the Russian Communists."[95]

At the end of June, Chiang ordered his troops in Manchuria not to engage in offensive action.[96] In essence, Chiang had reverted to the strategy that he had initially taken in Manchuria back in November 1945: he would remain on the defensive in the Northeast, eliminate the Communists in China Proper, and then turn his attention back to Manchuria.[97] For the moment, it seemed that Marshall had finally succeeded.

8

Visions of the Past and Future

The brown cement Martyrs Monument to the Four Battles of Siping stands quietly in a small park in the middle of a traffic roundabout west of the railway station. Children play happily nearby, unaware of whatever the monument might mean. Old folks play there too, endless games of cards and *xiangqi* on tables in the shade of the trees. Even in the summer of 2010, some of them remember those bitter times when the city was torn by war, but they are reluctant to talk about them. Why ruin a perfectly nice afternoon and a fine game of Chinese chess with unhappy memories?

A few minutes' walk away in Martyrs Park, the Memorial Hall of the Four Battles of Siping struggles to keep the memory of the events of 1946 alive and to give them significance in a world that seems to have changed beyond recognition. The Memorial Hall, opened in 2007, and the monument, which dates back to the 1950s, are both attempts to capture the memory of the past and to preserve it in concrete, steel, inscriptions, and (in the case of the Memorial Hall) displays of artifacts and illustrations. But despite the best attempts of the architect and the museum designer, memory cannot be captured and preserved. The meaning of events changes from generation to generation, from decade to decade, even, at times, from year to year. Incidents buried deep in the past and seemingly forgotten may be brought to life again and given new significance in a new context.

FIGURE 8.1. Siping Martyrs Monument. *Photograph by the author.*

FIGURE 8.2. Battle of Siping Memorial Hall. *Photograph by the author.*

So it has been with the battle which took place at Siping in April–May 1946. In Taiwan, where it is called the Battle of Siping, and in the United States, where it has no name, the Second Battle of Siping has been represented as a turning point—a chance for complete victory that Chiang Kai-shek failed to seize, and which consequently became a moment of opportunity for Mao Zedong, Lin Biao, and the Northeast Democratic United Army. Remembered in China as the Battle to Defend Siping, it has been seen both as a victory and as a defeat, a strategic turning point and a strategic error. The competing interpretations of the Second Battle of Siping all carry with them different lessons from the past and different visions of the future. All of them are not only based on the events that took place at Siping itself; the events of that time and place are also interpreted in the context of what happened next—the Northeast Democratic Army's recovery of strength, its counterattack against and then destruction of the Nationalist forces in Manchuria, and the Communist Party's ultimate defeat of Chiang Kai-shek. In order to understand the shifting and competing significances of the Second Battle of Siping, we too must look, if only briefly, at what happened after Lin Biao retreated to Harbin and Chiang Kai-shek and the Communists signed on to Marshall's June ceasefire agreement.

THE TIPPING POINT: JUNE 1946–MARCH 1947

On 23 May, the Communist *Northeast Daily* reported the loss of Siping as a voluntary withdrawal after a month-long victorious defense.[1] Lin Biao and the leaders of the Northeast Bureau knew better. On 16 June 1946, the Central Committee of the Chinese Communist Party gave them the following stern directive:

> The current situation in the Northeast is grave. In order to unify leadership, it is decided that Lin Biao will serve as Secretary of the Northeast Bureau and concurrently as Commander-in-Chief and Political Commissar of the Northeast United Democratic Army. The four comrades Peng Zhen, Luo Ronghuan, Gao Gang and Chen Yun will serve concurrently as vice-secretaries and vice-political commissars. The Standing Committee of the Northeast Bureau will consist of five men: Lin, Peng, Luo and Chen. The Center believes that under the current conditions, this division of labor is not only necessary but also feasible; the Center is confident that said comrades will be able to act in concert with one another, unite around the new division of labor, work to overcome difficulties and strive for victory.[2]

This decision was a clear repudiation of Peng Zhen's leadership of the Northeast Bureau. For over nine months, Peng Zhen had wrestled with the challenges on the ground in Manchuria, with the shifting strategies coming out of Yan'an, and with increasingly vociferous criticism from Lin Biao and his supporters in the Northeast Bureau itself. Now, Peng was demoted to vice secretary and vice commissar—posts that he shared with three other men, two of whom (Gao Gang and Chen Yun) were clearly aligned with Lin Biao. But while demoting Peng Zhen, the Party Center also wanted the opposing factions in the Northeast Bureau to end their squabbling and work effectively with each other. Mao Zedong himself added the last lines of the directive, calling on all concerned to "act in concert with one another."[3] One of Lin Biao's first actions as Secretary of the Northeast Bureau was to call a meeting to assess the overall situation and to lay out strategic principles to guide

FIGURE 8.3. Lin Biao leading a meeting of the Northeast Bureau in Harbin, 1946. *Courtesy of the Liao-Shen Campaign Memorial Hall.*

the Communists on their way forward. Chen Yun drafted the resulting document, which was approved on 7 July—but only after Mao Zedong had made extensive revisions.

Chen Yun's draft of this "7–7 Resolution" used carefully chosen words and phrases to suggest that Peng Zhen's lack of vision and unrealistic hopes for peace had led to irresponsible decisions and to the serious setbacks that had brought the Northeast Democratic Army to its present, battered state. Chen Yun emphasized the Communists' lack of mass support, their military weaknesses, the strengths of the Nationalists, and the need to recognize clearly that peace was not waiting around the corner. The resolution concluded that the Communists would need to use the techniques of class struggle to build strong rural base areas and to prepare for a protracted armed struggle with the Kuomintang. The search for a climactic decisive battle and Peng Zhen's "Three Big Cities" strategy were no longer parts of the Communist strategy for the Northeast.[4]

When Chairman Mao saw the 7–7 Resolution, he felt obliged to make substantial changes. Mao smoothed out much of the language, removing phrases that were implicitly critical of Peng Zhen (and which could also be read as being critical of Mao himself, since Peng's fundamental strategy in the Northeast, including both the attempt to control the entire area and the optimism about the chances for peace had simply been reflections of strategy set in Yan'an). Where Chen Yun had focused on the past and called attention to Communist weaknesses and Nationalist strengths, Mao shifted the emphasis to the positive: contradictions were building between the Americans and the British and within the United States itself, Chiang Kai-shek's government was facing economic difficulties and losing popular support, and the government military forces were over-extended. Looking toward the future, Mao's revised version of the 7–7 Resolution pointed out that Chiang's armies were stretched too thin to be able to launch a new offensive in the Northeast, but that if they did (which they would, as soon as they had enough troops in place), the Communists could and should be determined to fight, "gaining peace through victory in war." And while Mao certainly agreed with the call to build rural base areas and recognized that this implied a certain degree of class struggle against wealthy landlords, he advised the Northeast Bureau not to explicitly use the phrase "class struggle" as a slogan. Instead, the Northeast Bureau should conduct land reform in a way calculated to build broad-based support among the people of a wide range of social classes.[5]

The 7–7 Resolution, as revised by Mao Zedong, gave Lin Biao a clear set of strategic principles on which to act: on the one hand, send Communist party cadres and combat units into the countryside, build base areas, and conduct land reform; on the other hand, publicly present Communist military action in Manchuria in terms of defending existing liberated areas from unprovoked Kuomintang aggression, strengthen the NDUA, and prepare to use the principles of mobile warfare to annihilate Nationalist units. Rather than defend positions, Lin should "draw the enemy in deep, wait until the enemy is dispersed, and use superior numbers to annihilate the enemy."[6]

In China, the Second Battle of Siping, Marshall's June ceasefire, and the 7–7 Resolution together are seen as a key turning point in the Communist Party's war against the Nationalists in Manchuria. The battle and consequent ceasefire assured that the Communists would have the space

(Manchuria north of the Songhua) and the time to re-build their forces. With the 7–7 Resolution, Lin Biao and the Northeast Bureau, acting with the guidance of Mao and the Central Committee, laid out the strategic principles that would allow them to make the most of this opportunity. From June through October, Lin was able to send cadres and combat units deep into the North Manchurian countryside to suppress a variety of local armed forces (which the Communists lumped together under the generic title of "bandits"), establish Communist political power at the grass-roots level, carry out land reform, and recruit new soldiers.

In the meantime, Chiang Kai-shek was not standing still. He had ended offensive operations against Lin Biao's main force in North Manchuria as called for by the June ceasefire agreement. But putting those operations on hold gave Chiang an opportunity to shift the focus to China Proper. On 26 June, he launched an ambitious "General Offensive" against Communist base areas from the Yangzi Valley in the south to Hebei province in the north and Shandong in the east. Although the fighting was difficult, Chiang's armies made considerable progress, pushing the Communists out of key parts of Anhui, Jiangsu, and Shandong provinces.[7]

At the same time, in Manchuria, Chiang Kai-shek ordered Du Yuming to adopt a "first south, then north" strategy. Chiang's intent was to secure southern Manchuria and the border provinces of Rehe and Chahar first; then, with the Communists in Manchuria isolated from the Communist base areas in North China, and with his rear area in South Manchuria secure, Du Yuming could turn his complete attention to a campaign to expel Lin Biao from the north. The strategy of focusing first on China Proper and South Manchuria and then turning to North Manchuria was similar to Chiang's (and Albert Wedemeyer's) thinking back in August–September 1945.

The first step of the "first south, then north" strategy was to secure the crucial Bei-Ning railway line (from Shenyang to Shanhaiguan), which was still vulnerable to Communist guerrilla attack, and to capture Rehe and Chahar. Du Yuming assigned these tasks to General Zheng Dongguo. Zheng's armies went into action on 21 August, and by the twenty-ninth, they had captured Chengde, the capital of Rehe province. It took until 4 October to defeat the Communists at Chifeng in Chahar. Six days later, another Nationalist army captured the border city of Zhangjiakou (then known as Kalgan). These victories severed the connection between Manchuria and the Communist base areas in northern and northwestern China, including the Communist headquarters in Yan'an.

In Manchuria itself, there were a number of small Communist units scattered across Liaoning province, but there was only one real Communist base area left south of the Songhua. This "South Manchurian Base Area" consisted of a chunk of territory in the Changbai Mountains, backing onto the Yalu River—the border with North Korea. In order to complete the "first south, then north" strategy, Du Yuming would need to eliminate both the scattered Communist guerrilla units and, most importantly, this small Communist stronghold, which centered on the rural county town of Linjiang.

Du began his offensive on 9 October. The extensive road and railway system of South Manchuria worked to Du's advantage, allowing him to move troops and equipment quickly and efficiently to staging points from which his troops began their operations. Lin Biao's response was to order his men in South Manchuria not to be forced into passive defensive positions in which they would have to take hits from the enemy: "From here on out," he instructed them, "victory in the Northeast will mainly rely on this kind of combat style [concentrating superior force to annihilate isolated enemy units] and on thorough upholding of rural guerrilla operations and work among the masses."[8] Above all, Lin warned, the Communist forces in South Manchuria should not try to defend positions against superior Nationalist armies: "In that kind of situation, if we fight we will still lose those places, like Siping, Benxi, and Qingyuan, if we didn't fight we'd have lost them, but the result of fighting was to add to it that the army took a heavy hit."[9] Having learned the lesson of Siping, Lin now insisted that his men use mobile and guerrilla tactics against the Nationalists. There would be no more "Madrids."

Du's operations went very well at first. He recovered territory on the Liaodong Peninsula, forcing some of the Communist units there to take refuge in the Soviet-controlled area around the Port of Dalian.[10] The offensive against the Communists at Linjiang compressed the South Manchuria Base Area into four small, rural counties deep in the Changbai Mountains, cutting it off completely from Lin Biao's North Manchuria base area. Kuomintang control of territory in the Northeast had now reached its highest point. But as winter set in, Lin was determined to defend Linjiang and prevent Du Yuming from successfully completing the "first south, then north" strategy. Between 17 December 1946 and 3 April 1947 Lin sent troops from North Manchuria south across the frozen Songhua River three times to attack Nationalist positions and draw Nationalist strength away from Linjiang. At the same time, the Communist troops in the South Manchuria Base Area conducted four defensive operations, using mobile and guerrilla warfare to harass the enemy both at the front and in his rear areas. As a result of the Three Expeditions/Four Defenses Campaign, the Communists held on to their small base area at Linjiang, and Du Yuming was unable to concentrate his full force against Communist positions in either South or North Manchuria.

With civil war raging, first in China Proper and then, in October 1946, once again in Manchuria, General Marshall grew frustrated and depressed. In September 1946, he reported to President Truman, "As the Government campaign in Jehol [Rehe] continues to develop favorably the Government's stand has become more implacable regarding the conditions for the termination of hostilities."[11] On 31 December, Marshall's staff forwarded him a report from a Lieutenant Colonel McQuillen of the U.S. Marine Corps. McQuillen stated:

> On conclusion of tour of China I am convinced peaceable solution of Chinese difficulties is impossible. Communists fear to give up control of independent army lest they be decimated. Kuomintang refuses to permit Communists to participate in government without integration of CCP forces. Communists using negotiations to delay advances of government troops without real intention making any agreement or keeping any made. Long range objective of Communists is to sap strength government and wait for Kuomintang to discredit itself throughout China.[12]

The Kuomintang had already discredited itself in Marshall's and Truman's eyes. Marshall deplored the "rottenness and corruption in the lower echelon of the Kuomintang" and opined that "there was little hope for correcting such a condition except on the basis of a genuine two-party government."[13] Truman, for his part, was deeply disillusioned by Chiang's style of government, which included the assassination of opposition figures. With the Nationalists clearly set on a military resolution of their conflict with the Communists, and the Communists unwilling to accept American negotiation and increasingly critical of Marshall and the United States, Marshall had to admit defeat. He left China on 8 January 1947.

THE THIRD AND FOURTH BATTLES OF SIPING

By the time he left China, Marshall's presence or absence was utterly insignificant to the development of the civil war in Manchuria. The Three Expeditions/Four Defenses Campaign of winter 1946–1947 had done more than just preserve the Communists' small South Manchuria base area centered on Linjiang: it had allowed Lin Biao's Northeast Democratic United Army to move from the defensive to the counteroffensive. In October 1946, the Communists' main concern had been to prevent any further loss of strength and territory. By the spring of 1947, the Nationalists had lost the initiative and were increasingly limited to defending their "points and lines" against the mobile and increasingly aggressive Communist armies. At the same time, Lin Biao had been consolidating control over the land, the resources, and the population of the South and especially the North Manchuria base areas, establishing political control, carrying out land reform, mobilizing the farmers to produce more grain, and building his armies.[14]

The success of the Three Expeditions/Four Defenses Campaign and the ongoing achievements of base-building and army-building made it possible for Lin Biao to mount a series of offensives: the Summer Offensive (1 May–13 July 1947), the Autumn Offensive (14 September–5 November 1947), and the Winter Offensive (15 December 1947–15 March 1948). The Third Battle of Siping (14–30 June 1947) and the Fourth Battle of Siping (12–13 March 1948) took place during the Summer and Winter Offensives, respectively.

The Summer Offensive began on a strong note for the Communists. Using their accustomed tactics of attacking weak and isolated enemy strongholds and either blocking or annihilating relief forces, the NDUA inflicted serious damage on Nationalist positions south of the Songhua. But in June, Lin Biao overreached with an attempt to further isolate Nationalist-held Changchun by recapturing Siping.[15]

Lin Biao's commander on the ground at Siping was Li Tianyou, the Soviet-trained leader of the First Column. Acting on Lin's orders, Li Tianyou began by eliminating Nationalist positions in the smaller towns on the periphery of Siping and by capturing the airport. These operations (which took place from 11–13 June) were clearly meant to simplify the process of attacking Siping itself by eliminating bases from which Nationalist units might harass the attackers from the rear and to make it impossible for the Nationalist command to reinforce Siping by air. All this corresponded to Lin Biao's emphasis on the need for intelligence work and thorough preparation and planning for the assault itself. But unfortunately for Li Tianyou, the extended process of deployment, preparation, and peripheral operations clearly signaled Communist intent, and thus gave the Nationalists in Siping about a month to strengthen their already very imposing defenses.

In command at Siping was General Chen Mingren, with the main force (two divisions) of the Seventy-first Army, one division of the Sixteenth Army, and miscellaneous forces, a total of thirty-five thousand to thirty-seven thousand men. Chen's approach to the defense of Siping was quite different from that of Lin Biao. In the Second Battle of Siping in 1946, Lin had established long lines of defense south of the city, extending tens of kilometers east and west. He had placed relatively few troops in Siping. Chen Mingren, on the other hand, had few troops outside the city. Instead, he built a wall of earth, a dry moat, and barbed-wire emplacements around the city and stationed the main strength of his troops inside. Within Siping itself, he incorporated streets and buildings into a multi-layered defensive network, linked with trenches and punctuated by bunkers and pill-boxes. The city was divided into five sectors, with a command post for each sector. This method of defense was to have devastating effects both on the Communist attackers and on the city and its people.

Li Tianyou's intelligence led him to believe that he was facing fifteen thousand to twenty thousand men, not the force of thirty-five thousand or more that Chen Mingren actually had at his disposal. Intelligence also indicated (correctly) that Chen's main headquarters and his strongest units were in the Tiexi district, west of the railway tracks. The Communists decided to tackle the hardest job first, while their troops were still fresh. Thus the offensive began at eight o'clock on the night of 14 June 1947 with an all-out assault on Nationalist positions in Tiexi. At first, things went well for the Communists. For their breakthrough point, they had chosen a sector manned by a Peace Preservation regiment, not by the regular soldiers of the Seventy-first Army. When the regimental commander fled, the line collapsed and the Communists broke through.[16] But as the battle continued, the Communists' lack of preparation, poor tactical skills, and insufficient numbers began to tell. An overconfident Li Tianyou had begun the attack with too few men and before all his artillery was in position. Li's men, unused to fighting in an urban environment, failed to divide the enemy into manageable segments. Instead, they pushed forward along a single front, bulldozer-style. When they got bogged down, instead of changing tactics Li Tianyou simply poured in more troops. What had been envisaged as a three-day operation stretched into sixteen days of bitter combat. Although they were lacking in tactical skill and vulnerable to Nationalist airpower, the Communist soldiers fought with determination. By 23 June they had pushed the Nationalists out of Tiexi and had crossed the railway tracks into the Tiedong district.

As the battle raged across the city, civilian lives and property were caught in the crossfire. There is no way to accurately determine the number of civilian casualties or the scale of physical destruction. However, the reports and reminiscences of the Canadian Catholic missionaries in Siping once again give us a small window onto the suffering of war. As they had a year earlier, the Sisters of the Immaculate Conception and an assortment of priests, Chinese Catholic laypeople, and refugees—some two hundred in all—took refuge in the cellar of the Bishop's residence at the Catholic Church compound in Tiedong. But this time, the battle came up to their doorstep. As a priest from the Missions Étrangéres later recalled:

> On the morning of 22 June, we had to think of leaving the bishopric. We were in the southwest of the city. There was gunfire at night. On the morning of 23 June, the Communists had crossed the railway, and were in the compound of our neighbor. We decide to leave immediately. We were on the firing line. But God was watching.... Suddenly, there comes a young officer, a Christian from Liaoyuan.... He warns us to depart and he conveys us to the College of the Clerics of St. Viator. We leave. We leave everything.... Along the way, sentries

stopped us three times . . . but, thanks to our officer, we arrive at the street where the college is. . . . Everything is mined, then by another street, then we are there. What a relief! The next day, the taking of the bishopric by the Communists.[17]

But even as the Communist troops were occupying the Catholic bishop's residence, the overall situation was shifting in favor of Chen Mingren and his Seventy-first Army. Chen's experienced soldiers, resupplied with ammunition by airdrop, were now concentrated in the remaining sector of Tiedong. Nationalist airpower played a significant role in preventing the Communists from operating by day, while on the ground, reinforcements were drawing near. On 30 June, the Communist troops withdrew. They had failed to capture the city, and while they had inflicted (by their own count) seventeen thousand casualties on the enemy, they had lost some thirteen thousand men in the process.[18] When the Catholic missionaries returned to their compound in Tiedong, they reported that "the city itself is a heap of rubble." Of their own buildings and belongings, "absolutely nothing [could] be salvaged."[19] With the nearly complete destruction of their buildings, the missionaries abandoned Siping. One can only imagine the difficulties and suffering that the ordinary citizens of the city faced.

At the end of the Summer Offensive, Lin Biao's men returned to their refuge north of the Songhua River. Despite the failure at Siping, in strategic terms the Summer Offensive had been a success: the Communists had weakened the enemy and blunted his ability to attack. Lin's armies returned south again in the Autumn and then the Winter Offensives. All the while, they were gaining in strength, building new stockpiles of weapons and ammunition, and acquiring new technical and tactical skills to enable them to attack and capture well-defended Nationalist positions. The Nationalists, for their part, had been thrown on the defensive. The Nationalist commanders in the Manchurian theater simply did not have enough troops both to defend all the key positions that needed to be defended and to initiate offensive operations against the Communists at the same time. In the Autumn and Winter Offensives, Lin Biao continued on the offensive, first weakening and then attacking and capturing one Nationalist position after another. During the Winter Offensive, this brought Lin's armies to Siping for a fourth and final battle for control of the city.

By the time of the Fourth Battle of Siping in March 1948, the strategic situation had changed dramatically. Base-building, training, recruitment (including the incorporation of captured Nationalist soldiers), experience, and the cumulative effects of nearly a year of successful operations had given the Communists a distinct advantage over the increasingly dispirited Nationalist armies. In North Manchuria, the Nationalists were now isolated in the cities of Jilin and Changchun. The Nationalist forces at Siping played an important role in maintaining the line of communication between the Nationalist stronghold at Shenyang and the outposts of Changchun and Jilin to the north. This made Siping a natural target for the last phase of Lin Biao's Winter Offensive.

The Fourth Battle of Siping was a relatively simple affair. With Li Tianyou once again in command, the Communist forces moved into positions around the city on 28 February. From 4 to 8 March, they eliminated Nationalist positions on the edge of Siping and placed troops to the north and the south of the city to prevent the Nationalist soldiers in Siping from retreating and to block any relief forces that might be sent from Shenyang. Siping itself was lightly defended: worried about a Communist attack on Shenyang and confident that Lin Biao would not attack Siping again, the Nationalists had left the city with a garrison of only seventeen thousand. Li Tianyou began his assault at six-thirty on the morning of 12 March. By seven o'clock the next morning, the battle was over. The K M T forces had been trapped and annihilated (killed, wounded, and captured).

While Li Tianyou was preparing for the Fourth Battle of Siping, Communist units also captured the Nationalist position at Jilin. This, combined with the fall of Siping, left the Nationalists in defensive positions in and around the three major cities of Changchun, Shenyang, and Jinzhou and along the Bei-Ning railway from Jinzhou to Shanhaiguan. The Communists controlled everything else.

END-GAME: THE LIAO-SHEN CAMPAIGN

As they moved from the defensive to the counteroffensive to the offensive, the Communists began looking, once again, for that "decisive battle" that would put a quick and dramatic end to the fight for control of Manchuria.[20] The opportunity finally came with the Liao-Shen Campaign of the autumn of 1948.

As envisioned by Mao Zedong and implemented by Lin Biao, the goal of the Liao-Shen Campaign was to "close the door and beat the dog." That is, to sever the Bei-Ning (Shanhaiguan–Shenyang) railway and capture the remaining Manchurian ports in order to cut off the Nationalists' lines of retreat, attack them in their remaining urban strongholds, and thoroughly annihilate them. This was a huge and very risky operation. The Nationalist-held city of Changchun had been under siege since 23 May. During the summer, Mao Zedong encouraged Lin Biao to set Changchun aside and deploy all available resources on cutting the Bei-Ning line and attacking the Nationalists at Jinzhou and Shenyang, while still keeping Changchun under siege. Lin hesitated, concerned about the logistical challenges and worried about sending his crack troops and all their assets so far from their base area in the north.

Under pressure from Mao, Lin initiated the Liao-Shen Campaign on 12 September. Communist infantry supported by tanks and artillery cut the railway line and attacked the Nationalists at Jinzhou—the same city from which Lin Biao had retreated without a fight three years earlier. While Jinzhou was under attack, Communist units successfully blocked two Nationalist relief forces, one sent from Shenyang, the other advancing from the coast. The Communist Northeast People's Liberation Army captured Jinzhou on 14 October. The Nationalist garrison at Changchun surrendered on 21 October, after a long siege in which over one hundred thousand civilians had died of starvation. Shenyang fell on 1 November, and by 12 November, Lin Biao had cleared all the remaining Nationalist resistance from Manchuria. The Nationalists had lost some 300,000 to 472,000 men and the largest industrial base in China.

The Liao-Shen Campaign was the first of the "Three Big Campaigns" which determined the outcome of the Chinese Civil War. After the Liao-Shen Campaign, Lin Biao's Northeast People's Liberation Army entered China Proper through Shanhaiguan and participated in the second of the Three Big Campaigns, the Ping-Jin (Beiping-Tianjin) campaign, which lasted from 28 November 1948 to 31 January 1949. In this campaign, the Communists captured Tianjin after a bitter fight, and Fu Zuoyi, the Nationalist commander at Beiping (Beijing) negotiated the surrender of his 260,000 troops. To the south, in the area of the Huai River, just north of the Yangzi, the PLA's East China and Central Plains Field Armies inflicted a decisive defeat on the Nationalists in the third of the Three Big Campaigns, the Huai-Hai Campaign (6 November 1948 to 10 January 1949).

After the Ping-Jin Campaign, Lin Biao and his Northeast People's Liberation Army—now called the Fourth Field Army—continued to fight all the way into South China. The battle-hardened men from Manchuria ended the Civil War by capturing the subtropical island of Hainan. Lin Biao's comrade-in-arms Gao Gang, however, stayed behind in Shenyang to exercise overall control over the Communist Party's work in the Northeast. The fields, mines, and factories of Manchuria were an important source of war materiel for the Communist armies as they advanced southward to and across the Yangzi River. Railways had to be repaired, production restored, and the economy guided through the transformation from a market economy to socialism. Gao Gang set up a highly centralized military government to accomplish these tasks—so centralized that he became known as "king of the Northeast." When Chairman Mao Zedong announced the establishment of the People's Republic of China on 1 October 1949, Gao Gang's position in Manchuria made him one of the most powerful and high-ranking members of the Chinese Communist Party.

SIPING REMEMBERED: STRATEGIC VICTORY OR STRATEGIC ERROR?

One of the tasks of Gao Gang's administration was to define and memorialize the historical process by which the Communists had fought and won the civil war in the Northeast. As a part of that effort, the local authorities in Siping decided in April 1948 to construct the Martyrs Monument in remembrance of those who had sacrificed their lives in the Four Battles of Siping. When the monument was completed in 1953, the four sides of the tower were decorated with inscriptions by four of the leaders of the Communist Party's Northeast Bureau and Northeast Democratic United Army. There were inscriptions by NDUA commander Lin Biao, his political ally Gao Gang, and two less well-known leaders, Lin Feng (at the time serving as vice chairman of the Northeast People's Government) and Tao Zhu (assistant director of the political department of the Northeast Field Army). Peng Zhen's calligraphy was notably absent from the memorial. Lin Biao's contribution was the rather unimaginative "Eternal glory to the martyrs who sacrificed their lives to liberate the people." Tao Zhu's inscription was the most poetic of the four: "Cherishing the ambition to fulfill humaneness, flowers anticipate martyr's blood; the fragrance of those who killed the enemy and remain in the red-stained soil lingers on."[21]

Like any other monument to battle, the Martyrs Monument in Siping was not meant to simply commemorate an event—its purpose was to shape the memory of those events, in this case by streamlining four separate battles, two of them defeats, into a single, smooth narrative of Communist victory. But, as we have seen already, the Second Battle of Siping was controversial from the beginning. While it was officially represented as having played a glorious part in the Communist Party's historically inevitable march to victory over Chiang Kai-shek, some men within the People's Liberation Army and the Communist Party still questioned the wisdom of the decision to defend Siping. Those reservations were expressed most dramatically in a brief conversation between Huang Kecheng and Mao Zedong at the famous Lushan Plenum in 1959.

Lushan is a refreshingly cool mountain resort just south of the Yangzi River—a pleasant retreat from the summer swelter of Shanghai and Nanjing. Lushan had been a favorite summer spot of Chiang Kai-shek, and also of General and Mrs. Marshall during Marshall's frustrating mission to China. Marshall described in his papers the complicated process of getting to Lushan—a combination of airplane, motor vehicle, and, for the final leg of the journey, nearly three hours in a sedan chair borne on the shoulders of Chinese "coolies" who carried important guests up the tortuous stone stairs to the mountaintop.[22] Once there, Chiang, Marshall, and other important guests lived in charming bungalows and enjoyed the cool climate and mountain scenery.

Communist Party leaders, too, like their creature comforts. And so it was to Lushan that the Communist Party's Central Committee repaired in July 1959 for a plenary meeting. Unfortunately, the circum-

stances of the meeting were nowhere near as pleasant as the natural sur-
roundings of Lushan. The leading members of the Chinese Communist
Party had gathered to discuss and propose solutions to the disastrous
results of Party Chairman Mao Zedong's recent economic policy, the
Great Leap Forward. Instead of bringing about miraculous economic
growth, the Great Leap had caused chaos, waste, violence, environmental degradation, a man-made famine, and waves of refugees fleeing the
countryside to search for jobs and food in the cities. Once at Lushan, the
notoriously undiplomatic defense minister Marshal Peng Dehuai had
circulated an open letter criticizing Chairman Mao's policies as "infan-
tile leftism" (a serious charge in Communist circles). In response, the
Chairman had transformed the Lushan Plenum into a denunciation of
the "right opportunism" (another, even more serious charge to bring
against a Communist Party member) of Peng Dehuai and anyone who
supported him.

Huang Kecheng was one of the few men to speak out in support of
Peng Dehuai at Lushan. Huang, like Peng, was noted for his bluntness.
Back in Siping, when his men were in danger of being outflanked and
annihilated, Huang Kecheng had sent telegrams, first to Lin Biao and
then directly to the Party Center, recommending that the NDUA retreat.
His telegrams had never been answered. Even in 1959, Huang still did
not know the political background to the Second Battle of Siping. Now,
at Lushan, the topic of Siping came up in a conversation with Mao Zedong—evidently a conversation about errors that, in Huang's opinion,
the Communist Party leadership had been guilty of in the past. Huang
had already made his position clear, and had been labeled a "rightist."
As he described it in his memoirs, the conversation went something
like this:

MAO ZEDONG: Surely, the Battle to Defend Siping wasn't a mistake?
HUANG: At the beginning, as the enemy was advancing on Siping, if we'd
             hit him once to slow his advance, there would have been nothing
             wrong with that. But afterwards, when the enemy concentrated
             his heavy troops and looked for a chance to fight our main force
             to the finish, we shouldn't have stubbornly defended Siping.
MAO: To stubbornly defend Siping at the time was my decision.
HUANG: Even if it was your decision, it was wrong.
MAO: Well, let history and posterity be the judges of that.[23]

Historians and posterity are notoriously fickle judges. In addition, their verdicts are often deeply influenced by the political climate of their time and place. Nevertheless, from the 1950s to the present, a minority of Chinese military historians have expressed skepticism or even outright criticism of the Battle to Defend Siping. Soon after the battle, even the Communist Party's Central Committee noted that "the battle to defend Siping was the product of the particular circumstances of the time: it cannot become our general operational principle."[24] Skepticism about the battle was evident in internal histories compiled by the People's Liberation Army in the 1950s. Much of the criticism expressed in these documents concerns tactical issues, and is clearly meant to provide practical lessons for the PLA's future reference. For instance, the preliminary draft of the PLA Forty-third Army's combat history in the Civil War period (1945–1949), compiled in 1956, praised the professionalism of the Kuomintang armies and laid out a series of criticisms of the way in which the battle had been fought, including poor planning, poor coordination of forces and of firepower, and lack of in-depth defenses.[25]

In 1959 in a draft manuscript on the battle, authors at the Training Bureau of the PLA's Institute of Advanced Military Studies praised the Nationalists at Siping for their effective use of flanking tactics, their ability to identify and focus their attack on weak points in the Communist lines, their bravery, their ability to fight both day and night, their ability to use the terrain to their advantage, and their coordinated use of artillery and machine-gun fire in order to prepare the way for, and then cover, infantry charges.[26] The authors of this analysis noted certain Nationalist weak points as well: lack of spirit when attacking and ineffective conduct of some night operations.[27] But their harshest criticism was for their own troops. The Communist soldiers at Siping, they observed, only knew how to fire their weapons straight ahead at the enemy: they were incapable of coordinating with each other to create crossfire in order to support their fellow units to the left and the right. Artillery units fired at will, exhausting large numbers of shells with very little effect. The defensive lines were poorly planned—too long, lacking in depth, and without sufficient reserve forces to reinforce areas that came under intense pressure from the enemy.[28]

It was clearly a lot safer to criticize tactics than to criticize the strategic decision to defend Siping in the first place. Nonetheless, criticisms were made. The authors of the draft manuscript on the Battle to Defend Siping began by praising the month-long defense for having successfully repelled three assaults on the city and for having forced the Nationalists to expend a large number (three hundred thousand rounds) of artillery shells. But later, they concluded that "under the circumstances of the time, it was not advantageous to stage a large-scale defensive battle; the Battle to Defend Siping developed due to an incorrect assessment of the situation, in which it was believed that the defense of Siping would lead to peace."[29] General Han Xianchu, a veteran of the civil war in the Northeast, put it more bluntly: "Too much emphasis was placed on the gain or loss of a city, so that they [the Communist forces] fought the battle under disadvantageous conditions. In strategic terms, it was a mistake."[30]

This criticism has been echoed—carefully—by some authors, but it remains a minority opinion in China. To question the soundness of the decision to defend Siping is to question the leaders who made that decision: first and foremost, Mao Zedong and Zhou Enlai. In a more open society, such questioning would not be a problem. In China, debate about the past was a part of a series of intense political struggles that took place from the mid-1950s to the early 1980s. Many of the men who had been involved with the battle found themselves on the losing side of the vicious factional struggles that characterized the first three decades of the People's Republic of China. For example, all four of the men whose inscriptions graced the Martyrs Monument in Siping fell into disgrace. Gao Gang fell first, in 1954, when he committed suicide after a failed attempt to push Zhou Enlai and Liu Shaoqi out of power. Tao Zhu and Lin Feng both fell in the Cultural Revolution, a mass movement in which Mao Zedong engineered the overthrow of scores of high-ranking Communist Party members whom he regarded as enemies. Finally, in 1971, Lin Biao became involved in an attempt to overthrow Chairman Mao. When the plot was discovered, Lin commandeered an airplane and fled the country. The airplane crashed in Mongolia, killing all aboard.

In Mao's China, when people came under a political cloud, their entire careers were reviewed to prove that they had been traitors to the revolution from the beginning. As Gao Gang, Peng Zhen, Lin Feng, and then Lin Biao fell from grace, history was re-written to condemn them, as it was for many others as well. Their inscriptions were removed one by one from the Martyrs Monument in Siping and replaced by a single dedicatory inscription from Mao Zedong: "Eternal Glory to the People's Martyrs!" In addition to Gao Gang, Peng Zhen, Lin Feng,, and Lin Biao, many of the other men who were in positions of responsibility at the Second Battle of Siping—either as commanders on the ground or as leaders of the Northeast Bureau—were among the victims of the Cultural Revolution. But as these men were condemned and every stage of their careers reassessed, the Battle to Defend Siping remained off limits. Even in 1971, when it was suggested that the Second Battle of Siping be brought up as part of the criticism of Lin Biao, Zhou Enlai issued a directive stating, "If it is all right not to write about it then don't write about it."[31] Zhou Enlai's directive prevented the Battle to Defend Siping from becoming an object of the politicized debate of the Cultural Revolution—a debate that surely would have touched Zhou Enlai himself, as his optimism about the chances of Marshall forcing Chiang Kai-shek to sign a ceasefire agreement contributed to Mao Zedong's decision to defend Siping in the first place.

Since the end of the Cultural Revolution, the Battle to Defend Siping has been the subject of both scholarship and propaganda. Professional historians, both those associated with the People's Liberation Army and those working for the Chinese Academy of Social Sciences, have written thoughtfully and incisively about the battle. For the broader public, the battle has been celebrated in a feature film and in the form of popular books written for the mass market. In Siping itself, the Four Battles of Siping are celebrated in the Revolutionary Martyrs Cemetery (established on a hilltop north of the city in 1951 but completely refurbished in 1989), in a television documentary in 2008, and in the Siping Battle Memorial Hall.

The books and articles of the historians, the memoirs of men who fought at Siping, and even the television documentary and the displays in the Memorial Hall acknowledge and discuss the controversial nature of Mao Zedong's decision to defend Siping and the criticisms of the way in which the battle was fought. But the official verdict remains positive.

In the words of the official PLA history of Lin Biao's Fourth Field Army, the battle "deflated the Nationalist Army's rampant arrogance and co-ordinated with the struggle with the Nationalists in the negotiations, so that after the Nationalists occupied Changchun and Jilin they no longer had the strength to attack Harbin, winning four months of ceasefire in the Northeast, which gave the Northeast Bureau and the Northeast Democratic United Army precious time to go in deep to mobilize the masses and build a solid base area in the Northeast."[32] Zhang Yanhua, an assistant director of the Siping Battle Memorial Hall, laid down the bottom line in an interview for Siping Television's documentary: "Mao Zedong [and] the Party Center, they fought this battle from the vantage point of the overall strategic situation. . . . To fight the Battle to Defend Siping was absolutely correct."[33]

WHOSE LESSONS OF HISTORY?

Chinese debates about the Second Battle of Siping are ultimately de-bates about the personal responsibility of Mao Zedong, Peng Zhen, and Lin Biao. Critics of the decision to defend Siping imply that Mao's strategy of combining ceasefire negotiations with an emphasis on the control of major cities (an emphasis shared by Peng Zhen) and with the search for decisive battle led to an unnecessary loss of soldiers' lives. They suggest that Lin Biao's NDUA forces were not ready to make the transition from a guerrilla style of combat to a conventional one. In their view, the Second Battle of Siping, Peng Zhen's fall from power, and the 7–7 Resolution were a turning point in the Civil War because they ushered in a change in strategy: a retrenchment, a temporary return to a greater emphasis on guerrilla and small-scale mobile operations and base-building, and then a more gradual transition to conventional war-fare as Lin Biao, his officers, and his men drew practical lessons from the defense of Siping and other operations.

Mao's defenders, on the other hand, suggest that if the NDUA had not taken a stand at Siping, Chiang's forces would have advanced unop-posed through Siping to Changchun, Harbin, and beyond. As they see it, Marshall's negotiations alone would never have stopped the Nationalist armies. The Communists would have had to stand and fight *somewhere*, or retreat to the deserts of Inner Mongolia or all the way to the Soviet Union. As Liu Shaoqi is said to have remarked in the days before the battle, "We continuously retreat to the north; how far will we retreat before we have to stop?"[34] In the final analysis, the bitter month-long defense of Siping, in combination with the Marshall negotiations and events on the ground both in South Manchuria and in China Proper, did halt Du Yuming's northern advance and give Lin Biao and the NDUA time to rebuild. Seen from this point of view, it may not have been a victory, but it was a success.

If the Second Battle of Siping was in some sense a success and a turning point for Lin Biao and the Chinese Communist forces in Manchuria, was it also a turning point for the Nationalists? In the eyes of commentators ranging from Chiang Kai-shek and Joseph McCarthy to Ramon Myers, Jung Chang, and Jon Halliday, the answer is an emphatic "yes." As they see it, the Second Battle of Siping could have been the decisive encounter that led to the complete annihilation of Communist forces in Manchuria and then to the defeat of the Communists throughout China. But for this to have happened, Du Yuming would have had to follow the advice of Raimondo Montecuccoli: "The remnants of the routed army must be hunted down and annihilated."[35] Instead, George Marshall forced Chiang Kai-shek to accept a ceasefire, and Siping became an entirely different sort of turning point: one which gave Lin Biao and the Communists the space and time to recover, rebuild, and then come back to defeat the Nationalists. For those who espouse this point of view, China's fate rested on the outcome of the Second Battle of Siping. By intervening to determine the final results of that battle, George Marshall ensured that China would be ruled not by the American-leaning regime of Chiang Kai-shek, but by Mao Zedong and his Chinese Communist Party.

This interpretation of the Second Battle of Siping and the June ceasefire implies a particular "lesson of history": The forces of evil are inherently aggressive and cannot be negotiated with. Any compromise with such people is simply appeasement and will always fail. Bullies only understand force, and therefore, the only realistic way to deal with them is to draw a metaphorical "line in the sand." If the enemy does not cave, the appropriate response is to use overwhelming military force to completely eliminate him.

The trouble with deriving this particular lesson of history from the Second Battle of Siping is that it is based on a seriously flawed understanding of what actually happened in Manchuria in 1946 and how it fit into the context of events in China as a whole. The idea that George Marshall saved Mao Zedong and the Chinese Communist Party from certain defeat requires us to accept a "what if" scenario in which Du Yuming's armies follow up their hard-won battle at Siping and continue to advance triumphantly northward to Harbin, Qiqihaer, and onward to the Mongolian, Soviet, and North Korean frontiers. This, of course, is what Du Yuming confidently imagined in 1946 and what Chiang had in mind ten years later when he wrote that if not for the June ceasefire, "Communist remnants in northern Manchuria would have been liquidated" and "a fundamental solution to the problem of Manchuria would have been at hand."[36]

History is not a laboratory science. Neither Marshall's critics nor I can run experiments to prove our hypotheses. But we do have enough evidence to cast serious doubt on the optimistic "what if" scenario in which Du Yuming's forces wipe out Lin Biao's NDUA in Manchuria, Chiang Kai-shek goes on to win the Civil War, and China is, as a result, administered by a more democratic, efficient, and pro-American government than the Chinese Communist Party. The "what if" scenario in which Siping becomes the start of the utter defeat of Communism assumes that Lin Biao's main force had been crushed, as Chiang Kai-shek believed at the time, or (as a later historian asserted) had suffered "40,000 dead."[37] As we have seen, this was not the case. Lin's main force had certainly suffered heavy casualties and high rates of desertion, and was low on supplies and ammunition. They were substantially weakened and glad of the respite offered by the ceasefire, which was certainly to their advantage. But Communist historical sources and American intelligence reports of the time suggest that Lin's main force, though weakened, had survived. In addition (as discussed in chapter 7), Lin still had some important strengths: both the Communist forces in the small South Manchuria base area and the presence of substantial Communist armies in China Proper placed limits on Chiang Kai-shek and Du Yuming's freedom of movement, making it unlikely that they could achieve complete victory in either North China or Manchuria without enduring significant losses in one or the other.

A second problem with the "what if" scenario is that it makes some very questionable assumptions about the competence of Du Yuming and his armies. By June 1946, Du Yuming had already missed two chances to annihilate Lin Biao's main force. First, Chiang's strategic vision and Du's own plan of battle called for the KMT forces to penetrate the Communist left (east) flank and sweep rapidly north of Siping to cut off Lin Biao's route of retreat. In practice, Du's armies were unable to execute the planned penetration and envelopment. Second, even when the Communist retreat collapsed into a chaotic rush toward the Songhua River, the Nationalist forces did not sweep around and cut them off. Instead, Du chose to pursue the Communists along a broad, fan-shaped front. In this way, the Nationalist armies swept forward, triumphantly capturing towns and cities. The Communists, in spite of their disorganization and massive desertions, had a clear route to Harbin. Chiang Kai-shek himself observed in 1962 that as a result of Du Yuming's mishandling of the battle and the pursuit, Lin Biao's main force "easily withdrew from the battlefield."[38]

A third problem with the rosy vision of Chiang Kai-shek achieving a crucial victory in the Northeast is that it requires an exaggeration of Nationalist troop strength. The armchair strategist can easily imagine Du Yuming's American-trained, American-equipped armies sweeping north, their tanks, armored vehicles, and airplanes giving them speed and mobility, their weapons, including artillery, supplying an overwhelming advantage in firepower, and trucks and railways providing seamless logistical support. The reality was a great deal messier.

American training and equipment did not give the Nationalists a significant advantage on the Manchurian battlefield, and particularly not in North Manchuria.[39] The American style of fighting in which Nationalist units such as the Thirteenth, the Fifty-second, and the Seventy-first Armies had been trained required an emphasis on artillery, automatic weapons, and mechanical transport (motor vehicles and trains) for both combat mobility and logistics. In South Manchuria, the Nationalists' superior equipment, training, and combat experience had given them some advantage. Communist sources praised the Nationalists for their professionalism and consistently warned against underestimating the enemy. But even in South Manchuria, where the terrain and the infrastructure (roads and railways) were most conducive to the Nationalists' modern style of warfare, the Nationalist units encountered significant problems. The Liaoxi Corridor Campaign of November 1945 was marred by logistical shortcomings, lack of ammunition, and poor communications. As a result, Du Yuming failed in his several attempts to pin and annihilate Communist units. Lin Biao withdrew to fight another day.

By the time they got to Siping in April 1946, the inherent weaknesses of Chinese armies' attempting to adopt American technology were becoming more acute. As an American intelligence report of 1948 described it, "American-made heavy equipment . . . has failed to produce the desired effects in the past two years of fighting because it was never meant for such terrain."[40] American vehicles bogged down in the spring mud, bayonets (a crucial weapon for the Nationalist troops when they faced determined Communist soldiers in hand-to-hand combat) were not supplied with the new American weapons, ammunition was in short supply, and artillery pieces and shells were not available when they were most needed. This was primarily a problem of logistics. The further they got from the most highly developed core areas of South Manchuria, the more severe became the gap between a primitive logistics system and the Nationalists' attempt to fight an American-style war with American weapons. The deep-set problems plaguing even the strongest, most modernized Nationalist armies cast serious doubt on the argument that if he had not been restrained by George Marshall, Chiang Kai-shek could have maintained the initiative in the field and gone on to use overwhelming modern firepower to eliminate Lin Biao's NDUA. As Victor Cheng observes, "The chance to defeat the CCP armies in mobile warfare [in May 1946] virtually did not exist."[41]

A fourth objection to the idea that George Marshall deprived Chiang Kai-shek of his victory in the Northeast and thus sealed China's fate is that it ignored the national and international context in which the Second Battle of Siping and subsequent events took place. Mao Zedong did not see the Northeast theater in isolation, and neither should we. In the summer of 1946, Chiang's troops were already stretched thin across North China and parts of Manchuria up to the Songhua River. After the Second Battle of Siping, successful Nationalist operations in North China, Chahar, Rehe, and South Manchuria captured even more territory, which simply made the situation worse.

The fact that Chiang Kai-shek's armies devoted most of their energy to capturing territory (especially cities and transportation lines) was not random or unexplainable: it was a deliberate strategy which grew out of a particular historical background. Chiang's government armies had fought warlords in the 1920s and 1930s, driven the Communists out of their old Jiangxi base area in South China in 1934, and fought the Japanese from 1937 through 1945. In doing so, they had developed a particular style of warfare based on the lessons of their own experiences.[42] Warlords were highly dependent on cities and railway lines, and the key to defeating a warlord was to capture these key positions. With that done, his army would collapse, with many of his units changing sides. In the Fifth Extermination Campaign, Chiang had found a successful formula for destroying a Communist base area: First, achieve absolute superiority in numbers. Second, surround the base area with a system of blockhouses and roads. Third, draw the circle tighter and tighter in order to constrict the enemy in a small area. Here too, the emphasis was first on controlling territory; destruction of the enemy forces themselves would follow—except in this case, when the Communists took advantage of a weak point in the encirclement to break out on what would become their famous "Long March." The Kuomintang's battles against the Japanese were battles over cities and railway lines. And finally, in fighting warlords and the Japanese, Chiang Kai-shek could also conduct a reasonably successful political struggle, appealing to patriotism in order to mobilize popular support.

Chiang and his armies took the lessons and techniques of these past struggles and applied them to the civil war against the Communists. Unfortunately for the Kuomintang, the old techniques did not translate well to a new situation. The Communists did not depend on cities and railway lines. Mao Zedong and his generals combined warfare and rural revolution in a way that allowed them to draw human and material resources from China's smaller cities, towns, and rural areas. In Manchuria, the Communists had the additional advantage that their base areas, however hastily thrown together, were adjacent to the Soviet Union, North Korea, and the Soviet-controlled part of the Liaodong Peninsula. Even if he had many more troops (which he did not), Du Yuming would not have been able to fully encircle these base areas. Since they failed, repeatedly, to outflank and destroy Communist units, the Nationalists could do no more than capture places like Siping and Changchun. The Communist armies, even when beat up as badly as Lin's forces were at Siping, could withdraw to safety and rebuild. And even when they were outclassed on the battlefield, the Communists were consistently victorious in the political realm. In towns and cities all across China, even in the capital of Nanjing and the port city of Shanghai, Communist front organizations, newspapers, student and worker activists, intellectuals, and spies steadily undermined the Nationalist government's legitimacy and built sympathy, if not support, for the Communists.

It seems highly unlikely that all of the many factors which contributed to the Kuomintang's weakness throughout the Civil War would have magically disappeared if Du Yuming had simply been allowed to advance north of the Songhua to Harbin and beyond in 1946. Just in terms of the military struggle, any further commitment of Nationalist forces to North Manchuria would have led to Nationalist weakness in South Manchuria and/or North China. Mao Zedong was aware of this and ready to take advantage of any opportunity that it might lead to. As we have seen, while Lin Biao's main force had been significantly weakened and had withdrawn to Harbin, the NDUA still had some units in South Manchuria. These units were strong enough to take advantage of the weaknesses in the Nationalists' rear areas to carry out successful attacks on Anshan, Haicheng, and Yingkou, forcing Du Yuming to transfer troops from the front in North Manchuria to redress his weakness in the south. At the same time, Mao Zedong ordered PLA units to step up their operations in North China in order to prevent Chiang from transferring more troops to Manchuria—troops which Du Yuming would need if he were to continue to press north. In short, the national context of the Chinese Civil War in the summer of 1946 casts serious doubt on the idea that an advance north of the Songhua would have led to complete Nationalist control of the Northeast, much less China as a whole.

The international context, too, poses difficulties for Du Yuming's hypothetical victory. Chiang Kai-shek's concern about the Soviet Union's attitude had made him reluctant to commit military force to the Northeast from the outset. The same concerns appear to have contributed to his initial caution about advancing any farther north than Harbin, and then to his decision to accept Marshall's ceasefire proposal and stop Du Yuming at the Songhua River. Caution about the Soviet Union also played a role in American decision-making. The Truman administration had decided that while the United States would support Chiang Kai-shek, there would be limits to the extent of that support. Chiang desperately wanted the United States to take a more active role in supporting his government and his army in their struggle against what Chiang portrayed as the Soviet Union's imperialist designs on Chinese territory. The Truman administration, however, was determined not to get directly involved in the Chinese Civil War, and especially not to challenge the Soviet Union by getting drawn into the struggle in Manchuria. America was willing to transport Nationalist armies and to supply substantial amounts of weapons and ammunition, but, as we have seen above, American equipment alone could not give the Nationalists a substantial advantage on the battlefields of Manchuria. Even if the United States had been willing to do so, extending unlimited military aid to an army that was pursuing a fundamentally flawed strategy and a government that was proving incapable of winning the political struggle is not likely to have changed failure into success.

In any event, the United States did not have unlimited resources to expend on Chiang's government. Truman's decision to limit support for Chiang was based on his assessment of American interests and capabilities, including American commitments elsewhere around the globe, and the very real possibility that American embroilment in China could lead to conflict with the Soviet Union. Marshall's decision to push for a ceasefire in June 1946 was made in this context, as well as on the basis of his assessment (backed up by the intelligence reports available to him) that the Nationalist Army was simply not capable of achieving victory in Manchuria. Chiang agreed to the ceasefire not only because Marshall was pressuring him to do so (although this was certainly an important factor), but also because he was aware of the limitations of his own armies, the challenges of further operations in North Manchuria, and the possibility that military operations north of the Songhua could elicit a dangerous reaction from the Soviet Union.

Whether or not the outcome of Marshall's mediation was in the best interests of the Chinese people and whether or not the American people had a moral responsibility to prop up Chiang Kai-shek's government regardless of the sacrifice in American and Chinese lives and treasure are questions that scholars may continue to debate. What is not debatable is that the Truman administration's policy of placing limits on American involvement in the Chinese Civil War meant that American blood and treasure were not expended in an attempt to defend Chiang Kai-shek's government. In addition, it is clear that the establishment of the People's Republic of China in 1949 did not prevent the United States from enjoying a period of unprecedented wealth and power in the second half of the twentieth century.

As a consequence, we might suggest that if Americans are to learn a lesson from the Second Battle of Siping and George Marshall's conduct of diplomacy in China, it is that decisions regarding involvement in foreign civil wars should be made on the basis of a careful assessment of American strength, capabilities, and national interests. But before that, there is one other simple lesson that historians, pundits, and policymakers might consider: if you want to draw a "lesson of history" from some event that occurred in the past, the first step might be to understand what actually happened.

NOTES

1. SIPING, 1946

1. "Zhongguo renmin jiefangjun disi yezhanjun zhanshi" bianxiezu, *Zhongguo renmin jiefangjun disi yezhanjun zhanshi*, 80.

2. Zhang, *Xuebai*, 144.

3. Westad, *Decisive Encounters*, 46–47.

4. On the Huai-Hai Campaign, see Bjorge, *Moving the Enemy*.

5. Chiang, *Soviet Russia in China*.

6. Ibid., 343–49.

7. Ibid., 23.

8. For a general overview of this historical background, see Tanner, *China: A History*.

9. Chiang, *Soviet Russia in China*, 166–67. Chiang's estimate of three hundred thousand Communist troops at Siping and his statement that more than half of those three hundred thousand became casualties are both inaccurate. Numbers of troops present and casualties incurred are discussed in chapter 7.

10. Ibid., 166–68; Jiang, *Su E zai Zhongguo*, 336.

11. Chiang, *Soviet Russia in China*, 167–68.

12. McCarthy, *America's Retreat From Victory*, 95, 102, 107, 112–13.

13. Waldron, "China Without Tears," 379–80.

14. Gillin and Myers, "Introduction," 48–52, 58.

15. Chang and Halliday, *Mao: The Unknown Story*, 289–90.

16. Beevor, *The Spanish Civil War*, 129–40.

17. Hills, *The Battle for Madrid*, 86–88, 92.

18. For a discussion of the ways in which the Communist leaders used Madrid as an example both in rhetoric and in strategic thinking, see Cheng, "Imagining China's Madrid." On the Madrid-Wuhan connection, see MacKinnon, *Wuhan, 1938*, 3, 4, 79, 93, 94, 95, 113.

19. Harari, "The Concept of 'Decisive Battles,'" 251–66.

20. Montecuccoli, quoted in Rothenburg, "Maurice of Nassau," 56.

21. Ibid., 62.

22. Paret, "Napoleon and the Revolution in War," 131, 138.

23. Weigley, *The Age of Battles*, xii.

24. Ibid., xv.

25. Dreyer, *China at War*, 182, 191–92.

26. Rosenfeld, "Why Do We Ask 'What If?'" 90–103.

27. Weinberg, Germany, Hitler, and World War II, 111, 119; Weinberg, *The Foreign Policy of Hitler*, 461–62.

28. Howard, *The Lessons of History*, 12.

29. This list of questions is drawn from Black, *Rethinking Military History*, 134, 206.

2. THE MANCHURIAN CHESSBOARD, AUGUST–SEPTEMBER 1945

1. Both *xiangqi* and Western chess are thought to have been derived from the Indian game of *chanturanga*. See "Xiangqi."

2. For an up-to-date map of the People's Republic of China, see the Central Intelligence Agency, "East and Southeast Asia: China."

3. Jiumenkou had recently played a major role in the warlord conflicts of the 1920s. See Waldron, *From War to Nationalism*, 106–18.

4. Duara, *Sovereignty and Authenticity*, 43; Lattimore, Manchuria, 36–48.

5. Historians distinguish the Ming "Great Wall" which we see today from the "Great Wall" of the Qin dynasty (221–206 BCE). For further discussion, see Waldron, *The Great Wall of China*.

6. The Qing empire, the largest of all of the dynastic empires in Chinese history, was the only one to include China Proper, Manchuria, Inner and Outer Mongolia, Xinjiang in the northwest, Tibet, Qinghai, and the island of Taiwan. The modern People's Republic of China is, with the loss of Outer Mongolia, Taiwan, and a few peripheral areas, the successor state of the Qing Empire.

7. Duara, *Sovereignty and Authenticity*, 41–42.

8. This description and the accompanying map are based on Glantz, *The Soviet Strategic Offensive in Manchuria*, 47–48, 55–56.

9. The following discussion of the Trans-Siberian and Chinese Eastern Railways draws on Paine, "The Chinese Eastern Railway."

10. Marks, *Road to Power*.

11. Russia had secured its influence in Manchuria the previous year when the "Triple Intervention" of Russia, France, and Germany forced Japan to withdraw from the Liaodong Peninsula, which it had captured during the Sino-Japanese War (1894–1895).

12. On Harbin, the Russian community there, and its interaction with the Chinese, see Wolff, *To the Harbin Station*; and Carter, *Creating a Chinese Harbin*.

13. The Russians named the new railway junction town after a nearby village called Siping. The village became "Old Siping," while the new town was called "Sipingjie" (Siping Street), or just "Siping" for short.

14. Siping shi, *Siping shizhi*, 26.

15. Gottschang and Lary, *Swallows And Settlers*, 3; Schumpeter, "Japan, Korea, and Manchukuo," 382.

16. Paine, "The Chinese Eastern Railway," 27.

17. Westwood, *Russia Against Japan*, 37.

18. For a Russian point of view, see Kuropatkin, *The Russian Army and the Japanese*. General Kuropatkin attributes Japanese victories partly to the greater moral strength of the Japanese and argues that his army, strengthened by the addition of fresh reserves

and having learned valuable lessons regarding the attack, the use of terrain, and the employment of artillery, was ready to fend off any further Japanese advance. While highly critical of the Russian Army in many respects, Kuropatkin argues that "though the war was brought to an end, the army was not beaten" (vol. 2, 32). He also excoriates the press for their ignorance, inaccuracy, and a pronounced tendency to dwell too much on "the orgies and dissipation that went on in Harbin" rather than on the sacrifices that his soldiers made in battle (vol. 1, xix–xx).

19. Kuropatkin, *The Russian Army and the Japanese War*, vol. 1, 229, 231; vol. 2, 183–85, 193–94, 287. Jeremy Black agrees that the Russian Army could have defeated the Japanese if they had sent in new forces in mid-1905. Black, *War and the World*, 234.

20. Sipingshi, *Siping shizhi*, 27.

21. Japan, its armies exhausted and facing severe shortages of ammunition and its government burdened by an increasing war debt, was also ready to come to the negotiating table. Westwood, *Russia Against Japan*, 154–55.

22. Sipingshi, *Siping shizhi*, 27.

23. McClain, *Japan*, 436. The following description of Japanese policy in Manchuria follows McClain, 435–36.

24. The Kwantung Army in fact had a difficult relationship with zaibatsu and at times tried to keep them out of Manchuria. In the end, the zaibatsu were invited in simply because they were the only source of the substantial investment capital that the Kwantung Army was seeking. See chapter 5, "Uneasy Partnership: Soldiers and Capitalists in the Colonial Economy" in Young, *Japan's Total Empire*. I thank Andrew Hall for pointing this out.

25. Schumpeter, "The Mineral Resources of the Japanese Empire and Manchukuo," 385, 390–91.

26. McClain, *Japan*, 460. Also on the economic development of Manchukuo, see Katsujji, "Manchukuo and Economic Development."

27. Taylor, *The Generalissimo*, 94. Chiang's decision was reasonable from a strategic point of view, but it was politically disastrous, as it left him open to accusations that he was unwilling or unable to defend China's territorial sovereignty.

28. Gottschang and Lary, *Swallows*, 129; Mitter, *The Manchurian*, 72–73.

29. Mitter, *The Manchurian Myth*, 189–94.

30. Junshi kexueyuan, *Zhongguo renmin jiefangjun zhanshi di yi juan*, 379.

31. Ibid.

32. Guan, "Lun dongbei ge minzu," 72–73.

33. Duara, *Sovereignty and Authenticity*, 70.

34. Guan, "Lun dongbei ge minzu," 74.

35. Li and Wang, "Dongbei kangri lianjun," 142.

36. Junshi kexueyuan, *Zhongguo renmin jiefangjun zhanshi di yi juan*, 389.

37. Li and Wang, "Dongbei kangri lianjun de douzheng licheng," 147.

38. Lee, *Counter-insurgency in Manchuria*.

39. Li and Wang, "Dongbei kangri lianjun," 166–67.

40. Li and Wang, "Dongbei kangri lianjun," 167–68; Lee, "The Chinese Communist Party and the Anti-Japanese Movement"; Lee, *Revolutionary Struggle in Manchuria*; Coogan, "Northeast China and the Origins of the Anti-Japanese United Front"; Pan, *Dongbei kang-Ri yiyongjun shi*.

41. For an example of Communist Party claims regarding the strength and record of resistance to the Japanese occupation of the Northeast, see "Zhongguo renmin jie-

fangjun disi yezhanjun zhanshi" bianxiezu, *Zhongguo renmin jiefangjun disi yezhanjun zhanshi*, 30–31.

42. See Glantz, *The Soviet Strategic Offensive In Manchuria, 1945* and Glantz, *Soviet Operational and Tactical Combat in Manchuria*, 1945.

43. Tian, *Peng Zhen zhuchi*, 13.

44. Glantz, *The Soviet Strategic Offensive In Manchuria*, 311–23.

45. Shi, *Feng yu gu*, 17. The respective roles of the atomic bombings of Hiroshima and Nagasaki and the Soviet invasion of Manchuria in the Japanese decision to surrender are hotly debated among historians. The consensus among Japanese and Chinese historians is that the Soviet invasion of Manchuria was the key factor. For example, see Hasegawa, *Racing the Enemy*. For an overview of the debate, see H-Diplo Roundtable, *Racing the Enemy Roundtable*.

46. MIS 267921 "Soviet Looting of the Manchurian Hitachi Works, Ltd.," 7 May 1946, Army Intelligence File RG 319, Box 1797; MIS 267922 "Looting and Destruction of Manchurian Electic Wire Co., Ltd.," 7 May 1946, Army Intelligence File RG 319, Box 1797.

47. Liu, *Dongbei jiefang zhanzheng*, 145. While the Northeast Bureau objected to the Soviet Union's behavior, the Party Center in Yan'an urged its men on the ground in the Northeast to see the Soviet Union's actions in the context of the big picture, which was that overall, the Soviet presence in the Northeast was good for the Communist Party.

48. Jin, *Sulian chubing Zhongguo dongbei*, 147–48.

49. MIS 276809 "Strategic Services Unit, Intelligence Dissemination A-6904," 10 May 1946, Army Intelligence File RG 319, Box 1855.

50. Ibid.

51. Conversation with an elderly resident of Jinzhou, 8 July 2010.

52. MIS 276809 "Strategic Services Unit, Intelligence Dissemination A-6904," 10 May 1946, Army Intelligence File RG 319, Box 1855; "The Consul General at Kunming (Langdon) to the Secretary of State, Tientsin," 8 October 1945, FRUS 1945 VII, 1030–32; Zhang, *Xuebai*, 87–89.

53. Liu, *Dongbei jiefang zhanzheng*, 24.

54. One hundred had already been parachuted into the Northeast in July to gather intelligence, which they transmitted back to the Soviet Union by radio. Tian, *Peng Zhen zhuchi*, 6.

55. Zhao, *Dongbei jiefang daquanjing*, 5.

56. Van Slyke, "The Battle of the Hundred Regiments."

57. Takeshi, "The Ichigō Offensive."

58. Cheng, "The Escalation of Hostilities in Manchuria," 78.

59. The following description of Chinese Communist strategic thinking and actions draws on Lew, *The Third Chinese Revolutionary Civil War*, 16–34, and on Tanner, "Guerilla, Mobile, and Base Warfare in Communist Military Operations in Manchuria," as well as on the Chinese primary and secondary sources cited below.

60. Lew, *The Third Chinese Revolutionary Civil War*, 6.

61. Ibid., 5.

62. Tian, *Peng Zhen zhuchi*, 4–5.

63. Mao Zedong, "Speech on the Problem Concerning Electing Alternate Members of the CCP Central Committee, 10 June 1945," quoted in Yang, "The Soviet Factor," 22. The idea that the Soviet Union might enter the war against Japan by invading Manchu-

kuo, and that such an invasion would be followed by a transfer of the Communist Party's main forces from China Proper into the Northeast was advanced as early as 1942. See Zhao, *Dongbei jiefang daquanjing*, 3–4; Tian, *Peng Zhen zhuchi*, 2–3.

64. Yang Kuisong suggests that the Communist Party "had decided as early as July 1945 that they would focus their postwar strategy on the competition for the Northeast with the backing of the Soviet Union." Yang, "The Soviet Factor and the CCP's Policy Toward the United States," 23. Nonetheless, the Communists' troop deployments in July and August suggest that they were not expecting the war against Japan to end and the struggle for the Northeast to begin as soon as it did.

65. Shi, *Zai lishi juren shenbian*, 305.

66. Zhonggong zhongyang dang'anguan, *Zhonggong zhongyang wenjian xuanji dishiwu ce*, 217–25.

67. Dong, *Tingjin Dongbei*, 7–8.

68. Zhao, *Dongbei jiefang daquanjing*, 5.

69. Tian, *Peng Zhen zhuchi*, 11.

70. Ibid.

71. Ibid., 12.

72. Tian, *Peng Zhen zhuchi*, 23. This and the following account of Zeng Kelin and Tang Kai's advance into the Northeast and the capture of Shanhaiguan draw primarily on Dong, *Tingjin Dongbei*, 8–48; on the accounts of Li Yunchang, Zeng Kelin, Tang Kai, and Zhang Zhikui in Yuan, *Shanhaiguan zhi zhan*, 5–53, 85–88; and on Zhao, *Dongbei jiefang daquanjing*, 8.

73. "Zhongyang guanyu xunsu jinru dongbei kongzhi guangda xiangcun he zhongxiao chengshi de zhishi" [Party Center directive on rapidly entering the Northeast and controlling the vast rural areas and medium and small cities], 29 August 1945, in Zhonggong zhongyang dang'anguan, *Zhonggong zhongyang wenjian xuanji dishiwu ce*, 257–59.

74. Dong, *Tingjin dongbei*, 30.

75. Zhang, *Xuebai*, 40.

76. Chen, "Jiefang zhanzheng guodu jieduan," 53.

77. The following account draws on Zhang, *Xuebai, xuehong*, 61–62; Chen, "Jiefang zhanzheng guodu jieduan," 53–54; Du, "Kangzhan shengli chuqi guogong liangdang," 62–63; Jin et al., "Kangri zhanzheng shengli hou zai dongbei wenti shang," 162–63; Heinzig, *The Soviet Union and Communist China*, 83–84.

78. Chen, "Liu Shaoqi zhidao wojun jinjun dongbei," 36–42.

79. Heinzig, *The Soviet Union and Communist China*, 83–84; Tian, *Peng Zhen zhuchi*, 27.

80. Huang, "Cong Subei dao dongbei," 57–58.

81. Christopher Lew argues that Liu Shaoqi was personally responsible for this decision, which he interprets as evidence of Liu's strategic acumen. So too does Shiu Chiang Cheng: in his memoirs, Shi Zhe recalls it as a collective decision. Lew, *The Third Revolutionary Chinese Civil War*, 20–22; Cheng, "The Escalation of Hostilities in Manchuria," 153–54; Shi, *Zai lishi juren shenbian*, 310.

82. The Soviet Union encouraged the Communist Party to put more troops in Rehe and Chahar and stated that if the Nationalists pushed the Communist forces out of these areas, they could take refuge in Outer Mongolia. Tian, *Peng Zhen zhuchi*, 35–36.

83. Wu, *Wu Yuzhang huiyilu*, 217–18; Cheng, "The Escalation of Hostilities in Manchuria," 94.

84. Chen, "Jiefang zhanzhengguodu jieduan," 54.

3. THE COMMUNIST RETREAT, OCTOBER–DECEMBER 1945

1. Heinzig, *The Soviet Union and Communist China*, 76; Wang, *Cong kangzhan shengli*, 38; Yang, Guomindang de "liangong," 534.

2. Chiang Kai-shek to Mao Zedong, 14 August 1945, quoted in Liu, *Dongbei jiefang zhanzheng*, 11.

3. Ibid.

4. Taylor, *The Generalissimo*, 315.

5. Shi, *Zai lishi juren shenbian*, 308, 312; Cheng, "The Escalation of Hostilities in Manchuria," 67.

6. Sheng, *Battling Western Imperialism*, 104.

7. The following description of the Treaty of Friendship and Alliance and the agreement on the Manchurian railways draws on Atkinson, "The Sino-Soviet Treaty of Friendship and Alliance."

8. Wang, "Guo Gong neizhan chuqi de dongbei zhanchang," 520.

9. Quoted in Wang, *Cong kangzhan shengli*, 34.

10. Taylor, *The Generalissimo*, 319; Wang, *Cong kangzhan shengli*, 50.

11. Cheng, "The Escalation of Hostilities in Manchuria," 131.

12. Shi, *Zai lishi juren shenbian*, 324.

13. Tian, *Peng Zhen zhuchi*, 65.

14. Zhonggong zhongyang, *Liu Shaoqi nianpu* (shang), 246 (26 September 1946).

15. Quoted in Tian, *Peng Zhen zhuchi*, 94.

16. Yang, *Mao Zedong yu Mosike*, 156.

17. Tian, *Peng Zhen zhuchi*, 48; Zhonggong zhongyang, *Liu Shaoqi nianpu* (shang), 246–47 (20, 22 September 1945).

18. Quoted in Ding, Ge, and Wang, *Dongbei jiefang zhanzheng dashiji*, 12.

19. Zhonggong zhongyang, *Liu Shaoqi nianpu* (shang), 251 (9 October 1945).

20. Dong Ge and Wang, *Dongbei jiefang zhanzheng dashiji*, 9.

21. Tian, *Peng Zhen zhuchi*, 7.

22. Peng Zhen, "Guanyu dizhanqu de chengshi gongzuo."

23. Tian, *Peng Zhen zhuchi*, 7–8, 39, 61; Tanner, "Railways in Communist Strategy and Operations in Manchuria," 151; Peng, "Dongbei jiefang zhanzheng," 255, 351.

24. Tian, *Peng Zhen zhuchi*, 52.

25. Wang Hongqi, "Jinjun dongbei haiyun ji," 469.

26. Tian, *Peng Zhen zhuchi*, 42.

27. MIS 260492 "Strategic Services Unit, War Department, Military Information: General Condition," Army Intelligence File RG 319, Box 1746; "Type 38 Rifle": Absolute astronomy.com, "Type 38 rifle."

28. Wetzel, "From the Jaws of Defeat," 174–75; "The Charge in China (Robertson) to the Secretary of State, Chungking," 9 October 1945, FRUS 1945 VII, 578–79.

29. "The Charge in China (Robertson) to the Secretary of State, Chungking," 29 September 1945, FRUS 1945 VII, 572–73.

30. Yang, *Mao Zedong yu Mosike*, 194. For similar figures, claimed by a Soviet general in 1967, see Wetzel, "From the Jaws of Defeat," 173–74. Wetzel suggests that some weapons may have been counted twice, once by the Soviets and a second time by the Chinese Communists, thus leading to inflated estimates of the numbers of weapons held in Kwantung Army warehouses ("From the Jaws of Defeat," 16). The Soviet sources also report eight hundred airplanes, but this claim is particularly dubious. The Communist

forces in Manchuria had about thirty working aircraft, which they used for training purposes; they made no combat use of airpower (Liu Tong, "Jiefang zhanzheng zhong dongbei yezhanjun wuqiliayuan tantao," 79). A Japanese officer interviewed by American intelligence in June 1946 stated that he believed that Communist forces were using some Japanese gunners and machine gunners, but that any airplanes that they may have laid hands on would not be maintainable over half a year without spare parts. MIS 277211 "Daily Intelligence Extracts" 25 June 1946, Army Intelligence File RG 319, Box 387; MIS 0249521 "Col. William Mayer to Military Intelligence Service, War Department," 12 March 1946, Army Intelligence File RG 319, Box 1661.

31. Yang, *Mao Zedong yu Mosike*, 184. Liu Tong takes issue with Yang Kuisong's use of Soviet data and with his conclusions about the amount and significance of Soviet support for the Communists in the Northeast. See Liu Tong, "Jiefang zhanzheng zhong dongbei yezhanjun wuqiliayuan," 76–80 and Yang's response in Yang, "Guanyu jiefang zhanzheng zhong de Sulian junshi yuanzhu."

32. Ibid. The following draws on Yang's article.

33. In mid-September, for instance, when the Soviet Union was trying to maintain a facade of neutrality in the developing military confrontation between Nationalists and Communists, Soviet commanders refused to transfer Japanese weapons to Chinese Communist troops. Heinzig, *The Soviet Union and Communist China*, 87; Garthoff, "Soviet Intervention in Manchuria," 72; Westad, *Cold War and Revolution*, 83–87, 89–90, 119; Cheng, "The Escalation of Hostilities in Manchuria, 1945–47," 149. At times the Soviets shipped out or even destroyed weapons or other military supplies because the Communists did not have enough troops to take the materiel. Tian, *Peng Zhen zhuchi*, 93.

34. American weapons, ammunition, and other equipment captured from the Nationalists or brought over by surrendering Nationalist units also played a role. Mao Zedong deliberately drew attention to the Communists' use of captured American weapons and downplayed the assistance received from the Soviet Union, telling a Soviet diplomat in February 1949, "The Chinese Communist Party wants to use this to prove that Chiang Kai-shek used American technology to arm the Chinese People's Liberation Army." Quoted in Yang, *Mao Zedong yu Mosike*, 185. Analysis of the relative amounts and significance of equipment supplied by the Soviets as compared to that of captured American equipment is beyond the scope of this study.

35. Liu, *Dongbei jiefang zhanzheng*, 42–43.

36. Tian, *Peng Zhen zhuchi*, 53–54; Wang, "Jinjun dongbei haiyunji," 467–70.

37. Mao Zedong to Peng Zhen, 16 October 1945, quoted in Tian, *Peng Zhen zhuchi*, 66; Zhang, *Mao Zedong junshi nianpu*, 456.

38. Tian, *Peng Zhen zhuchi*, 161–62.

39. Sheng, *Battling Western Imperialism*, 109; Heinzig, *The Soviet Union and Communist China*, 87–89.

40. Tian, *Peng Zhen zhuchi*, 52. Peng reportedly asked for, and received, three hundred thousand rifles, one thousand machine guns, and fifteen heavy artillery pieces. Ibid., 56.

41. Liu Shaoqi to Peng Zhen, 9 October 1945, quoted in Tian, *Peng Zhen zhuchi*, 59.

42. "Zhongyang guanyu quanli kongzhi dongbei juzhi Jiang jun denglu zhuolu gei dongbeiju de zhishi" [Central directive to the Northeast Bureau on sparing no effort to control the Northeast and check the Jiang armies' attempts to land or touch down], 28 October 1945, in Zhonggong zhongyang dang'anguan, *Zhonggong zhongyang wenjian xuanji di shiwu ce*, 319.

43. "Zhongguo renmin jiefangjun disi yezhanjun zhanshi" bianxiezu, *Zhongguo ren-min jiefangjun disi yezhanjun zhanshi,* 50.

44. Wang, "Quanmian neizhan chuqi," 99.

45. Cheng, "Guo Gong neizhan," 78–79.

46. Taylor, *The Generalissimo,* 310.

47. Ibid., 320.

48. "The Joint Chiefs of Staff to the Commanding General, United States Forces, China Theater (Wedemeyer)," 18 September 1945, FRUS 1945 VII, 565.

49. "The Joint Chiefs of Staff to the Commanding General, United States Forces, China Theater (Wedemeyer)," 10 August 1945, FRUS 1945 VII, 527; "Memorandum by the Acting Secretary of State (Acheson) to President Truman," 13 September 1945, FRUS 1945 VII, 559–61; "Suggested Oral Statement to Dr. Soong Concerning Assistance to China," 14 September 1945, FRUS 1945 VII, 561–62.

50. Wedemeyer, *Wedemeyer Reports!,* 348–49.

51. Taylor, *The Generalissimo,* 325; "The Commanding General, United States Forces, China Theater (Wedemeyer) to the Chief of Staff, United States Army (Marshall), Chungking," 14 November 1945, FRUS 1945 VII, 627–29; "State-War-Navy Coordinating Committee Directive U.S. Policy Toward Manchuria and North China," 16 November 1945, Marshall Mission Records, Box 1.

52. Taylor, *The Generalissimo,* 321.

53. Tian, *Peng Zhen zhuchi,* 75.

54. Elleman, "Soviet Sea Denial and the KMT-CCP Civil War."

55. MIS 242469 "Intelligence Report, Assistant Military Attache, Manchuria," 28 February 1946, Army Intelligence File RG 319, Box 1673.

56. "Memorandum from Strategy and Policy Group, Operations Division, War Department General Staff Gen. Lincoln/umb 5032," 19 October 1945, Marshall Mission Records, Box 1.

57. Tian, *Peng Zhen zhuchi,* 70.

58. "The Navy Department to the Department of State, Washington," 14 November 1945, FRUS 1945 VII, 625–26; "The Consul General at Shanghai (Josselyn) to the Secretary of State, Shanghai," 7 November 1945, FRUS 1945 VII, 678.

59. Zhang, *Xuebai,* 96. Zhang suggests that Shi Jue, apparently basing his position on this intelligence, advised against an attack on Shanhaiguan.

60. *Shilue gaoben,* Guoshiguan file no. 002000000686A, 7 November 1945.

61. Zhang, *Xuebai,* 67.

62. Boorman, *Biographical Dictionary,* vol. III, 326–28.

63. Zhang, *Xuebai,* 96–97.

64. Li Yunchang, "Kongzhi zhanlue shuniu," 20. The following paragraph draws on Li's account of the preparations for the defense of Shanhaiguan.

65. Tian, *Peng Zhen zhuchi,* 88–91.

66. Zhang Heming, "Guanyu Shanhaiguan baoweizhan," 175.

67. Li Yunchang to Lin Biao and Mao Zedong, 9 November 1945, quoted in Liu, *Dong-bei jiefang zhanzheng,* 65.

68. Yang, *Wushier jun,* 5; Du, "Jingong dongbei shimo," 511–12.

69. Yang, *Wushier jun,* 6. In his reminiscences, Shi Jue, commander of the Thirteenth Army, does not tell the story in the precisely the same way. He chooses not to offer any explanation as to why the Communists escaped being pinned to the

beaches of Bohai and wiped out. See Chen and Zhang, *Shi Jue xiansheng fangwen jilu*, 210–11

70. Yang, *Wushier jun*, 7–10. The following paragraph draws on Yang's account and analysis of the weaknesses of the Kuomintang forces.

71. Yang, *Wushier jun*, 6–7. Shi Jue, for his part, says that the Thirteenth Army's pursuit of the Communists was slowed down when Du Yuming insisted on reviewing the troops on the morning of 17 November—a process which took three hours. Chen and Zhang, *Shi Jue xiansheng fangwen jilu*, 123.

72. Wang Chaoguang, "Guo Gong neizhan chuqi de dongbei zhanchang," 526.

73. Quoted in Zhang, *Xuebai*, 101.

74. Ibid.

75. Chen, "Zong xu," 3.

76. Liu, *Dongbei jiefang zhanzheng*, 69–70.

77. Yang, *Wushier jun*, 15. The following paragraph draws on Yang's account and analysis of the capture of Xingcheng, Jinxi, and Huludao on pages 15–30.

78. Du, "Jingong dongbei shimo," 514.

79. Chen and Zhang, *Shi Jue xiansheng fangwen jilu*, 123–124.

80. Yang, *Wushier jun*, 27.

81. "Zhongguo renmin jiefangjun disi yezhanjun zhanshi" bianxiezu, *Zhongguo renmin jiefangjun disi yezhanjun zhanshi*, 55.

82. Zhang, *Xuebai*, 111–112.

83. "Zhongguo renmin jiefangjun disi yezhanjun zhanshi" bianxiezu, *Zhongguo renmin jiefangjun disi yezhanjun zhanshi*, 56.

84. Tian, *Peng Zhen zhuchi*, 102–103; "Peng Zhen zhuan" bianxiezu, *Peng Zhen nianpu* (shang), 322–323.

85. Yang, *Wushier jun*, 31–32; Cheng, "The Escalation of Hostilities in Manchuria," 242; Du, "Jingong dongbei shimo," 515.

86. Zhongguo renmin jiefangjun, *Zhongguo renmin jiefangjun di sishisan jun*, 15.

87. "Zhongguo renmin jiefangjun disi yezhanjun zhanshi" bianxiezu, *Zhongguo renmin jiefangjun disi yezhanjun zhanshi*, 58; "Lin Biao de liuge zhanshu yuanze."

88. Ding, Ge, and Wang, *Dongbei jiefang zhanzheng dashiji*, 25–26.

89. Party Center to Northeast Bureau, 28 November 1945, Zhonggong zhongyang dang'anguan, *Zhonggong zhongyang wenjian xuanji di shiwu ce*, 447–48.

90. Ibid.; Northeast Bureau's Directive on Policy and Tasks, 29 November 1945, Zhonggong zhongyang dang'anguan, *Zhonggong zhongyang wenjian xuanji di shiwu ce*, 449–52; Party Center to Northeast Bureau, 3 December 1945, ibid., 460; Ding, Ge, and Wang, *Dongbei jiefang zhanzheng dashiji*, 28; Zhang, *Xuebai*, 116.

91. Xu Yongchang to Chiang Kai-shek, 16 December 1945, Guoshiguan file no. 002-020400-00001-132.

92. Du Yuming to Chiang Kai-shek, 4 December 1946; Chiang Kai-shek to Du Yuming, 4 December 1946, Guoshiguan file no. 002000000405A; "Geming wenxian—jieshou dongbei yu dui Su jiaoshe (yi)" [Documents of the revolution—transfer of sovereignty over the Northeast and dealings with the Soviets (1)], 101, 104.

93. *Shilue gaoben*, 15 November 1945, Guoshiguan file no. 002000000686A.

94. Party Center to Northeast Bureau, 7 December 1945, in Zhonggong zhongyang dang'anguan, *Zhonggong zhongyang wenjian xuanji di shiwu ce*, 465–67.

95. Party Center to Northeast Bureau, 7 December 1945, ibid., 466.

4. GEORGE MARSHALL'S MISSION, DECEMBER 1945–MARCH 1946

1. Beal, *Marshall in China*; Bland, *George C. Marshall's Mediation Mission*; Levine, "A New Look at American Mediation"; "May, 1947–48: When Marshall Kept the U.S. Out of War in China." The report and essential documents of the Marshall Mission are published in van Slyke, *Marshall's Mission to China*.

2. van de Ven, "Stilwell in the Stocks."

3. Tuchman, *Stilwell and the American Experience*, 504.

4. "The Ambassador to China (Hurley) to President Truman, Washington," 26 November 1945, FRUS 1945 VII, 722–26.

5. "Department of State on 3 April 1945," FRUS 1945 VII, 585–87.

6. Donavan, *Conflict and Crisis*, 152.

7. Quoted in Donavan, *Conflict and Crisis*, 156.

8. Ibid., 154.

9. Pogue, *George Marshall: Statesman*, 60.

10. Ibid., 65.

11. See Levine, "A New Look at American Mediation."

12. "The Commanding General, United States Forces, China Theater (Wedemeyer), to the Chief of Staff, United States Army (Eisenhower), Shanghai," 23 November 1945, FRUS 1945 VII, 662–65.

13. "The Acting Secretary of State to the Charge in China (Robertson), Washington," 20 December 1945, FRUS 1945 VII, 786.

14. "Memorandum: The President's Directive to General of the Army George C. Marshall for the Latter's Mission to China in December 1945," Marshall Mission Records, Box 1, File "Marshall Mission-China," Tab A.

15. *Shilue gaoben*, 16 December 1945, Guoshiguan file no. 02000000687A.

16. This and the following discussion of Marshall's early experiences in China draw on Wang, "George Marshall in Early Republican China."

17. Pogue, *George C. Marshall: Education of a General*, 228–46.

18. George Marshall, "To Major General John L. Hines, September 21, 1924," quoted in Wang, "George C. Marshall in Early Republican China," 17.

19. Pogue, *George C. Marshall: Organizer of Victory*, 284–85, 387, 478–79.

20. "HQ China Theater Admin Shanghai to War Department," 20 November 1945, Marshall Mission Records, Box 1.

21. For example see the anonymous "top secret" "Memo to General Marshall," 29 November 1945, Marshall Mission Records, Box 1.

22. Marshall was not a man who easily revealed his feelings or opinions. Consequently, it is often difficult to ascertain what his point of view may have been on this and a number of other issues.

23. Levine, "A New Look at American Mediation in the Chinese Civil War," 354.

24. "General of the Army George C. Marshall to Fleet Admiral William D. Leahy, Chief of Staff to the Commander in Chief of the Army and Navy, Washington," 30 November 1945, FRUS 1945 VII, 747–48.

25. Quoted in Myers, "Frustration, Fortitude, and Friendship," 153. The following paragraph draws on Myers.

26. *Shilue gaoben*, 28 November 1945, Guoshiguan file no. 002–060100–00206–028; Myers, "Frustration, Fortitude and Friendship," 153; Huang, *Wo zuo Jiang Jieshi 'Teqin zongguan'*, 133.

27. Zhou Enlai, "Guanyu Guo Gong tanpan" [Regarding the Nationalist-Communist negotiations], 5 December 1945, in Zhonggong zhongyang wenxian yanjiushi, *Zhou Enlai yijiusiliu nian tanpan wenxuan*, 1–16. The following paragraph draws on this document.

28. Yang, *Zouxiang polie*, 234.

29. Zhang, "Zhou Enlai and the Marshall Mission," 207–208.

30. He, "Mao Zedong and the Marshall Mission," 176.

31. Wedemeyer, *Wedemeyer Reports!*, 363.

32. Taylor, *The Generalissimo*, 332–33. The files of the Marshall Mission and Marshall's own personal files contain numerous documents concerning the social events and gifts which Chiang and his wife Song Meiling used in their handling of the relationship with Marshall and Mrs. Marshall.

33. Tao Xisheng and Xu Yingchang to Chiang Kai-shek, 28 November 1945, Guoshi-guan file no. 002000000408A.

34. Myers, "Frustration, Fortitude, and Friendship," 153.

35. Guo and Jia, *Bai Chongxi xiansheng fangwen jilu* (xia), 874.

36. Marshall, "Report," 8; Zhou Enlai, "Huanying Maxieer lai Hua cujin Zhongguo heping" [Welcome Marshall to China to advance peace in China], 23 December 1945, in Zhonggong zhongyang wenxian yanjiushi, *Zhou Enlai yijiusiliu nian tanpan wenxuan*, 22–24.

37. Marshall, "Report," 8.

38. Tian, *Peng Zhen zhuchi*, 118–19.

39. "Party Center to Northeast Bureau," 24 December 1945, Zhonggong zhongyang dang'anguan, *Zhonggong zhongyang wenjian xuanji di shiwu ce*, 512–14.

40. Wetzel, "From the Jaws of Defeat," 137.

41. "Zhongguo renmin jiefangjun disi yezhanjun zhanshi" bianxiezu, *Zhongguo renmin jiefangjun disi yezhanjun zhanshi*, 64–65.

42. Mao Zedong, "Build Stable Base Areas in the Northeast," 28 December 1945, in *Selected Works of Mao Tse-tung*, vol. 4, 81–85.

43. Ding, Ge and Wang, *Dongbei jiefang zhanzheng dashiji*, 35; "Military Affairs Commission to Cheng Zihua, Xiao Ke, Luo Ruiqing, Lin Biao, Nie Rongzhen and Liu Lantao," 29 December, 1945, in Zhonggong zhongyang dang'anguan, *Zhonggong zhongyang wenjian xuanji di shiwu ce*, 526–27.

44. Ding, Ge, and Wang, *Dongbei jiefang zhanzheng dashiji*, 35; Zhang, *Xuebai*, 133–34.

45. Liu, *Dongbei jiefang zhanzheng*, 111. The following paragraph draws on Liu's account.

46. Zhou Enlai, "Shouyao wenti shi liji tingzhan" [The main question is an immediate ceasefire], 9 January 1946, in Zhonggong zhongyang wenxian yanjiushi, *Zhou Enlai yijiusiliu nian tanpan wenxuan*, 47–48.

47. Jiang, *Kanluan jianshi* (yi), 25; Li, Dongbei kanluan, 59.

48. Zhengzhi xueyuan diyi junshi jiaoyanshi, *Zhanyi zhanli xuanbian (er)*, 9.

49. Heinzig, *The Soviet Union and Communist China*, 95.

50. Zhou Enlai, "Ying liji wutiaojian tingzhi neizhan" [There should be an immediate, unconditional end to the civil war], 27 December 1945, in Zhonggong zhongyang wenxian yanjiushi, *Zhou Enlai yijiusiliu nian tanpan wenxuan*, 25–26.

51. Cessation of Hostilities order, released 10 January 1946, in van Slyke, *Marshall's Mission to China*, vol. 2, 23–25.

52. Quoted in Yang and Bai, *Luo Ronghuan zai dongbei*, 67.

53. Ibid.

54. Tian, *Peng Zhen zhuchi*, 147.

55. Jiang, *Kanluan jianshi*, 23.

56. Ibid., 24; Zhang, *Xuebai*, 120.

57. Ibid. The following account of the battle for Yingkou follows Zhang, *Xuebai*, 120–21 and MIS 230376, Strategic Services Unit, "War Department Intelligence Dissemination A-65148," 16 January 1946, Army Intelligence File RG 319, Box 1533.

58. A Nationalist source claims that the Soviet commander, Malinovsky, purposely scheduled the transfer of authority over Shenyang for 13 January in order to further stretch the already over-extended Nationalist forces. See Yang, *Wushier jun kanluan*, 57.

59. Michael Sheng argues that Communist commitment to the ceasefire in Manchuria was at least partly due to Soviet advice. In mid-January 1946, the Soviet Union, concerned that the United States would become involved if civil war broke out, urged the Communist Party to avoid war and work with Chiang Kai-shek to democratize China. Sheng, *Battling Western Imperialism*, 123.

60. Quoted in Zhang, *Xuebai*, 134.

61. Sheng, *Battling Western Imperialism*, 123; Niu, *Cong Yanan zouxiang shijie*, 219; Yang, "1946 nian guogong liangdang douzheng"; and He, "1945–1949 nian zhongguo gongchandang duimei zhengce."

62. Zhou, "Tanpan jue bu ying zai xia yi ji polie." Zhonggong zhongyang wenxian yanjiushi, *Zhou Enlai yijiusiliu nian tanpan wenxuan*, 91.

63. Zhang, "Zhou Enlai and the Marshall Mission," 216; Zhonggong zhongyang wenxian yanjiushi, *Zhou Enlai yijiusiliu nian tanpan wenxuan*, 92–94.

64. Zhonggong zhongyang wenxian yanjiushi, *Zhou Enlai yijiusiliu nian tanpan wenxuan*, 92–94; "Draft of message from Marshall to John Carter Vincent," 29 May 1946, Marshall Mission Records, Box 16.

65. Liu, *Dongbei jiefang zhanzheng*, 112.

66. Lin Biao to Party Center, January 15, 1946, quoted in Liu, *Dongbei jiefang zhanzheng*, 112. The document is in "Peng Zhen zhuan" bianxiezu, *Peng Zhen nianpu* (shang), 358.

67. Tian, *Peng Zhen zhuchi*, 149, 156. "Peng Zhen zhuan" bianxiezu, *Peng Zhen nianpu* (shang), 353–54.

68. "Zhongguo renmin jiefangjun disi yezhanjun zhanshi" bianxiezu, *Zhongguo renmin jiefangjun disi yezhanjun zhanshi*, 68.

69. Liu Shaoqi to Peng Zhen, January 27, 1946, quoted in Liu, *Dongbei jiefang zhanzheng*, 120–21; "Peng Zhen zhuan" bianxiezu, *Peng Zhen nianpu* (shang),154–55.

70. Chiang Diaries, 23 January 1946, Box 45, Folder 2.

71. Liu Shaoqi for the Party Center to Peng Zhen and Lin Biao, 5 February 1946, quoted in Tian, *Peng Zhen zhuchi*, 156–57.

72. The following description of the Battle of Xiushuihezi draws on Yang, *Wushier jun kanluan*, 66–72; *Siye zhanshi*, 75–79; Zhang, *Xuebai*, 122–26; and Zhongguo renmin jiefangjun disishisanjun silingbu, *disishisanjun disanci guonei geming zhanzhengshi*, 19–22.

73. "Peng Zhen zhuan" bianxiezu, *Peng Zhen nianpu* (shang), 376.

74. Zhongguo renmin jiefangjun, *Zhongguo renmin jiefangjun di sishiyijun*, 23.

75. The following draws on Zhang, *Xuebai*, 126–29; Zhongguo renmin jiefangjun, *Zhongguo renmin jiefangjun di sishiyijun*, 23–27; and Liu, *Dongbei jiefang zhanzheng*, 125–29.

76. Quoted in Zhang, *Xuebai*, 128.

77. Zhang, *Xuebai*, 126–27; "Zhongguo renmin jiefangjun disi yezhanjun zhanshi" bianxiezu, *Zhongguo renmin jiefangjun disi yezhanjun zhanshi*, 78–79.

78. Clubb, "Manchuria in the Balance," 381–83.

79. Tian, *Peng Zhen zhuchi*, 92.

80. "Zhongyang guanyu tingzhan hou wodang dui Manzhou de zhengce wenti gei Dongbeiju de zhishi" [Central directive to the Northeast Bureau on questions of policy toward Manchuria following the cease-fire], 11 January 1946. Zhongyang dang'anguan, *Zhonggong zhongyang wenjian xuanji di shiliu ce*, 20–21.

81. MIS 276809 "Strategic Services Unit, Intelligence Dissemination A-6904," 10 May 1946, Army Intelligence File RG 319, Box 1855.

82. Wu, *Wode licheng*, 172.

83. Tian, *Peng Zhen zhuchi*, 166.

84. Chen Jiazhen, "Changchun diyici jiefang qianhou de qingkuang," 768.

85. Zhang, *Mao Zedong junshi nianpu*, 474; van Slyke, *Marshall's Mission to China*, vol. 1, 53.

86. Shi, *Zai lishi juren shenbian*, 318–19.

87. Qin, *Zongtong Jiang gong dashi changbian*, 135–36.

88. Zhou Enlai, "Maxieer zhongshi guanyu dongbei wenti de tanpan" [Marshall emphasizes negotiation on the Northeast problem], 19 March 1946, in Zhonggong zhongyang wenxian yanjiushi, *Zhou Enlai yijiusiliu nian tanpan wenxuan*, 124.

89. Zhou Enlai, "Daibiaotuan yu dongbei wenti de duice" [The representative mission and countermeasures on the Northeast issue], 10 March 1946, in Zhonggong zhongyang wenxian yanjiushi, *Zhou Enlai yijiusiliu nian tanpan wenxuan*, 131–32.

5. THE SECOND BATTLE OF SIPING: PHASE ONE

1. Wetzel, "From the Jaws of Defeat," 139.

2. Heinzig, *The Soviet Union and Communist China*, 96, 98; Yang, *Zouxiang polie*, 202.

3. Wang, *Cong kangzhan shengli dao neizhan baofa*, 456–57.

4. Zhongyang dang'anguan, *Zhonggong zhongyang wenjian xuanji di shiliu ce*, 89–91.

5. Sheng, *Battling Western Imperialism*, 126.

6. Yang, *Zhongjian didai de geming*, 428–29.

7. Heinzig, *The Soviet Union and Communist China*, 98. Sheng, *Battling Western Imperialism*, 132–33.

8. Tian, *Peng Zhen zhuchi*, 166; Yang, *Zouxiang polie*, 202.

9. Tian, *Peng Zhen zhuchi*, 167.

10. Zhongyang dang'anguan, *Zhonggong zhongyang wenjian xuanji di shiliu ce*, 89–91; Zhonggong zhongyang wenxian yanjiushi, ed., *Zhou Enlai nianpu* (xia), 667.

11. Yang, *Mao Zedong yu Mosike*, 202.

12. Zhonggong zhongyang wenxian yanjiushi, ed., *Zhou Enlai nianpu* (xia), 668.

13. Mao to Zhou, 16 March 1946, in Zhang, *Mao Zedong junshi nianpu*, 475.

14. Ibid.

15. Qin, *Zongtong Jiang gong dashi changbian*, 77.

16. "The Precursor," November–December 1946, 731; "La Societé en Chine pendant la montée communiste (1945–1954)," Missions Étrangéres.

17. *Sizhan Siping*, Episode 2.

18. Yang, *Zhongjian didai de geming*, 431.

19. Zhang, "Zhou Enlai and the Marshall Mission," 221.

20. Zhou, "Jiang Jieshi liangmianpai de zuofa he women de duice" [Chiang Kai-shek's two-faced policy and our countermeasures], 19 March 1946, Zhonggong zhongyang wenxian yanjiushi, *Zhou Enlai yijiusiliu nian tanpan wenxuan*, 155–56.

21. Quoted in Zhang, *Xuebai*, 138–39.

22. Yang, *Zhongjian didai de geming*, 431.

23. Tian, *Peng Zhen zhuchi*, 171.

24. Ibid.

25. "Zhongyang guanyu kongzhi Changchun, Haerbin ji zhongdong lu baowei bei-man gei Dongbeiju de zhishi" [Party central directive to the Northeast Bureau on controlling Changchun, Harbin and the China Eastern railway and defending north Manchuria], 24 March 1946, in Zhongyang dang'anguan, *Zhonggong zhongyang wenjian xuanji di shiliu ce*, 100–101.

26. "Liujie erzhong quanhui diwuci huiyi sujilu" [Shorthand record of the fifth meeting of the second plenary session of the sixth central committee], 5 March 1946, Dangshiguan file no. 6.2/10.1.2; "Liujie sanzhong quanhui disici huiyi sujilu" [Shorthand record of the fourth meeting of the third plenary session of the sixth central committee], 19 March 1946, Dangshiguan file no. 6.2/57.2.

27. Zheng, *Wode rongma shengya*, 413–14.

28. Jiang, *Kanluan jianshi*, 29; "Zhongguo renmin jiefangjun disi yezhanjun zhanshi" bianxiezu, *Zhongguo renmin jiefangjun disi yezhanjun zhanshi*, 79.

29. Zhonggong zhongyang wenxian yanjiushi, *Zhou Enlai yijiusiliu nian tanpan wenxuan*, 161.

30. "Zhongguo renmin jiefangjun disi yezhanjun zhanshi" bianxiezu, *Zhongguo renmin jiefangjun disi yezhanjun zhanshi*, 79, 89; Wetzel, "From the Jaws of Defeat," 141.

31. "Zhongguo renmin jiefangjun disi yezhanjun zhanshi" bianxiezu, *Zhongguo renmin jiefangjun disi yezhanjun zhanshi*, 90–91.

32. Qin, *Zongtong Jiang gong dashi changbian*, 79; Chiang Diaries, 21 March 1946, Box 45, Folder 4. Diary entries made in mid-April also indicate Chiang's awareness that his forces in Manchuria would be hard-pressed to perform the tasks that he was demanding of them. Chiang Diaries, 18 April 1946, Box 45, Folder 5.

33. Qin, *Zongtong Jiang gong dashi changbian*, 100–103; Chiang Kai-shek to Northeast Command, 6 April 1946, Guoshiguan file no. 002000001941A, 38, 39.

34. *Shilue gaoben*, 6 April 1946, Guoshiguan file no. 002000000691A.

35. *Shilue gaoben*, 13 April 1946, Guoshiguan file no. 002000000691A.

36. Ibid.

37. The main sources from which we can derive a preliminary understanding of this issue are: Lin, "Lin Biao tongzhi guanyu dongbei luxian fenqi wenti zhi Mao zhuxi, Liu Shaoqi dian"; and Peng, "Dongbei jiefang zhanzheng tou jiuge yue." Some insights may also be gleaned from Liu, *Dongbei jiefang zhanzheng*, and from Zhang, *Xuebai*.

38. Lew, *The Third Chinese Revolutionary Civil War*, 34.

39. Tian, *Peng Zhen zhuchi*, 160–61.

40. Lin, "Lin Biao tongzhi guanyu dongbei luxian fenqi wenti."

41. Tian, *Peng Zhen zhuchi*, 161.

42. Lin, "Lin Biao tongzhi guanyu dongbei luxian fenqi wenti." The following paragraphs summarize this document.

43. Zhang, *Xuebai,* 136.

44. Yang and Bai, *Luo Ronghuan zai dongbei,* 67

45. Qiu and Cao, *Zhongguo yongshi,* 50.

46. Ibid.; Yang and Bai, *Luo Ronghuan zai dongbei,* 68.

47. Hu, "Guanyu Siping baoweizhan de yixie wenti," 22.

48. Quoted in Tian, *Peng Zhen zhuchi,* 173; see also"Zhongguo renmin jiefangjun disi yezhanjun zhanshi" bianxiezu, *Zhongguo renmin jiefangjun disi yezhanjun zhanshi,* 51.

49. Communist Party Central Committee, "Guanyu dui Jiang dui fei fangzhen" [Regarding strategy toward Chiang and toward bandits], 27 March 1946, quoted in Ding, Ge, and Wang, *Dongbei jiefang zhanzheng dashiji,* 47. The Northeast Bureau Bureau established its "Deployment of troops for major battle in the Northeast " ("dongbei dahuizhan bushu") on 26 March 1946. See Yang and Bai, *Luo Ronghuan zai dongbei,* 67.

50. Liu, *Dongbei jiefang zhanzheng,* 166.

51. Mao Zedong to Lin Biao and Peng Zhen, 6 April 1946, in *Mao Zedong junshi wenxuan (neibuben),* 274–75.

52. "Dui dongbei zuozhan wenti de buchong zhishi" [Supplemental directive regarding questions of battle in the Northeast], 8 April 1946, in *Mao Zedong junshi wenji,* 161.

53. Ibid.

54. Hu, "Guanyu Siping baoweizhan de yixie wenti," 18.

55. Wetzel, "From the Jaws of Defeat," 144.

56. "Zhonggong zhongyang guanyu zhengqu dasheng Siping Benxi liangge zhanyi zhi Lin Biao bing Peng Zhen dian" [Party Center telegram to Lin Biao and Peng Zhen on fighting to victory in the two battles of Siping and Benxi], 6 April 1946, in Gao, *Sizhan Siping,* 28.

57. Zhengzhi xueyuan diyi junshi jiaoyanshi, ed., *Zhongguo renmin jiefangjun zhanyi zhanli xuanbian,* 9–16.

58. Wetzel, "From the Jaws of Defeat," 141–42; Huang, "Some Observations on Manchuria in the Balance," 163.

59. Liu, *Dongbei jiefang zhanzheng,* 167.

60. "Zhongguo renmin jiefangjun disi yezhanjun zhanshi" bianxiezu, *Zhongguo renmin jiefangjun disi yezhanjun zhanshi,* 91.

61. *Sizhan Siping,* Episode 3.

62. Wan, "Huiyi Siping," 189–90.

63. Lin Biao to the Party Center, 11 April 1946, quoted in Liu, *Dongbei jiefang zhanzheng,* 168.

64. Zhou Enlai to Party Center, 11 April 1946, in Zhonggong zhongyang wenxian yanjiushi, *Zhou Enlai nianpu* (xia), 674.

65. At the same time, the Soviets were denying the Nationalist armies use of the railway under the excuse that there was not enough rolling stock available. Roberts to Marshall, 17 May 1946, Marshall Mission Records, Box 43, File "Messages—Vol. VII, 17 May 1946–2 June 1946."

66. Zhongguo renmin jiefangjun, *Zhongguo renmin jiefangjun di sishisan jun,* 23–25.

67. Ibid., 25.

68. Mao Zedong to Northeast Bureau, 20 April 1946, quoted in Liu, *Dongbei jiefang zhanzheng,* 170.

69. Chen, "Siping baowei zhan," 217.

70. *Sizhan Siping,* Episode 3.

71. Zhongguo renmin jiefangjun gaodeng junshi xuexiao, "Siping baoweizhan," 2.

72. Wan, "Huiyi Siping," 190; "Zhongguo renmin jiefangjun disi yezhanjun zhanshi" bianxiezu, *Zhongguo renmin jiefangjun disi yezhanjun zhanshi*, 92.

73. Ibid.

74. Wetzel, "From the Jaws of Defeat," 147; Pepper, *Civil War in China*, 202.

75. Zuo, "Huiyi yizhan Siping," 278.

76. Zhang, *Xuebai*, 158.

77. "The Precursor," November–December 1946, 731; "La Societé en Chine pendant la montée communiste (1945–1954)," 602, Missions Étrangéres.

78. Zhongguo renmin jiefangjun gaodeng junshi xuexiao, "Siping baoweizhan," 2.

79. Ibid.

80. *Sizhan Siping*, Episode 3.

81. Conversations with residents of Siping and Jinzhou, Summer 2010; *Sizhan Siping*, Episode 4.

82. Conversation with an elderly resident of Siping, 18 July 2010.

83. Conversations with elderly residents of Siping, July 2008.

84. Conversations with elderly residents of Siping, 2008 and 2010.

85. "The Precursor," November–December 1946, 731; "La Societé en Chine pendant la montée communiste (1945–1954)," 585, 602, Missions Étrangéres.

86. Rigg, *Red China's Fighting Hordes*, 217; Zhongguo Gongchandang Jilin sheng Siping shi zuzhi shiliao, 14–17.

87. Liu, *Shidai de yinxiang*, 100.

88. "Zhanling Changchun hou de dongbei junzheng gongzuo bushu" [Disposal of military and political work in the northeast following the occupation of Changchun], 19 April 1946, in *Mao Zedong junshi wenji*, 171.

89. Liu, *Shidai de yinxiang*, 100.

90. "Siping baowei heping minzhu dahui tongdian" [Telegram from the Siping rally in defense of peace and democracy]. Originally published in *Shengli bao* [Victory news], 12 April 1946, excerpt in Gao, *Sizhan Siping*, 329.

91. "Siping baowei heping minzhu dahui tongdian" [Open telegram from the Siping peace and democracy defense rally], Shenglibao, 12 April 1946, in Gao, *Sizhan Siping*, 125.

92. Zhao, *Dongbei jiefang daquanjing*, 57. Zhao suggests that Zheng Dongguo, Zhao Jiaxiang, and Zhao Gongwu, in light of Xiong's incompetence, and worried that Fan Hanjie would come to the Northeast and use Hu Zongren's methods of rectifying the commanders there, hurriedly asked Du Yuming to return and take command as quickly as possible.

93. Zhao, *Dongbei jiefang daquanjing*, 58; Wang, *Cong kangzhan shengli dao neizhan baofa*, 471.

94. *Shilue gaoben*, 19 April 1946, Guoshiguan, file no. 002000000691A.

95. Qin Xiaoyi, *Zongtong Jiang gong dashi changbian chugao*, 109.

96. Ibid, 114–67; *Shilue gaoben*, 20 April 1946, Guoshiguan, file no. 002000000691A.

97. Chiang to Xiong Shihui, 18 April 1946, Guoshiguan file no. 002000001941A, 64.

98. *Shilue gaoben*, 21 April 1946, Guoshiguan file no. 002000000691A.

99. Lin Biao, quoted in Hu, "Shilun Siping baoweizhan zhong de Mao Zedong yu Lin Biao," 6.

100. Wetzel, "From the Jaws of Defeat," 147–48.

101. "Zhongyang junwei guanyu jiangli Siping shoujun zhi Lin Biao dian" [Central military commission telegram to Lin Biao on rewarding the troops defending Siping], 27 April 1946, in Gao, *Sizhan Siping,* 33.

102. "Lin Biao, Peng Zhen, Luo Ronghuan tongling hejiang baowei Siping zhizhanyuan de dianbao" [Lin Biao, Peng Zhen, and Luo Ronghuan telegram of congratulations to the commanders at the battle to defend Siping], 29 April 1946, in ibid., 49.

103. This section draws on Liu, *Dongbei jiefang zhanzheng,* 175–76.

104. Cheng, "Modern War on an Ancient Battlefield," 45.

105. Jiang, *Kanluan jianshi,* 31.

6. THE SECOND BATTLE OF SIPING: PHASE TWO

1. Mao Zedong to Lin Biao, 1 May 1946, in *Mao Zedong junshi wenxuan,* 276.

2. Yang, *Wushier jun kanluan,* 81; "Zhongguo renmin jiefangjun disi yezhanjun zhanshi" bianxiezu, *Zhongguo renmin jiefangjun disi yezhanjun zhanshi,* 83.

3. Yang, *Wushier jun kanluan,* 90.

4. Zhongguo renmin jiefangjun, *Zhongguo renmin jiefangjun di sishiyijun,* 33.

5. Yang, *Wushier jun kanluan,* 91.

6. Zhongguo renmin jiefangjun, *Zhongguo renmin jiefangjun di sishiyijun,* 33–34.

7. Du, "Jingong dongbei shimo," 523.

8. Eastern Liaoning Military District to Northeast Bureau, 1 May 1946, quoted in Yang and Bai, *Luo Ronghuan zai dongbei,* 72; "Zhongguo renmin jiefangjun disi yezhanjun zhanshi" bianxiezu, *Zhongguo renmin jiefangjun disi yezhanjun zhanshi,* 85.

9. MIS 264430 "General Headquarters, United States Army Forces, Pacific, Military Intelligence Section, General Staff, Intelligence Summary," 15 May 1946, Army Intelligence File RG 319, Box 1772.

10. Zhongguo renmin jiefangjun, *Zhongguo renmin jiefangjun di sishiyijun,* 35.

11. Yang, *Wushier jun kanluan,* 91.

12. Chen et al., *Sizhan Siping shi,* 74.

13. Zhongguo renmin jiefangjun, *Zhongguo renmin jiefangjun di sishisan jun,* 27–28.

14. Quoted in Liu, *Dongbei jiefang zhanzheng,* 181.

15. Liu, *Liu Baiyu dongbei zhanchang,* 18–20.

16. *Sizhan Siping,* Episode 2.

17. "Lin Biao zong siling jiejian jizhe" [Commander Lin Biao meets with reporters]. *Mudanjiang ribao,* 18 June 1946, 2.

18. Zhongguo renmin jiefangjun, *Zhongguo renmin jiefangjun di sishisan jun,* 18.

19. Mao Zedong to Lin Biao on behalf of the Military Affairs Commission, 27 April 1946, in Gao, *Sizhan Siping,* 33.

20. Mao to Lin Biao, 28 April 1946, quoted in Tian, *Peng Zhen zhuchi,* 195.

21. Cheng, "Escalation of Hostilities in Manchuria," 309–10.

22. Lin Biao to the Party Center and the Northeast Bureau, 29 April 1946, in Gao, *Sizhan Siping,* 48.

23. Mao Zedong to Lin Biao and Peng Zhen, 30 April 1946, in "Peng Zhen zhuan" bianxiezu, ed. *Peng Zhen nianpu* (shang), 418.

24. Tian, *Peng Zhen zhuchi,* 195.

25. Mao to Lin Biao, 1 May 1946, quoted in Cheng, "The Escalation of Hostilities in Manchuria," 309.

26. Mao Zedong to Lin Biao, 1 May 1946, in Gao, *Sizhan Siping,* 34.

27. Mao Zedong to Lin Biao, 1 May 1946, in Gao, *Sizhan Siping*, 34.

28. Lin, "Lin Biao tongzhi guanyu dongbei luxian fenqi wenti zhi Mao zhuxi, Liu Shaoqi dian."

29. On the second front operation, see Liu, *Dongbei jiefang zhanzheng*, 181–82; Hu, "Guanyu Siping baoweizhan de yixie wenti," 7–8; Cheng, "Escalation of Hostilities in Manchuria," 310–11; and Yang, "1945 nian Guo Gong Siping," 147. The discussion in the following two paragraphs draws on these sources.

30. Tian, *Peng Zhen zhuchi*, 197.

31. On the preparedness and the high morale of the New Sixth Army, see MIS 242469 "Intelligence Report, Assistant Military Attache, Manchuria," 28 February 1946, Army Intelligence File RG 319, Box 1673.

32. Liu, *Dongbei jiefang zhanzheng*, 182.

33. Luo, *Jiqing suiyue*, 79, 80, 90.

34. van Slyke, *Marshall's Mission to China*, vol. 1, 19–23; vol. 2, 126–28.

35. Ibid., vol. 1, 51.

36. Ibid., vol. 1, 54.

37. Melby, *Mandate of Heaven*, 125.

38. Zhonggong zhongyang wenxian yanjiushi, ed., *Zhou Enlai nianpu* (xia), 670; van Slyke, *Marshall's Mission to China*, vol. 2, 319.

39. Ibid., vol. 1, 96; MIS 255372 "Intelligence Dissemination #A-67923," 19 April 1946, Army Intelligence File RG 319, Box 1707.

40. Zhonggong zhongyang wenxian yanjiushi, ed., *Zhou Enlai nianpu* (xia), 671, 672.

41. Ibid., 168; Sheng, *Battling Western Imperialism*, 127; Zhang, *Xuebai*, 138–39.

42. He Di, "Mao and the Marshall Mission," 193–94; Zhang, "Zhou and the Marshall Mission," 223.

43. Zhonggong zhongyang wenxian yanjiushi, *Zhou Enlai nianpu* (xia), 676.

44. Quoted in Westad, "Could the Chinese Civil War Have Been Avoided," 511. See also Mao to Lin Biao and Peng Zhen, 21 April 1946, in Ding, Ge, and Wang, *Dongbei jiefang zhanzheng dashiji*, 53.

45. Zhou Enlai to Mao Zedong, 22 April 1946, in Zhonggong zhongyang wenxian yanjiushi, ed., *Zhou Enlai nianpu* (xia), 676.

46. Account of meeting between Zhou Enlai and Marshall, 22 April 1946, in ibid., 676; Zhonggong zhongyang wenxian yanjiushi, *Zhou Enlai yijiusiliu nian tanpan wenxuan*, 265–67; account of meeting between Zhou and Marshall, 29 April 1946, Zhonggong zhongyang wenxian yanjiushi, ed., *Zhou Enlai nianpu* (xia), 678.

47. Myers, ""Frustration, Fortitude, and Friendship," 155.

48. Chiang Diaries, 22 April 1946, quoted in Qin, *Zongtong Jiang gong dashi changbian*, 116; Chiang Diaries, 23 April 1946, 27 April 1946, Box 45, folder 5.

49. Chiang Diaries, quoted in Qin, *Zongtong Jiang gong dashi changbian*, 116.

50. Chiang Diaries, 28 April 1946, quoted in Qin, *Zongtong Jiang gong dashi changbian*, 124.

51. Chiang Diaries, 23 April 1946, quoted in ibid., 124.

52. Chiang Diaries, 28 April 1946, quoted in ibid., 124.

53. Carter to Marshall, 2 May 1946, in Marshall Mission Records, Box 43. Carter is quoting an SSU report of 13 April.

54. Van Slyke, *Marshall's Mission*, vol. 1, 99.

55. Ibid., 106–107.

56. Melby, *Mandate of Heaven,* 142, 144.

57. Marshall to Truman, 6 May 1946, Marshall Mission Records, Box 16.

58. Marshall to Chiang Kai-shek (draft), 10 May 1946, Marshall Mission Records, Box 16.

59. Ibid.

60. van Slyke, *Marshall's Mission,* vol. 1, 111; Qin, *Zongtong Jiang gong dashi changbian,* 135–36; Zhonggong zhongyang wenxian yanjiushi, ed., *Zhou Enlai nianpu* (xia), 681.

61. Zhou to Party Center, 13 May 1946, in ibid., 682.

62. Ibid.; Sheng, *Battling Western Imperialism,* 140.

63. Huang, "Observations on Manchuria," 165.

64. *Shilue gaoben* 5, 12, and 15 May 1946, Guoshiguan file no. 002000000692A.

65. "Siping baowei zhanyi'an" [Report on the battle to defend Siping], Guojia dang'an guanliju file no. 0035/543.6/6021.2, 5.

66. Huang Kecheng to Party Center, 12 May 1946, quoted in Huang, *Huang Kecheng zishu,* 204–205.

67. Mao Zedong to Peng Zhen and Lin Biao, 15 May 1946, cited in Yang Kuisong, "Yijiusiliu nian Guo Gong Siping," 148.

68. Mao Zedong to the Party Bureaus, Zhou Enlai, Ye Jianying, et al., 15 May 1946, Zhongyang dang'anguan, *Zhonggong zhongyang wenjian xuanji di shiliu ce,* 161–63.

69. Cheng, "The Escalation of Hostilities in Manchuria," 312–13.

70. "Zhongyang guanyu shiju ji duice de zhishi" [Center's directive regarding the situation and countermeasures], 15 May 1946, in Zhongyang dang'anguan, *Zhonggong zhongyang wenjian xuanji di shiliu ce,* 161–63.

71. Cheng, "China's Madrid in Manchuria," 97.

72. Zhou Enlai to Party Center, 16 May 1946, Zhonggong zhongyang wenxian yanjiushi, *Zhou Enlai yijiusiliu nian tanpan wenxuan,* 137–39.

73. Liu, *Dongbei jiefang zhanzheng,* 184.

74. Ibid., 184–85.

75. Chen, "Siping baoweizhan," 224; Liu, *Dongbei jiefang zhanzheng,* 185. The following draws on Chen and Liu.

76. Chen, "Siping baoweizhan," 224.

77. Liu, *Dongbei jiefang zhanzheng,* 187. The following description of the fight for Tazishan draws on Liu and on *Sizhan Siping,* Episode 5; Chen, "Siping Baoweizhan"; Hu Zhefeng, "Shilun Siping baoweizhan"; interview with Wang Yongxing (director of *Sizhan Siping*), 21 July 2010; and discussions with personnel at the Siping zhanyi jinianguan, also in July 2010.

78. Conversation with an elderly resident of Siping, 18 July 2010.

79. Interview with Wang Yongxing, 21 July 2010.

80. Lin Biao to Northeast Bureau, Party Center, quoted in Liu, *Dongbei jiefang zhanzheng,* 188.

81. *Sizhan Siping,* Episode 5.

82. Conversation with an elderly resident of Siping, 18 July 2010.

83. Luo, *Jiqing suiyue,* 93.

7. THE CHASE AND THE CEASEFIRE, MAY–JUNE 1946

1. Zheng et al., *Du Yuming jiangjun,* 65; Du, "Jingong dongbei shimo," 526–27.

2. Chiang Diaries, 19 April 1946, Box 45, Folder 5.

3. Zheng et al., *Du Yuming jiangjun*, 65; Du, "Jingong dongbei shimo," 526–27.

4. "Jiang Jieshi de liangmian zuofa he women de fangzhen" [Chiang Kai-shek's two-faced methods and our strategy], 13 May 1946, in *Zhou Enlai yijiu siliu nian tanpan wenxuan*, 323–26; Mei Jiang zai dongbei wenti shang de juli yi bu xiangyuan [America and Chiang now not far apart on the Northeast question], 13 May 1946, ibid., 327–28.

5. Zhou Enlai to Party Center, 22 May 1946, in Zhonggong zhongyang wenxian yanjiushi, *Zhou Enlai yijiusiliu nian tanpan wenxuan*, 351–53.

6. Ibid.

7. Ibid.

8. Beal, *Marshall in China*, 65.

9. Cheng, "Modern War on an Ancient Battlefield," 47.

10. Draft of Memorandum from Marshall to Chiang Kai-shek, Subject: "Possible basis for agreement regarding Manchurian issues," 10 May 1946, Marshall Mission Records, Box 16.

11. Zhou, "Guomindang jiji beizhan yi biaomianhua," Zhonggong zhongyang wenxian yanjiushi, *Zhou Enlai yijiusiliu nian tanpan wenxuan*, 351–53

12. Taylor, *The Generalissimo*, 351.

13. Chiang Diaries, 21 May 1946, Box 45, Folder 6.

14. Chiang Diaries, 22, 24, 27, 29 April 1946, Box 45, Folder 5.

15. Herzstein, *Henry R. Luce*, 59. Lauterbach was later fired when Henry Luce purged the *Time* staff of suspected Communists. Ibid., 82.

16. Richard Lauterbach to General Marshall, 29 May 1946, Marshall Mission Records, Box 43, File "Messages—Vol. VII, 17 May–2 June 1946."

17. Ibid.

18. Qin Xiaoyi, *Zongtong Jiang gong dashi changbian*, 146–47.

19. Richard Lauterbach to General Marshall, 29 May 1946, Marshall Mission Records, Box 43, File "Messages—Vol. VII, 17 May–2 June 1946."

20. *Shilue gaoben*, 23 May 1946, Guoshiguan file no. 002000000692A.

21. Marshall, "Report," 118.

22. Chiang Diaries, 24 May 1946, Box 45, Folder 6.

23. Chiang Diaries, 25 May 1946, Box 45, Folder 6.

24. Ibid.

25. Qin, *Zongtong Jiang gong dashi changbian*, 150.

26. Ibid.

27. Marshall, "Report," 123.

28. *Shilue gaoben*, 26 May 1946, Guoshiguan file no. 002000000692A.

29. Qin, *Zongtong Jiang gong dashi changbian*, 153; Marshall to Chiang, 26 May, 1946, quoted in Marshall, "Report," 125–26.

30. *Shilue gaoben*, 25 May 1946, Guoshiguan, file no. 002000000689A.

31. Zhou Enlai, "Jiang Jieshi suo ti tiaojian yizai kuoda zhanzheng" [Chiang Kai-shek's goal in raising conditions is to expand the war], 30 May 1946. Zhonggong zhongyang wenxian yanjiushi, *Zhou Enlai yijiusiliu nian tanpan wenxuan*, 375–76; *Shilue gaoben*, 27 May 1946, Guoshiguan file no. 002000000692A; Chiang Diaries, 28 May 1946, Box 45, Folder 6.

32. Marshall to Chiang, 29 May 1946, in Marshall, "Report," 128.

33. "Guojun yue Siping beijin," [National Army leaps past Siping, advances north], *Qianjinbao*, 20 May 1946, 1; "Beishang guojun jinqu Hashi" [Northward-advancing National Army presses toward Harbin], *Qianjinbao*, 6 June 1946, 1; "Changchun gongjun xi kuibai bingfei zidong chetui" [The Communist army at Changchun was defeated; it did not retreat voluntarily], *Qianjinbao*, 21 May 1946, 1; "Guojun yuyue Siping zhuijiao canfei" [The National Army leaps past Siping to pursue and annihilate bandit remnants], *Xinbao*, 20 May 1946, 2.

34. "Dongbei guojun fen qilu tingjin" [National Army in the Northeast advances along seven vectors], *Dagongbao*, 4 June 1946, 2.

35. Chen, "Dongbei minzhu lianjun chechu Siping," 83.

36. Elleman, *Modern Chinese Warfare*, 182–85.

37. "China: 400 Million Humiliations."

38. Chen, "Dongbei Minzhu Lianjun chechu Siping," 83. Chiang himself, in discussions with Marshall on 23 April, seems to have been willing to consider a ceasefire line to the north of Changchun. Taylor, *The Generalissimo*, 348. This conversation, however, took place while the Communists were still successfully holding off Chiang's troops at Siping and is more consistent with Chiang's caution of March–April 1946 rather than the more confident attitude that he evinces in his diaries after 19 May.

39. Chiang Diaries, 25 May 1946, Box 45, Folder 6.

40. Qin, *Zongtong Jiang gong dashi changbian*, 151.

41. Communist Party Center to Lin Biao and the Northeast Bureau, "Tuichu Siping hou de junshi bushu" [Military deployment after the retreat from Siping], 19 May 1946, in *Mao Zedong junshi wenji*, vol. 3, 226–27.

42. The following description of the Wang Jifang affair draws on Zhang, *Xuebai*, 172–73 and on the report on Wang Jifeng's interrogation, Guoshiguan file no. 008000001300A.

43. MIS 268149 General Headquarters, United States Army Forces, Pacific, Military Intelligence Section, General Staff, "Intelligence Summary 1508," 29 May 1946, Army Intelligence File RG 319, Box 1799.

44. Beal, *Marshall in China*, 67.

45. Yang and Bai, *Luo Ronghuan zai dongbei*, 73; He, He Changgong huiyilu, 402–403.

46. Zhang, *Xuebai*, 179.

47. Wetzel, "From the Jaws of Defeat," 153.

48. Lieduofusiji (Ledovsky), *Sidalin yu Zhongguo*, 395. Ledovsky states that the Communist soldiers were down to three bullets (*sanfa zidan*) each, information that he attributes to a conversation between Zhou Enlai and the Soviet ambassador to China on 27 June 1946.

49. Huang, "Cong Subei dao dongbei," 74; Lew, "Becoming God(s)," 119.

50. Yang, *Mao Zedong yu Mosike*, 205. Elsewhere, Yang suggests the figure of twenty-five thousand dead and wounded in fighting from February 1946 through the withdrawal north of the Songhua River. See Yang, "Yijiusiliu nian Guo Gong Siping zhi zhan," 151. In yet another article, Yang gives the figure of around twenty thousand casualties in the battles of Benxi and Siping combined. Yang, "Guanyu jiefang zhanzheng zhong de Sulian junshi yuanzhu wenti."

51. Wang, *Cong kangzhan shengli dao neizhan baofa*, 474.

52. Beal, *Marshall in China*, 66.

53. Detwiler and Burdick, *War in the Pacific, 1937–1949*, 24.

54. Gillin and Meyers, "Introduction," 50; Waldron, "China Without Tears," 385.

55. "Counselor of the Embassy in China to the Secretary of State," 4 and 6 June 1946, in FRUS 1946 IX, 974–75, 995.

56. MIS 269236 General Headquarters, United States Army Forces, Pacific, Military Intelligence Section, General Staff, "Intelligence Summary 1509," 30 May 1946, Army Intelligence File RG 319, Box 1806. Taiwanese scholar Victor Cheng agrees that "the Nationalists failed to eliminate Lin Biao's forces in the battle of Sipingjie" and that the KMT armies had "never had a real chance to eliminate them [the CCP's main forces] on the field." Cheng, "Modern War," 46, 58.

57. Lin Biao to Party Center, 1 June 1946, quoted in Zhang, *Xuebai*, 184.

58. Ibid., 185–87.

59. Mikaberidze, *The Battle of Borodino* and *The Battle of Berezina*.

60. Mikaberidze, *The Battle of Borodino*, 222.

61. Conversation with an elderly resident of Siping, July 2008.

62. Dongbei baoan silingbu, *Jieshou dongbei zhounian jinian ce*; Zhu, *Du jiangjun zai dongbei*.

63. The following description of the capture of Anshan draws on *Siye zhanshi*, 103 and on Liu, *Dongbei jiefang zhanzheng*, 199.

64. Ibid.

65. "Zhongguo renmin jiefangjun disi yezhanjun zhanshi" bianxiezu, *Zhongguo renmin jiefangjun disi yezhanjun zhanshi*, 104.

66. Eastman, *Seeds of Destruction*, 38–40.

67. "Zhongguo renmin jiefangjun disi yezhanjun zhanshi" bianxiezu, *Zhongguo renmin jiefangjun disi yezhanjun zhanshi*, 104; Ma, "Dianjun di yibasi shi Haicheng qiyi," 799–800.

68. Liu, *Dongbei jiefang zhanzheng*, 200.

69. Ma, "Dianjun di yibasi shi Haicheng qiyi," 799–800.

70. Ibid, 801.

71. Liu, *Dongbei jiefang zhanzheng*, 200.

72. Chen, "Dongbei minzhu lianjun chechu Siping," 81.

73. Qin, *Zongtong Jiang gong dashi changbian*, 181.

74. MIS 269236 General Headquarters, United States Army Forces, Pacific, Military Intelligence Section, General Staff, "Intelligence Summary 1508," 29 May 1946, Army Intelligence File RG 319, Box 1799.

75. Marshall to Chiang Kai-shek, 31 May 1946, in van Slyke, *Marshall's Mission to China*, vol. 1, 129.

76. "Mei-Jiang miqie hezuo tusha Zhongguo renmin" [America and Chiang cooperate closely to butcher the Chinese people]. *Mudanjiang ribao*, 3 June 1946, 1.

77. Shepley to Marshall, 23 May 1946, Marshall Mission Records, Box 43, File "Messages—Vol. VI–X, May 1–July 3, 1946."

78. Zhou Enlai to Party Center, 25 May 1946, quoted in Chen, "Dongbei minzhu lianjun chechu Siping," 82.

79. "Fangqi Siping hou wo zhi xingdong fangzhen" [Our principles of operation after giving up Siping], 21 May 1946, in *Mao Zedong junshi wenji disanjuan*, 231.

80. Zheng, *Wode rongma shengya*, 429.

81. Liu, *Dongbei jiefang zhanzheng,* 203. A U.S. Navy intelligence summary forwarded to Marshall reported on 5 June that "present indications CCP intends to fight for Harbin." See "Administrative Office, Commander Seventh Fleet to AL USNA Nanking, copy to Marshall," 5 June 1946, Marshall Mission Records, Box 43, File "Messages—Vol. VIII, 2 June 1946–15 June 1946."

82. Pogue, *George C. Marshall,* 115.

83. Draft of memorandum from Marshall to Wedemeyer, 1 June 1946, Marshall Mission Records, Box 16.

84. *Shilue gaoben,* 2 June 1946, Guoshiguan file no. 002000000693A.

85. Chiang Diaries, 3 June 1946, Box 45, Folder 7.

86. Chiang Diaries, 4 June 1946, Box 45, Folder 7.

87. Taylor, *The Generalissimo,* 353.

88. *Shilue gaoben,* 8 June 1946, Guoshiguan file no. 002000000693A.

89. Marshall to Truman (handwritten draft), 5 June 1946, Marshall Mission Records, Box 16.

90. Quoted in Zhang, "Zhou Enlai and the Marshall Mission," 224.

91. The following description and analysis of the battles of Lafa and Xinzhan draws on Liu, *Dongbei jiefang zhanzheng,* 201–202; and "Zhongguo renmin jiefangjun disi yezhanjun zhanshi" bianxiezu, *Zhongguo renmin jiefangjun disi yezhanjun zhanshi,* 101–102.

92. Marshall to T. V. Soong, undated memorandum, Marshall Mission Records, Box 16. The context places this sometime around mid-June; Chiang Kai-shek to Du Yuming, 12 June 1946, Guoshiguan file no. 002000001941A.

93. Marshall to Truman, 17 June 1946, FRUS 1946 IX, 1099–1101.

94. Marshall to Truman, 30 June 1946, Marshall Mission Records, Box 9, File "Negotiations."

95. Chiang Kai-shek, 26 June 1946, quoted in Wang, "Guo Gong neizhan chuqi," 551.

96. Marshall to Truman, 30 June 1946, Marshall Mission Records, Box 9, File "Negotiations."

97. Wang, "Guo Gong neizhan chuqi," 549.

8. VISIONS OF THE PAST AND FUTURE

1. "Wojun zidong chechu Siping" [Our army voluntarily withdraws from Siping]. *Dongbei ribao,* 23 May 1946, 1.

2. Communist Party Central Committee to Northeast Bureau, 16 July 1946, quoted in Liu, *Dongbei jiefang zhanzheng,* 208.

3. Tian, *Peng Zhen zhuchi,* 209.

4. See excerpts from Chen Yun's original draft quoted in Tian, *Peng Zhen zhuchi,* 210–15.

5. Tian, *Peng Zhen zhuchi,* 215.

6. Zhonggong zhongyang dongbeiju, "Guanyu xingshi he renwu de jueyi" [Decision on the situation and tasks], 7 July 1946, in "Liao-Shen juezhan" bianxie xiaozu, *Liao-Shen juezhan* (shang), 47.

7. Lew, *The Third Chinese Revolutionary Civil War,* 40, 50.

8. Northeast Bureau to Xiao Hua, Cheng Shicai et al., quoted in Liu, *Dongbei jiefang zhanzheng,* 291–92.

9. Ibid.

10. Ibid., 304.

11. Marshall to Truman, undated draft memorandum, probably September 1946, Marshall Mission Records, Box 16.

12. Secretary General Staff Carter to Marshall, 31 December 1946, Marshall Mission Records, Box 16.

13. Marshall to Truman, undated draft memorandum, probably September 1946, Marshall Mission Records, Box 16.

14. For descriptions of land reform, base-building and army-building, see Levine, *Anvil of Victory,* chapters 3, 5, and 6, and Liu, *Dongbei jiefang zhanzheng,* 219–87, 372–441.

15. The following description of the Fourth Battle of Siping draws on Zhongguo renmin jiefangjun disi yezhanjun zhanshi bianxiezu, *Zhongguo renmin jiefangjun disi yezhanjun zhanshi,* 197–202; Liu, *Dongbei jiefang zhanzheng,* 459–72; Zhongguo renmin jiefangjun, *Zhongguo renmin jiefangjun di sishisan jun,* 53–58.

16. Sanjun daxue, *Guomin gemingjun zhanyishi diwubu—kanluan,disice kanluan qianqi (shang),* 718.

17. "Un Sejour en Chine . . . en Mandchourie," 5, Missions Étrangéres.

18. "Zhongguo renmin jiefangjun disi yezhanjun zhanshi" bianxiezu, *Zhongguo renmin jiefangjun disi yezhanjun zhanshi,* 203.

19. *The Precursor,* September-October 1947, 276–77.

20. Lew, *The Third Chinese Revolutionary Civil War,* 69.

21. "*Cheng ren you zhi hua ying bi; sha di liu hong tu yi xiang.*" This couplet includes a number of classical allusions suggesting the continuity of martyrs' sacrifice (their "fulfillment of humaneness," in Confucius' words) in the natural realm. The allusions are difficult, if not impossible, to translate fully. While accepting responsibility for any errors in the translation above, I thank the following who contributed their insights to a Facebook discussion on the couplet: Tim Chan, Michael A. Fuller, Ji Hao, Joerg Henning Huesemann, Lu Yang, Andrew Meyer, Christopher Nugent, Julie Sullivan, and Ping Wang.

22. Pogue, *George Marshall: Statesman,* 111.

23. Huang, *Huang Kecheng zishu,* 205.

24. Communist Party Center to all military districts, 27 May 1946, *Mao Zedong junshi wenji,* vol. 3, 236.

25. Zhongguo renmmin jiefangjun, *Zhongguo renmin jiefangjun disishisanjun,* 29–30.

26. Zhongguo renmin jiefangjun gaodeng junshi xueyuan, *Siping baoweizhan,* 4–5.

27. Ibid., 6.

28. Ibid., 8–10.

29. Ibid., 1, 6.

30. Han Xianchu, quoted in Yao and Li, *Liao-Shen zhanyi shilu,* 105.

31. He Zhefeng, "Guanyu Siping baoweizhan de yixie wenti," 17–18.

32. "Zhongguo renmin jiefangjun disi yezhanjun zhanshi" bianxiezu, *Zhongguo renmin jiefangjun disi yezhanjun zhanshi,* 99.

33. *Sizhan Siping,* Episode 5.

34. Ibid.

35. Montecuccoli, quoted in Rothenburg, "Maurice of Nassau," 56.

36. Chiang, *Soviet Russia in China*, 166–68.

37. Waldron, "China Without Tears," 385.

38. Jiang, *Kanluan jianshi*, 31.

39. Wang, "Quanmian neizhan chuqi," 98; Cheng, "Modern War on an Ancient Battlefield," 38–64. The following paragraphs draw on Cheng's article.

40. "A Japanese Looks at China." Records of General Headquarters, Box 1, Folder "China 0106 Military Operations."

41. Cheng, "Modern War on an Ancient Battlefield," 47.

42. The following draws on Sanjun daxue, *Guomin gemingjun zhanyi shi diwubu—kanluan, dijiuce: zong jiantao*, 70–73.

BIBLIOGRAPHY

ARCHIVAL SOURCES

Army Intelligence File   Army Intelligence File, Record Group 319. National Archives and Records Administration, College Park, MD.

Chiang Diaries   Chiang Kai-shek Diaries, Chiang Kai-shek Collection. Hoover Institution Archives, Stanford, CA.

Dangshiguan   Zhongguo Guomindang dangshiguan (Archives of the Chinese Nationalist Party), Taipei, Taiwan.

FRUS   Foreign Relations of the United States, various volumes and years. U.S. Government Printing Office, Washington, DC.

Guojia dang'an guanliju   National Archives Records Administration Office, Taipei, Taiwan.

Guoshiguan   Academia Historica (Guoshiguan), Taipei, Taiwan.

Marshall Mission Records   General Records of the Department of State, Marshall Mission Records, 1944–1948. Record Group 59. National Archives and Records Administration, College Park, MD.

Missions Étrangéres   Archives of the Missions Étrangéres, Laval, Quebec. I thank Gilles Dubé, p.m.é., Secrétaire general of the Societé des Missions-Étrangéres, for providing this material.

Records of General Headquarters   Records of General Headquarters, Far East Command, Supreme Commander Allied Powers, and United Nations Command Intelligence Reports, 1946–50 Burma-China 0106. Record Group 554, National Archives and Records Administration, College Park, MD.

Shilue gaoben   [Draft biographical sketch]. Academia Historica, Taipei.

NEWSPAPERS

Dagongbao   [The Impartial]. Shanghai.

Dongbei ribao   [Northeast Daily]. Various locations (Communist-controlled).

Mudanjiang ribao	[Mudanjiang Daily]. Mudanjiang, Heilongjiang Province (Communist-controlled).
Qianjinbao	[The Advance Gazette]. Shenyang (Nationalist-controlled).
Xinbao	[The New Paper]. Shenyang (Nationalist-controlled).

CHINESE-LANGUAGE SOURCES

Chen Cungong and Li Zhang, eds. *Shi Jue xiansheng fangwen jilu* [Record of interviews with Mr. Shi Jue]. Taipei: Zhongyang yanjiuyuan jindaishi yanjiusuo, 1986.

Chen Dejun. "Dongbei minzhu lianjun chechu Siping, Changchun hou bu bei zhizhui kao" [Why the Northeast Democratic United Army was not pursued after withdrawing from Siping and Changchun]. *Junshi lishi yanjiu* 2 (2007): 79–84.

Chen Jiazhen. "Changchun diyici jiefang qianhou de qingkuang" [The situation in Changchun around the time of its first liberation]. In Zhou, *Wenshi ziliao cungao xuanbian quanmian neizhan* (shang), 767–70.

Chen Lian. "Jiefang zhanzheng guodu jieduan zhonggong zhongyang luequ dongbei de zhanlue fangzhen yu bushu" [The Communist Party Center's strategy and deployment for capturing the Northeast in the transitional period of the Liberation War]. *Junshi lishi* 2 (2002): 53–57.

Chen Shoulin, Shi Yue, Zhang Qingfeng, Zhang Yanhu, and Ji Hanwen. *Sizhan Siping shi* [History of the Four Battles of Siping]. Changchun: Jilin wenshi chubanshe, 2007.

Chen Yi. "Siping baowei zhan" [The Battle to Defend Siping]. In Gao, *Sizhan Siping,* 216–25.

———. "Zong xu" [General introduction]. In Dong, *Tingjin dongbei,* 1–6.

Chen Ying. "Liu Shaoqi zhidao wojun jinjun dongbei de lilun yu shijian" [Theory and practice of Liu Shaoqi directing our forces to advance into the Northeast]. *Junshi lishi yanjiu* 3 (2007): 36–42.

Cheng Jiawen. "Guo Gong neizhan zhong de dongbei zhanchang" [The Northeast theater in the civil war between the Communists and Nationalists]. MA thesis, Taiwan National University, 1989.

Ding Xiaochun, Ge Fulu, and Wang Shiying, eds. *Dongbei jiefang zhanzheng dashiji* [Major events of the War of Liberation in the Northeast]. Beijing: Zhonggong dangshi ziliao chubanshe, 1987.

Dong Dianwen. *Tingjin Dongbei* [Advancing into the Northeast]. Shenyang: Liaoning renmin chubanshe, 1998.

Dongbei baoan silingbu. *Jieshou dongbei zhounian jinian ce* [Souvenir volume of the first anniversary of the transfer of sovereignty of the Northeast]. Liaoning Province Archives, n.d.

Du Weiwei. "Kangzhan shengli chuqi guogong liangdang weirao dongbei wenti de douzheng celue zhi bijiao" [Comparison of the Northeast strategies of the Nationalist and Communist parties on the early post–War of Resistance period]. *Junshi lishi yanjiu* 1 (2003): 60–67.

Du Yuming. "Jingong dongbei shimo" [The story of the attack on the Northeast]. In *Zhonghua wenshi ziliao wenku, zhengzhi junshi bian diliujuan (20–6) sanian juezhan* (shang) [Compendium of Chinese historical materials, part six, political and military affairs, (20–6), the three years of decisive battle (Vol. 1)], 504–32. Beijing: Zhongguo wenshi chubanshe, 1996.

Gao Yongchang, ed. *Sizhan Siping* [The Four Battles of Siping]. Changchun: Zhonggong Jilin shengwei dangshi gongzuo weiyuanhui, 1988.

Guan Wei. "Lun dongbei ge minzu kangri douzheng de tedian" [Characteristics of various ethnic groups' resistance to the Japanese in the Northeast]. *Junshi lishi yanjiu* 1 (2008): 71–81.

Guo Tingyi and Jia Tinghi, eds. *Bai Chongxi xiansheng fangwen jilu* [Record of interviews with Mr. Bai Chongxi]. Taipei: Zhongyang yanjiuyuan jindaishi yanjiusuo, 1984.

He Changgong. *He Changgong huiyilu* [Memoirs of He Changgong]. Beijing: Jiefangjun, 1987.

He Di. "1945–1949 nian Zhongguo gongchandang duimei zhengce de yanbian" [The development of the Chinese Communist Party's policy toward America, 1945–1949]. *Lishi yanjiu* [Historical research] 3 (1987): 15–23.

Hu Zhefeng. "Guanyu Siping baoweizhan de yixie wenti" [Some questions concerning the Battle to Defend Siping]. *Dangshi yanjiu ziliao* 9 (1996): 17–24.

———. "Shilun Siping baoweizhan zhong de Mao Zedong yu Lin Biao" [On Mao Zedong and Lin Biao in the Battle to Defend Siping]. *Junshi lishi yanjiu* [Research in Military History], 4 (1996): 1–12.

Huang Kecheng. "Cong Subei dao dongbei—xinsijun disan shi jinjun dongbei canjia dongbei jiefang zhanzheng de huigu" [From Subei to the Northeast—recollections of the New Fourth Army Third Division's deployment in the Northeast to join the War of Liberation in the Northeast]. *Zhonggong dangshi ziliao* 16 (1985): 56–81.

———. *Huang Kecheng zishu* [Huang Kecheng in his own words]. Beijing: Renmin chubanshe, 1994.

Huang Renlin. *Wo zuo Jiang Jieshi 'teqin zongguan' sishi nian—Huang Renlin huiyilu* [My forty years as Chiang Kai-shek's chief of special services—the memoirs of General Huang Renlin]. Beijing: Tuanjie chubanshe, 2006.

Jiang Jieshi (Chiang Kai-shek). *Su E zai Zhongguo* [Soviet Russia in China]. In Zhang, *Xian zongtong Jiang gong quanji*, 280–423.

Jiang Zhongzheng (Chiang Kai-shek). *Kanluan jianshi (yi)* [A short history of bandit suppression]. Taipei: Guofangbu shizhengju, 1962.

Jin Dongji, trans. *Sulian chubing Zhongguo dongbei jishi* [Record of Soviet operations in China's Northeast]. Chengdu: Sichuan chuban jituan, 2005.

Jin Yunfang, Sun Kewen, Ge Fulu, Ding Lisun, and Ding Xiaochun. "Kangri zhanzheng shengli hou zai dongbei wenti shang san guo sifang de guanxi he douzheng" [The relations and struggles of three countries and four parties on the Northeast question following victory in the War of Resistance Against Japan]. *Zhonggong dangshi ziliao* 28 (1988): 150–79.

Junshi kexueyuan junshi lishi yanjiubu, ed. *Zhongguo renmin jiefangjun zhanshi di yi juan tudi geming zhanzheng shiqi* [Battle history of the Chinese People's Liberation Army. Vol. 1, the period of the land revolution]. Beijing: Junshi kexue chubanshe, 1987.

Lieduofusiji (A. M. Ledovsky). *Sidalin yu Zhongguo*. Translated by Chen Cunhua and Liu Cunkuan. Beijing: Xinhua chubanshe, 2001.

Li Daren. *Dongbei kanluan huiyi* [Memoir of bandit suppression in the Northeast]. Taipei: Boxue chubanshe, 1979.

Li Hongwen and Wang Jing. "Dongbei kangri lianjun de douzheng licheng" [The Northeast anti-Japanese army's course of struggle]. *Zhonggong dangshi ziliao* 15 (1985): 128–72.

Li Yunchang. "Kongzhi zhanlue shuniu Shanhaiguan" [Control the strategic hub of Shanhaiguan]. In Yuan, *Shanhaiguan zhi zhan*, 5–30.

"Liaoshen juezhan" bianxie xiaozu. *Liaoshen juezhan* (shang, xia liangce) [The Liao-Shen Campaign. 2 vols.]. Beijing: Renmin chubanshe, 1988.

"Lin Biao de liuge zhanshu yuanze" [Lin Biao's six principles of tactics]. Accessed 8 July 2010. http://wangxudong99999.blog.163.com/blog/static/32271742200881911432162/

Lin Biao. "Lin Biao tongzhi guanyu dongbei luxian fenqi wenti zhi Mao zhuxi, Liu Shaoqi dian" [Comrade Lin Biao's telegram to Mao Zedong and Liu Shaoqi regarding disagreement on the line to be taken in the Northeast]. 13 March 1946. Copy in the author's possession.

Liu Baiyu. *Liu Baiyu dongbei zhanchang tongxunxuan* [Liu Baiyu's selected dispatches from the Northeast]. Beijing: Xinhua chubanshe, 1986.

———. *Shidai de yinxiang* [Impressions of an era]. Guanghua shudian, 1948.

Liu Tong. *Dongbei jiefang zhanzheng jishi* [True record of the War of Liberation in the Northeast]. Beijing: Renmin chubanshe, 2004.

———. "Jiefang zhanzheng zhong dongbei yezhanjun wuqilaiyuan tantao—jian yu Yang Kuisong xiansheng shangque" [An inquiry into the sources of the Northeast Field Army's weapons during the War of Liberation—a discussion with Mr. Yang Kuisong]. *Dang de wenxian* 4 (2000): 76–80.

Lü Fangshang, ed. *Jiang Zhongzheng riji yu Minguoshi yanjiu* [Jiang Zhongzheng's diary and research on Republican history]. Taipei: Shijie datong, 2011.

Luo Wei. *Jiqing suiyue: yiwei Xinhuashe nujizhe de dongbei riji* [Years of Passion: a female Xinhua new reporter's diary of the Northeast]. Beijing: Xinhua chubanshe, 2007.

Ma Mianfei. "Dianjun di yibasi shi Haicheng qiyi huiyi" [Memories of the Yunnan Army 184th Division's Haicheng Uprising]. In Zhou, *Wenshi ziliao cungao xuanbian*, 799–800.

Mao Zedong. *Mao Zedong junshi wenji* [Collected military writings of Mao Zedong]. Beijing: Junshi kexue chubanshe, 1993.

———. *Mao Zedong junshi wenxuan* (neibuben) [Selected military writings of Mao Zedong (internal edition)]. Beijing: Zhongguo renmin jiefangjun zhanshi chubanshe, 1981.

Niu Jun. *Cong Yan'an zouxiang shijie: Zhongguo gongchandang de duiwai guanxide qiyuan* [From Yan'an to the world: the origins of the Chinese Communist Party's foreign policy]. Fuzhou: Fujian renmin chubanshe, 1992.

Pan Xiting et al. *Dongbei kang-Ri yiyongjun shi* [History of the volunteer anti-Japanese army in the Northeast]. Shenyang: Liaoning renmin chubanshe, 1985.

"Peng Zhen zhuan" bianxiezu, ed. *Peng Zhen nianpu* [Chronology of Peng Zhen]. Beijing: Zhongyang wenxian chubanshe, 2002.

Peng Zhen. "Guanyu dizhanqu de chengshi gongzuo" [On urban work in enemy-occupied areas]. 3 May 1945. In Peng, *Peng Zhen wenxuan*, 79–80.

———. "Dongbei jiefang zhanzheng de tou jiuge yue" [The first nine months of the Liberation War in the Northeast]. In Tian, *Peng Zhen zhuchi*, 253–68.

———. *Peng Zhen wenxuan* [Selected writings of Peng Zhen]. Beijing: Renmin chubanshe, 1991.

Qin Xiaoyi, ed. *Zongtong Jiang gong dashi changbian chugao* (juan liu, shangce) [Major events of President Chiang Kai-shek, preliminary draft. Part 6, Vol. 1.]. Taipei: Caituan faren Zhongzheng wenjiao jijinhui, 1978.

Qiu Weijia and Cao Hong, eds. *Zhongguo yongshi: disi yezhanjun* [China's heroic forces: the Fourth Field Army]. Beijing: Zhonggong dangshi chubanshe, 2005.

Sanjun daxue, ed. *Guomin gemingjun zhanyishi diwubu—kanluan, dijiuce: zong jiantao* [Combat history of the National Revolutionary Army section five—rebellion suppression, part nine: general analysis]. Taipei: Guofangbu shizheng bianyiju, 1989.

———. *Guomin gemingjun zhanyishi diwubu—kanluan, disice kanluan qianqi (shang)* [Combat history of the National Revolutionary Army section five—rebellion suppression, part four, the early stages of rebellion suppression (Vol. 1)]. Taipei: Guofangbu shizheng bianyiju, 1989.

Shi Zhe. *Feng yu gu: Shi Zhe huiyilu* [Peaks and valleys: the memoirs of Shi Zhe]. Beijing: Hongqi chubanshe, 1992.

———. *Zai lishi juren shenbian: Shi Zhe huiyilu* [Beside the giants of history: the memoirs of Shi Zhe]. Beijing: Zhongyang wenxian chubanshe, 1995.

Siping shi difangzhi biancuan weiyuanhui, ed. *Siping shizhi* (shang) [Siping city gazetteer (Vol. 1)]. Changchun: Jilin renmin chubanshe, 1993.

Sizhan Siping: 15 ji lishi wenxianpian [The four battles of Siping: a 15-episode historical documentary]. DVD. Directed by Wang Yongxing. Siping, China: Siping wenhua xinwen chubanju, 2008.

Tian Youru. *Peng Zhen zhuchi dongbeiju* [Peng Zhen's leadership of the Northeast Bureau]. Beijing: Renmin chubanshe, 2007.

Wan Yi. "Huiyi Siping sici zuozhan" [Recalling the Four Battles of Siping]. In Gao, *Sizhan Siping*, 187–95.

Wang Chaoguang. *Cong kangzhan shengli dao neizhan baofa qianhou* [From the victory of the War of Resistance to the outbreak of civil war]. Beijing: Zhonghua shuju, 2000.

———. "Guo Gong neizhan chuqi de dongbei zhanchang yu Jiang Jieshi de junshi juece." In Lü, *Jiang Zhongzheng riji yu Minguoshi yanjiu*, 519–54.

———. "Quanmian neizhan chuqi Guomindang junshi shili yuanyin zhi bianxi" [Analysis of the reasons for the Nationalist loss of advantage in the preliminary stages of the Civil War]. *Minguo dang'an* [Republican archives] (January 2005): 97–105.

Wang Hongqi. "Jinjun dongbei haiyun ji" [Record of advancing into the Northeast by sea]. In Zhongguo renmin jiefangjun, *Houqin gongzuo shiliao*, 467–70.

Wu Xiuquan. *Wode licheng* [My journey]. Beijing: Jiefangjun chubanshe, 1984.

Wu Yuzhang. *Wu Yuzhang huiyilu* [Memoir of Wu Yuzhang]. Beijing: Zhongguo qingnian chubanshe, 1978.

Yang Jingbin, ed. *Wushier jun kanluan zhanyi jishi* [True record of the Fifty-second Army's bandit suppression campaigns]. Taipei: Beida shuju, 1956.

Yang Kuisong. "1946 nian guogong liangdang douzheng yu Marshall tiaochu" [The struggle between the Communist and the Nationalist parties and Marshall's mediation]. *Lishi yanjiu* [Historical research] 5 (1990): 52–67.

———. "Yijiusiliu nian Guo Gong Siping zhi zhan ji qi muhou" [Behind the scenes of the Communist vs. Nationalist Battle of Siping, 1946]. *Lishi yanjiu* 4 (2004): 132–52.

———. "Guanyu jiefang zhanzheng zhong de Sulian junshi yuanzhu wenti—jian tan zhixue taidu bing da Liu Tong xiansheng" [On the question of Soviet military aid during the Liberation War—together with a discussion of scholarship and a response to Mr. Liu Tong]. *Jindaishi yanjiu* 1 (2001): 285–306.

———. *Guomindang de "liangong," "fangong"* [Kuomintang: unity with Communists and anti-Communism]. Beijing: Shehui kexue wenxian chubanshe, 2007.

———. *Mao Zedong yu Mosike de enen yuanyuan* [Mao Zedong and Moscow: favor and frustation]. Nanchang: Jiangxi renmin chubanshe, 2009.

———. *Zhongjian didai de geming—Zhongguo geming de celue zai guoji beijing xia de yanbian* [Revolution in the middle realms—the unfolding of strategy in China's revolution in international context]. Beijing: Zhonggong zhongyang dangxiao chubanshe, 1992.

———. *Zouxiang polie: Mao Zedong yu Mosike de enen yuanyuan* [Walking toward a breakup: Mao Zedong and his frustrations and gratitude toward Moscow]. Hong Kong: Sanlian chubanshe, 1999.

"*Xiangqi*." Accessed 3 June 2009. http://www.chessvariants.com/xiangqi.html.

Yang Guoqing and Bai Ren. *Luo Ronghuan zai dongbei jiefang zhanzheng zhong* [Luo Ronghuan in the Liberation War in the Northeast]. Beijing: Jiefangjun chubanshe, 1986.

Yao Youzhi and Li Qingshan, eds. *Liaoshen zhanyi shilu* [True record of the Liao-Shen Campaign]. Shenyang: Baishan, 2007.

Yuan Wei, ed. *Shanhaiguan zhi zhan* [The Battle of Shanhaiguan]. Beijing: Junshi kexue chubanshe, 1989.

Zhang Jiayu, ed. *Mao Zedong junshi nianpu, 1925–1958* [Military chronology of Mao Zedong, 1925–1958]. Nanning: Guangxi renmin chubanshe, 1994.

Zhang Heming. "Guanyu Shanhaiguan baoweizhan de zongjie baogao" [Summary report on the Battle to Defend Shanhaiguan]. In Yuan, *Shanhaiguan zhi zhan*, 160–78.

Zhang Qiyun, ed. *Xian zongtong Jiang gong quanji* [Complete works of Former President Jiang]. Taipei: Zhongguo wenhua daxue, 1984.

Zhang Zhenglong. *Xuebai, xuehong: Guo Gong dongbei da juezhan lishi zhenxiang* [Snow white, blood red: the true history of the Communists' and Nationalists' decisive struggle for the Northeast]. Hong Kong: Dadi, 1991.

Zhao Qingxuan. *Dongbei jiefang daquanjing* [The liberation of the Northeast: the big picture]. Beijing: Zhonggong dangshi chubanshe, 1998.

Zheng Dongguo. *Wode rongma shengya—Zheng Dongguo huiyilu* [My military career—the memoirs of Zheng Dongguo]. Beijing: Tuanjie chubanshe, 1992

Zheng Dongguo, Hou Jingru, Tan Yizhi, Wen Qiang, Zheng Tingji, and Yang Baitao. *Du Yuming jiangjun* [General Du Yuming]. Beijing: Zhongguo wenshi chubanshe, 1986.

Zhengzhi xueyuan diyi junshi jiaoyanshi, ed. *Zhongguo renmin jiefangjun zhanyi zhanli xuanbian* (er) [Selected exemplary battles of the Chinese People's Liberation Army (2)]. Beijing: Jiefangjun zhengzhi xueyuan chubanshe, 1984.

Zhonggong zhongyang dang'anguan, ed. *Zhonggong zhongyang wenjian xuanji di shiwu ce (1945)* [Selected documents of the Chinese Communist Party Central Committee. Vol. 15 (1945).]. Beijing: Zhonggong zhongyang dangxiao chubanshe, 1991.

Zhongyang dang'anguan, ed. *Zhonggong zhongyang wenjian xuanji di shiliu ce (1946–1947)* [Selected documents of the Central Committee of the Chinese Communist Party. Vol. 16 (1946–1947)]. Beijing: Zhonggong zhongyang dangxiao chubanshe, 1992.

Zhonggong zhongyang wenxian yanjiushi, ed. *Liu Shaoqi nianpu* [Chronicle of Liu Shaoqi]. Beijing: Zhongyang wenxian chubanshe, 1996.

———, ed. *Zhou Enlai nianpu (1898–1949)* [Chronicle of Zhou Enlai (1848–1949)]. 2 vols. Beijing: Zhongyang wenxian chubanshe, 2007.

Zhonggong zhongyang wenxian yanjiushi, Zhonggong zhongyang Nanjingshi weiyuanhui, ed. *Zhou Enlai yijiusiliu nian tanpan wenxuan* [Selected documents from Zhou Enlai's 1946 negotiations]. Beijing: Zhongyang wenxian chubanshe, 1996.

Zhongguo Gongchandang Jilin sheng Siping shi zuzhi shiliao (1931–1987) [Historical materials on the organization of the Chinese Communist Party in the city of Siping, Jilin Province (1931–1987)]. Siping: Zhonggong Siping shiwei zuzhibu, n.d.

"Zhongguo renmin jiefangjun disi yezhanjun zhanshi" bianxiezu, ed. *Zhongguo renmin jiefangjun disi yezhanjun zhanshi* [Campaign history of the People's Liberation Army Fourth Field Army]. Beijing: Jiefangjun chubanshe, 1998.

Zhongguo renmin jiefangjun di sishisan jun silingbu, ed. *Zhongguo renmin jiefangjun di sishisan jun disanci guonei geming zhanshi* (chugao) [Campaign history of the People's Liberation Army Forty-third Army in China's Third Revolution (draft)]. n.p., 1956.

Zhongguo renmin jiefangjun di sishiyijun silingbu, ed. *Zhongguo renmin jiefangjun di sishiyijun disanci guonei geming zhanshi* (chugao) [Campaign history of the People's Liberation Army Forty-first Army in China's Third Revolution (draft)]. n.p., 1956.

Zhongguo renmin jiefangjun gaodeng junshi xuexiao xunlianbu. "Siping baoweizhan (chugao)" [The Battle to Defend Siping (draft)]. Document #000338. Liaoshen Campaign Memorial Hall Reference Room, Jinzhou, Liaoning Province, China.

Zhongguo renmin jiefangjun lishi ziliao bianshen weiyuanhui, ed. *Houqin gongzuo shiliao* (1) [Historical materials on logistics work (1)]. Beijing: Jiefangjun chubanshe, 1994.

Zhongguo renmin jiefangjun disi yezhanjun zhanshi bianxiezu, ed. *Zhongguo renmin jiefangjun disi yezhanjun zhanshi* [Campaign history of the People's Liberation Army Fourth Field Army]. Beijing: Jiefangjun chubanshe, 1998.

Zhou Hongyan, ed. *Wenshi ziliao cungao xuanbian quanmian neizhan* (shang) [Selected draft historical materials on the period of civil war. Vol. 1.]. Beijing: Zhongguo wenshi chubanshe, 2002.

Zhu Lun. *Du jiangjun zai dongbei* [General Du in the Northeast]. Liaoning Provincial Archives, n.d.

Zuo Ye. "Huiyi yizhan Siping he baowei Siping zhan" [Remembering the First Battle of Siping and the Battle to Defend Siping]. In Gao, *Sizhan Siping*, 277–79.

WESTERN-LANGUAGE SOURCES

Absoluteastronomy.com. "Type 38 rifle." Accessed 4 April 2010. http://www.absolute astronomy.com/topics/Type_38_rifle.

Atkinson, George W. "The Sino-Soviet Treaty of Friendship and Alliance." *International Affairs (Royal Institute of International Affairs 1944–)* 23, no. 3 (1947): 357–66.

Beal, John Robinson. *Marshall in China.* Toronto: Doubleday, 1970.

Beevor, Antony. *The Spanish Civil War.* New York: Peter Bedrick Books, 1983.

Bjorge, Gary J. *Moving the Enemy: Operational Art in the Chinese PLA's Huai Hai Campaign.* Fort Leavenworth, KS: Combat Studies Press, 2004.

Black, Jeremy. *Rethinking Military History.* London: Routledge, 2004.

———. *War and the World: Military Power and the Fate of Continents, 1450–2000.* New Haven, CT: Yale University Press, 1998.

Bland, Larry I., ed. *George C. Marshall's Mediation Mission to China, December 1945–January 1947.* Lexington, VA: George C. Marshall Foundation, 1998.

Boorman, Howard L., ed. *Biographical Dictionary of Republican China.* New York: Columbia University Press, 1970.

Carter, James Hugh. *Creating a Chinese Harbin: Nationalism in an International City, 1916–1932.* Ithaca, NY: Cornell University Press, 2002.

Central Intelligence Agency. "East and Southeast Asia: China." Accessed 4 April 2010. https://www.cia.gov/library/publications/the-world-factbook/geos/ch.html.

Chang, Jung and Jon Halliday. *Mao: The Unknown Story.* New York: Anchor Books, 2006.

Cheng, Shiu Chiang. "The Escalation of Hostilities in Manchuria, 1945–47: A Study of Strategic Realities and Normative Guidelines in Military Conflict in the Context of the Civil War." PhD diss., University of Melbourne, 2002.

Cheng, Victor Shiu Chiang. "Imagining China's Madrid in Manchuria: The Communist Military Strategy at the Onset of the Chinese Civil War, 1945–1946." *Modern China* 31, no. 1 (2005): 72–114.

———. "Modern War on an Ancient Battlefield: The Diffusion of American Military Technology and Ideas in the Chinese Civil War, 1946–1949." *Modern China* 35, no. 1 (2009): 38–64.

Chiang Chung-cheng (Chiang Kai-shek). *Soviet Russia in China: A Summing-up at Seventy.* New York: Farrar, Straus and Company, 1957.

"China: 400 Million Humiliations." *Time,* December 16, 1929. Accessed 10 May 2011. http://www.time.com/time/magazine/article/0,9171,881861,00.html.

Clubb, O. Edmund. "Manchuria in the Balance, 1945–1946." *Pacific Historical Review* 26, no. 4 (1957): 381–83.

Coogan, Anthony. "Northeast China and the Origins of the Anti-Japanese United Front." *Modern China* 20, no. 3 (1994): 282–314.

Coox, Alvin D. and Hilary Conroy, eds. *China and Japan: Search for Balance Since World War I.* Santa Barbara, CA: Clio, 1978.

Detwiler, Donald S. and Charles B. Burdick, eds. *War in the Pacific, 1937–1949, Volume 15: The Sino-Japanese and Chinese Civil Wars (Part III).* New York: Garland Publishing, 1980.

Cowley, Robert, ed. *What If? The World's Foremost Military Historians Imagine What Might Have Been.* New York: G. Putnam's Sons, 1999.

Donovan, Robert J. *Conflict and Crisis in the Presidency of Harry S. Truman, 1945–1948.* New York: Norton, 1977.

Dreyer, Edward L. *China at War, 1901–1949.* London: Longman, 1995.

Duara, Prasenjit. *Sovereignty and Authenticity: Manchukuo and the East Asian Modern.* Lanham, MD: Rowman and Littlefield, 2003.

Duus, Peter, Ramon H. Myers, and Mark R. Peattie, eds. *The Japanese Informal Empire in China, 1895–1937.* Princeton, NJ: Princeton University Press, 1991.

Eastman, Lloyd. *Seeds of Destruction: Nationalist China in War and Revolution, 1937–1949.* Stanford, CA: Stanford University Press, 1984.

Elleman, Bruce A. *Modern Chinese Warfare, 1795–1989.* London: Routledge, 2001.

———. "Soviet Sea Denial and the KMT-CCP Civil War on Manchuria, 1945–1949." In Elleman and Paine, *Naval Coalition Warfare,* 119–29.

Elleman, Bruce A. and Stephen Kotkin, eds. *Manchurian Railways and the Opening of China: An International History.* Armonk, NY: M. E. Sharpe, 2010.

Elleman, Bruce A. and S. C. M. Paine, eds. *Naval Coalition Warfare: From the Napoleonic War to Operation Iraqi Freedom.* London: Routledge, 2008.

Garthoff, Raymond L., ed. *Sino-Soviet Military Relations.* New York: Praeger, 1966.

Garthoff, Raymond L. "Soviet Intervention in Manchuria." In Garthoff, *Sino-Soviet Military Relations,* 57–81.

Gillin, Donald G. and Ramon H. Myers. "Introduction." In Gillin and Myers, *Last Chance in Manchuria*, 1–58.

Gillin, Donald G. and Ramon Myers, eds. *Last Chance in Manchuria: The Diary of Chang Kia-ngau*. Stanford, CA: Hoover Institution, 1989.

Glantz, David. *Soviet Operational and Tactical Combat in Manchuria, 1945: August Storm.* London: Frank Cass, 2003.

———. *The Soviet Strategic Offensive in Manchuria, 1945: "August Storm."* London: Frank Cass, 2003.

Gottschang, Thomas and Diana Lary. *Swallows And Settlers: The Great Migration from North China to Manchuria*. Ann Arbor: Michigan Monographs in Chinese Studies, 2000.

H-Diplo Roundtable. *Racing the Enemy Roundtable, Alperovitz on Hasegawa*. http://www.h-net.org/~diplo/roundtables/PDF/Alperovitz-HasegawaRoundtable.pdf.

Harari, Yuval Noah. "The Concept of 'Decisive Battles' in World History." *Journal of World History* 18, no. 3 (2007), 251–66.

Hasegawa, Tsuyoshi. *Racing the Enemy: Stalin, Truman, and the Surrender of Japan.* Cambridge, MA: Harvard University Press, 2006.

He Di. "Mao Zedong and the Marshall Mission." In Bland, *George C. Marshall's Mediation Mission to China*, 173–99.

Heinzig, Dieter. *The Soviet Union and Communist China, 1945–1950: The Arduous Road to the Alliance.* Armonk, NY: M. E. Sharpe, 2004.

Herzstein, Robert E. *Henry R. Luce, "Time," and the American Crusade in Asia.* Cambridge: Cambridge University Press, 2005.

Hills, George. *The Battle for Madrid.* London: Vantage Books, 1976.

Howard, Michael. *The Lessons of History.* New Haven, CT: Yale University Press, 1991.

Huang, Ray. "Some Observations on Manchuria in the Balance, Early 1946." *Pacific Historical Review* (May 1958): 159–69

Hunter, Janet, ed. *Japanese Economic History 1930–1960.* Vol. 8, *The Industrialization of Japan and Manchukuo, 1930–40.* London: Routledge, 2000.

Katsuji, Nakagane. "Manchukuo and Economic Development." In Duus, Myers, and Peattie, *The Japanese Informal Empire*, 133–57.

Kuropatkin, Aleksei Nikolaevich. *The Russian Army and the Japanese War, Being Historical and Critical Comments on the Military Policy and Power of Russia and on the Campaign in the Far East.* London: John Murray, 1909.

Lattimore, Owen. *Manchuria: Cradle of Conflict.* New York: Macmillan, 1932.

Lee, Chong-sik. *Counter-insurgency in Manchuria: The Japanese Experience, 1931–1940.* Santa Monica, CA: RAND Corporation, 1967.

———. "The Chinese Communist Party and the Anti-Japanese Movement: The Initial Stage." In Coox and Conroy, *China and Japan: Search for Balance*, 141–72.

———. *Revolutionary Struggle in Manchuria.* Berkeley: University of California Press, 1983.

Levine, Steven. "A New Look at American Mediation in the Chinese Civil War: the Marshall Mission and Manchuria." *Diplomatic History* 3, no. 4 (1979): 349–75.

———. *Anvil of Victory: The Communist Revolution in Manchuria, 1945–1948.* New York: Columbia University Press, 1987.

Lew, Christopher. "Becoming God(s): CCP Strategy and Hierarchy During the Third Revolutionary Civil War (1945–1949)." PhD diss., University of Pennsylvania, 2005.

———. *The Third Chinese Revolutionary Civil War, 1945–49: An Analysis of Communist Strategy and Leadership.* London: Routledge, 2009.

MacKinnon, Stephen R. *Wuhan, 1938: War, Refugees, and the Making of Modern China.* Berkeley: University of California Press, 2008.

Mao Zedong. *Selected Works of Mao Tse-tung.* Vol. 4. Peking: Foreign Languages Press, 1969.

McCarthy, Joseph. *America's Retreat from Victory: The Story of George Catlett Marshall.* New York: The Devin-Adair Company, 1951.

McClain, James L. *Japan: A Modern History.* New York: W. W. Norton & Co., 2002.

Marks, Steven G. *Road to Power: The Trans-Siberian Railroad and the Colonization of Asian Russia, 1850–1917.* Ithaca, NY: Cornell University Press, 1991.

Marshall, George. "Report." In van Slyke, *Marshall's Mission to China.* Vol. 1, 1–457.

May, Ernest R. "1947–48: When Marshall Kept the U.S. Out of War in China." *Journal of Military History* 166, no. 4 (2002), 1001–10.

Melby, John F. *Mandate of Heaven: Record of a Civil War, China 1945–49.* New York: Anchor Books, 1971.

Mikaberidze, Alexander. *The Battle of Borodino: Napoleon Against Kutuzov.* Barnsley, South Yorkshire: Pen and Sword, 2007.

———. *The Battle of Berezina: Napoleon's Great Escape.* Barnsley, South Yorkshire: Pen and Sword, 2010.

Missions Étrangéres, "Un Sejour en Chine . . . en Mandchourie," (n.d.), Missions Étrangéres.

Mitter, Rana. *The Manchurian Myth: Nationalism, Resistance, and Collaboration in Modern China.* Berkeley: University of California Press, 2000.

Myers, Ramon. "Frustration, Fortitude, and Friendship: Chiang Kai-shek's Reactions to Marshall's Mission." In Bland, *George C. Marshall's Mission to China,* 149–71.

Paine, S. C. M. "The Chinese Eastern Railway from the First Sino-Japanese War until the Russo-Japanese War." In Elleman and Kotkin, *Manchurian Railways,* 13–36.

Paret, Peter, ed. *Makers of Modern Strategy: From Machiavelli to the Nuclear Age.* Princeton, NJ: Princeton University Press, 1986.

Paret, Peter. "Napoleon and the Revolution in War." In Paret, *Makers of Modern Strategy,* 123–42.

Peattie, Mark, Edward J. Drea, and Hans van de Ven, eds. *The Battle for China: Essays on the Military History of the Sino-Japanese War of 1937–1945.* Stanford, CA: Stanford University Press, 2011.

Pepper, Suzanne. *Civil War in China: The Political Struggle, 1945–1949.* Berkeley: University of California Press, 1978.

Pogue, Forrest C. *George C. Marshall: Education of a General, 1880–1939.* New York: Viking Press, 1963.

———. *George C. Marshall: Organizer of Victory, 1943–1945.* New York: Viking Press, 1973.

———. *George Marshall: Statesman, 1945–1959.* New York: Viking Press, 1987.

"The Precursor." Material in the possession of the author. "The Precursor" is a publication of the Missionary Sisters of the Immaculate Conception, who had a mission in Siping from around 1927 through 1953. I am much indebted to Sister Huguette Turcotte, M.I.C., for her kind assistance in providing this and other material documenting the experiences of the Missionary Sisters in Siping in the 1940s.

Rigg, Robert. *Red China's Fighting Hordes*. Harrisburg, PA: Military Service Publishing Co., 1952.

Rosenfeld, Gavriel. "Why Do We Ask 'What If?': Reflections on the Function of Alternate History." *History and Theory* 41 (December 2002), 90–103.

Rothenburg, Gunther E. "Maurice of Nassau, Gustavus Adolphus, Raimondo Montecuccoli and the 'Military Revolution' of the Seventeenth Century." In Paret, *Makers of Modern Strategy*, 32–63.

Schumpeter, E. B. "Japan, Korea, and Manchukuo, 1936–1940." In Hunter, *Japanese Economic History*, 271–474.

———. "The Mineral Resources of the Japanese Empire and Manchukuo." In Hunter, *Japanese Economic History*, 362–474.

Sheng, Michael M. *Battling Western Imperialism: Mao, Stalin, and the United States*. Princeton, NJ: Princeton University Press, 1997.

van Slyke, Lyman P. "The Battle of the Hundred Regiments: Problems of Coordination and Control During the Sino-Japanese War." *Modern Asian Studies* 30, no. 4 (1996), 979–1005.

———, ed. *Marshall's Mission to China, December 1945–January 1947: The Report and Appended Documents*. 2 vols. Arlington, VA: University Publications of America, 1976.

Takeshi, Hara. "The Ichigō Offensive." In Peattie, Drea, and van de Ven, *The Battle for China*, 392–402.

Tanner, Harold M. *China: A History*. Indianapolis, IN: Hackett Publishing Company, 2009.

———. "Guerilla, Mobile, and Base Warfare in Communist Military Operations in Manchuria, 1945–1947." *Journal of Military History* 67 (October 2003): 1177–22.

———. "Railways in Communist Strategy and Operations in Manchuria, 1945–48." In Elleman and Kotkin, *Manchurian Railways and the Opening of China*, 149–70.

Taylor, Jay. *The Generalissimo: Chiang Kai-shek and the Struggle for Modern China*. Cambridge, MA: Harvard University Press, 2009.

Tuchman, Barbara. *Stilwell and the American Experience in China*. New York: Macmillan, 1971.

"Type 38 Rifle." Accessed 10 April 2010. http://en.wikipedia.org/wiki/Type_38_rifle.

van de Ven, Hans. "Stilwell in the Stocks: The Chinese Nationalists and the Allied Powers in the Second World War." In *Asian Affairs* 34, no. 3 (2003): 243–59.

Waldron, Arthur. "China Without Tears: If Chiang Kai-shek Hadn't Gambled in 1946." In Cowley, *What If?*, 377–92.

———. *From War to Nationalism: China's Turning Point, 1924–1925*. Cambridge: Cambridge University Press, 1995.

———. *The Great Wall of China: From History to Myth*. Cambridge: Cambridge University Press, 1992.

Wang, Peter Chen-main. "George Marshall in Early Republican China." Paper presented at the Annual Conference of the Chinese Military History Society, Richmond, BC, Canada, 9 May 2009. Cited by permission of the author.

Wedemeyer, Albert. *Wedemeyer Reports!* New York: Henry Holt and Company, 1958.

Weigley, Russell F. *The Age of Battles: The Quest for Decisive Warfare From Breitenfeld to Waterloo*. Bloomington: Indiana University Press, 1991.

Weinberg, Gerhard L. *The Foreign Policy of Hitler: Starting World War II, 1937–1939*. Chicago: University of Chicago Press, 1980.

———. *Germany, Hitler, and World War II: Essays in Modern German and World History.* Cambridge: Cambridge University Press, 1995.

Westad, Odd Arne. *Cold War and Revolution: Soviet-American Rivalry and the Origins of the Chinese Civil War, 1944–1946.* New York: Columbia University Press, 1993.

———. "Could the Chinese Civil War Have Been Avoided? An Exercise in Alternatives." In Bland, *George C. Marshall's Mediation Mission to China,* 501–13.

———. *Decisive Encounters: The Chinese Civil War, 1946–1950.* Stanford, CA: Stanford University, 2003.

Westwood, J. N., *Russia Against Japan, 1904–05: A New Look at the Russo-Japanese War.* Albany: State University of New York Press, 1986.

Wetzel, Carroll Robbins. "From the Jaws of Defeat: Lin Piao and the 4th Field Army in Manchuria." PhD diss., George Washington University, 1972.

Wolff, David. *To the Harbin Station: The Liberal Alternative in Russian Manchuria, 1898–1914.* Stanford:, CA Stanford University Press, 1999.

Yang Kuisong. "The Soviet Factor and the CCP's Policy Toward the United States in the 1940s." *Chinese Historians* 5, no. 1 (1992), 17–34.

Young, Louise. *Japan's Total Empire: Manchuria and the Culture of Wartime Imperialism.* Berkeley: University of California Press, 1999.

Zhang Baijia. "Zhou Enlai and the Marshall Mission." In Bland, *George C. Marshall's Mediation Mission to China,* 201–34.

INDEX

Acheson, Dean, 82
American arms and equipment: Communist use of, 229n33; limited value of, 63, 134, 168, 216–17, 220; Nationalist use of, 134, 135, 220
An-Hai Campaign, 185, 188
Anshan, battle of, 182, 183, 185
Autumn Offensive, 201, 204

Bai Chongxi, 61, 86, 166
Bandits: CCP recruitment of, 128; CCP regarded as by KMT, 2, 60, 112, 148, 169, 171; CCP suppression of, 89, 142, 198; KMT labeled as by CCP, 130
Beal, John, 179
Bei-Ning railway line, 98, 166, 191, 198, 205, 206
Belorussov, Dmitri, 44, 45, 53
Benxi: battle of, 136–38, 146, 243n50; Mao's determination to defend, 136, 144, 151; Nationalist decision to attack, 112, 131, 135
Bonaparte, Napoleon, 10, 180
Borodino, Battle of, 180, 181
Byrnes, James F., 79

Catholic missionaries, 110, 124, 126, 129, 163, 203, 204
Ceasefire (January 1946), 93, 94, 96, 234n59

Ceasefire (June 1946), 3, 6, 165, 189, 191; criticism of, 6, 7, 214
Chahar, 44, 46, 58, 88, 90, 91, 93, 109, 110, 123, 198, 218
Chamberlain, Neville, 13
Chang, Jung, 7, 12, 214; and Jon Halliday, *Mao: The Unknown Story*, 7
Changchun: Chiang Kai-shek's visit to, 188; Communist capture of, 123, 154; Communist decision to capture, 122–23; Du Yuming's determination to capture, 166–67, 170, 171; Lin Biao's decision not to defend, 176, 177; Marshall's plans for, 155, 169; Nationalist occupation of, 103; role in Communist strategy, 111, 124, 136, 147, 155, 157, 166, 167, 169, 170, 171, 176, 177, 179, 188, 191, 205; siege of, 206
Chen Lifu, 84, 170, 171, 174, 188, 189
Chen Mingren, 202, 204
Chen Yun, 52, 116, 195, 196, 197
Cheng, Victor, 143, 217, 244n56
Chengde, 18, 91, 146, 198
Chiang, Madame. *See* Soong Meiling
Chiang Kai-shek: agreement to June ceasefire, 188, 189, 243n38; conversation with Richard Lauterbach, 170; decision to send troops to the Northeast, 64, 74, 112; friction with Joseph Stilwell, 78; frustration with George Marshall,